CAMBRIDGE
UNIVERSITY PRESS

CAMBRIDGE ENGLISH

M000237727

Cambridge English

CAMBRIDGE
OFFICIAL
PREPARATION MATERIAL

Business
BENCHMARK

Pre-intermediate to Intermediate
Business Preliminary

Student's Book
Norman Whitby

2nd Edition

_ıBRIDGE
UNIVERSITY PRESS

University Printing House, Cambridge CB2 8BS, United Kingdom

Cambridge University Press is part of the University of Cambridge.

It furthers the University's mission by disseminating knowledge in the pursuit of
education, learning and research at the highest international levels of excellence.

www.cambridge.org
Information on this title: www.cambridge.org/9781107693999

© Cambridge University Press 2013

This publication is in copyright. Subject to statutory exception
and to the provisions of relevant collective licensing agreements,
no reproduction of any part may take place without the written
permission of Cambridge University Press.

First published 2006
Second edition published 2013
3rd printing 2014

Printed in the United Kingdom by Latimer Trend

A catalogue record for this publication is available from the British Library

ISBN 978-1-107-69399-9 Pre-intermediate to Intermediate Business Preliminary Student's Book
ISBN 978-1-107-69781-2 Pre-intermediate to Intermediate BULATS Student's Book
ISBN 978-1-107-66707-5 Pre-intermediate to Intermediate BULATS and Business Preliminary Teacher's Resource Book
ISBN 978-1-107-62848-9 Pre-intermediate to Intermediate BULATS and Business Preliminary Personal Study Book
ISBN 978-1-107-64481-6 Pre-intermediate to Intermediate BULATS Class Audio CDs (2)
ISBN 978-1-107-61103-0 Pre-intermediate to Intermediate Business Preliminary Class Audio CDs (2)

Cambridge University Press has no responsibility for the persistence or accuracy
of URLs for external or third-party internet websites referred to in this publication,
and does not guarantee that any content on such websites is, or will remain,
accurate or appropriate. Information regarding prices, travel timetables and other
factual information given in this work is correct at the time of first printing but
Cambridge University Press does not guarantee the accuracy of such information
thereafter.

Introduction

Business Benchmark Second edition Pre-intermediate to Intermediate, is a completely updated and revised course at CEFR B1 level, reflecting contemporary international business in a stimulating way both for people already working and for students who have not yet worked in business.

It teaches the reading, speaking, listening and writing skills needed in today's global workplaces together with essential business vocabulary and grammar.

Business Benchmark Second edition Pre-intermediate to Intermediate is also the most complete preparation material available for *Cambridge English: Business Preliminary,* also known as *Business English Certificate (BEC) Preliminary,* and is officially approved as an exam preparation course by Cambridge ESOL.

The book contains:

- **24 units for classroom study** covering all four skills in a dynamic and integrated way together with work on business vocabulary and grammar. It includes exercises which are informed by the Cambridge Learner Corpus (CLC) – see below.
- Interesting and stimulating listening and reading material, including interviews with real business people.
- Six **Grammar workshops** which revise and extend the grammar work covered in the units and which are informed by the Cambridge Learner Corpus (CLC).
- An eight-page **Writing reference** covering emails, memos, notes, letters and reports.
- A fully-referenced **Word list** with definitions covering key vocabulary from the units and the recording scripts.
- An **Exam skills and Exam practice** section which gives students detailed guidance on how to approach each exam task, the skills required and what the exam task is testing, together with exercises to build up students' exam skills. The Exam practice pages contain **a complete past Cambridge English: Business Preliminary exam**, with answers, **supplied by Cambridge ESOL.**
- A **full answer key** for all the exercises in the Student's book, including **sample answers** to all the writing tasks.
- **Complete recording transcripts.**

New features in the 2nd edition:

- **An expanded grammar syllabus** including six two-page Grammar workshops. These include exercises based on common grammar and vocabulary mistakes made by Business English students at this level, as shown by the CLC (see below). Exercises based on the CLC are indicated by this symbol: **⊙**
- **An expanded writing syllabus** including a new **Writing reference** section with guidance for each writing task and sample answers.
- **Authentic interviews** with real people working in business.
- New topics, texts and recordings reflecting the realities of contemporary international business.
- **Complete revision of all exam-style tasks,** making them closer to real exam tasks.

The Cambridge Learner Corpus (CLC)

The Cambridge Learner Corpus (CLC) is a large collection of exam scripts written by candidates taken from Cambridge ESOL exams around the world. It currently contains over 220,000 scripts, which translates to over 48 million words, and it is growing all the time. It forms part of the Cambridge International Corpus (CIC) and it has been built up by Cambridge University Press and Cambridge ESOL. The CLC currently contains scripts from over:

- 200,000 students
- 170 first languages
- 200 countries

Find out more about the Cambridge Learner Corpus at www.cambridge.org/corpus

Also available are:

- **2 audio CDs,** which include authentic interviews with real business people.
- **Teacher's Resource Book,** which includes photocopiable activities and case studies.
- **Personal Study Book,** which includes activities and exercises as well as a **self-study writing supplement.**

Map of the book

	Unit	Reading	Listening
Company profiles	**1** The working day 10–13	• Changing places: job swapping at work	• Being a PA
	2 Online communication 14–17	• The power of word of mouse: an article on the power of online customer opinions	• Email addresses
	3 Company growth 18–21	• Haier: an article about the history of a Chinese company • An article about how to think of good business ideas	• Growing pains: an interview with a business consultant about company growth
	4 Corporate culture 22–25	• What kind of company culture would suit you?: reading and answering a quiz	• Describing changes in a company: a conversation on the phone
	Grammar workshop 1 (Units 1–4) 26–27 Present simple and present continuous; Position of time phrases; Past simple and past continuous		
Production and selling	**5** Describing equipment 28–31	• Problems with equipment: emails and headings on a form	• Describing dimensions of products: conversations with colleagues and suppliers • The gizmo game: listening to the uses of a gadget
	6 Processes and procedures 32–35	• Waratah: an article on an Australian clothing company • Short texts: notices, notes and messages	• Chanel No. 5: an interview about a production process
	7 Distribution and delivery 36–39	• Selling your product abroad: an article • Workplace signs and notices	• Telephone conversations: information about orders and deliveries
	8 Advertising and marketing 40–43	• Descriptions of advertising media • Singapore Airlines: an article on the branding of an airline	• Description of how a product is advertised
	Grammar workshop 2 (Units 5–8) 44–45 Passive forms; Modal verbs; *because* and *so*		
Business travel	**9** Making arrangements 46–49		• Making and changing appointments: voicemail messages and phone conversations; Future intentions and predictions: short extracts
	10 Transport 50–53	• Travel arrangements: notices and short messages; Eurostar: an article on train travel	• A travel anecdote
	11 Working holidays 54–57	• Netflix: an article about a company's holiday policy; Thinking outside the box: an article on offsite meetings	• Half holidays: a conversation between two employees
	12 Conferences 58–61	• Short texts: feedback on conferences	• Discussing possible venues for a conference: a conversation between colleagues; A welcome speech at a conference
	Grammar workshop 3 (Units 9–12) 62–63 Future forms; Contrast words; Comparatives and superlatives		

Writing	Speaking	Vocabulary	Grammar
	• Describing jobs; asking other people about their job	• Job titles and describing jobs; names of company departments	• present simple and present continuous; time expressions; state verbs
• Set phrases for emails and letters • Writing emails: formal and informal styles		• Computer terms; email and website terms	
	• Asking about the history of a company: past simple questions		• Past simple: regular and irregular verbs and spelling of past simple forms; Past continuous
• An all staff email	• Asking questions about companies and jobs	• Finding and recording collocations	
	• Describing objects	• Vocabulary to describe objects: component parts, shapes, dimensions, materials; Describing problems with equipment	
• An email to your manager	• Passive forms: guessing true and false sentences	• Verbs to describe processes	• The present passive
	• Role-play: a telephone call to a supplier		• Modal verbs of obligation
• A promotional letter	• Describing a product and how it is advertised	• Vocabulary to talk about advertising and marketing; Language to describe cause and effect	• Words to describe causes and effects
	• Role-play: making an appointment; Role-play: planning a sales event	• Language for making appointments	• Present continuous for future arrangements; *will* and *going to* future forms
• A letter responding to an invitation		• Vocabulary for air travel	• Contrast words
	• Discussion: how to make decisions		• Comparatives: *as…as* structures
• *grateful* and *pleased*: an email confirming a booking	• Role-play: finding out about conference facilities		• Superlatives

	Unit	Reading	Listening
Business relationships	**13** New places, new people 64–67	• Career advice: letters to an advice column	• An interview with someone who has changed career
	14 Corporate gift-giving 68–71	• Promotional gifts: an article	• An interview about corporate gift giving
	15 Teamwork 72–75	• Descriptions of team building events; Kaizen: an article	• Creating good teams: a presentation
	16 Thinking globally 76–79	• Global HR management: an article	• Working in an international team: short extracts
	Grammar workshop 4 (Units 13–16) 80–81 Present perfect and past simple; *a/an* and *some*; Articles; Quantity expressions; Word types		
Finance	**17** Describing statistics 82–85	• Interpreting bar charts	• Listening to statistical information: short extracts
	18 Company finances 86–89	• Café Coffee Day: an article on the growth of the Indian coffee shop	• An interview with the employee of a company that helps failing businesses
	19 Investments 90–93	• Shares and the stock exchange: a web page; Short articles from the financial news; Men and women's investments: an article	• An interview with someone who works in investor relations
	20 Starting up 94–97	• Teenage entrepreneurs: reading and comparing two articles; Kalido: an article on funding	• Radio interview: the marketing director of a business support service
	Grammar workshop 5 (Units 17–20) 98–99 Adjectives and adverbs; Reference words; *which*, *what* and *that*; Prepositions		
Human resources	**21** Job applications 100–103	• Writing your CV: a book extract	• An interview with a careers adviser
	22 Recruitment 104–107	• Preparing for an interview: extract from a book giving advice; Interview questions: an article	• An interview with someone who works for a recruitment agency
	23 Staff development 108–111	• Advertisements for training courses: a memo and an advert; Sport and business: an article	• 360 degree feedback: a radio interview
	24 Employee productivity 112–115	• A business report	• An extract from a meeting; Radio interview on work situations: short extracts
	Grammar workshop 6 (Units 21–24) 116–117 Conditionals; Infinitive and *-ing* forms		

Writing	Speaking	Vocabulary	Grammar
	• Role-play: interviewing someone about a job change		• Present perfect: time expressions; Present perfect versus past simple
• A thank you letter to a business host			• Countable and uncountable nouns; Articles
	• Discussion: planning a team building event	• Suffixes: word building	
• An email requesting information	• Promoting a city: giving a speech	• Global management	• Expressions of quantity
• A description of a line graph	• Describing figures and trends	• Describing trends	• Adjectives and adverbs
	• Discussing company information	• Finance vocabulary	• Pronouns and reference words
		• Stocks and shares	
• Writing a letter to express an interest in a new product	• Giving a summary of an article	• Collocation sets: time and money	• *which/who/that/where* clauses
• Letter inviting a candidate for interview; Letter giving the result of an application; Letters giving good and bad news		• Headings for CVs; Describing application procedures	
• An email to a recruitment agency	• Discussing qualities needed in candidates for a job vacancy	• Employment vocabulary	• First and second conditionals
• Filling in a form; An email to book a place on a course		• Sports vocabulary in business	
• Completing a business report	• Ways to improve employee productivity		• Infinitive and *-ing* forms; Grammar revision

Acknowledgements

The author and publishers would like to thank the following teachers and consultants who commented on the material: Austria: Derek Callan; China: Bi Xuqiang; Poland: Andrzej Czaplicki; Russia: Wayne Rimmer; Spain: Inma Sánchez Ballesteros; Switzerland: Trant Luard; UK: Sharon Ashton, David Clark.

The author and publishers would also like to thank the following people for agreeing to be interviewed for this book: Matthew Beale and Steve Keley.

Thanks also to Michael Black, Susie-Fairfax Davies (interviewer), Ann Kennedy Smith (lexicographer), and Julie Moore (corpus researcher).

The author would also like to thank everyone who has worked on this book, particularly Ruth Cox for her editorial skills and patience.

Text acknowledgements
The author and publishers acknowledge the following sources of copyright material and are grateful for the permissions granted. While every effort has been made, it has not always been possible to identify the sources of all the material used, or to trace all copyright holders. If any omissions are brought to our notice, we will be happy to include the appropriate acknowledgements on reprinting.

The publisher has used its best endeavours to ensure that the URLs for external websites referred to in this book are correct and active at the time of going to press. However, the publisher has no responsibility for the websites and can make no guarantee that a site will remain live or that the content is or will remain appropriate.

p. 27: Levi Strauss & Co. for adapted text from http://www.levistrauss.com. Courtesy of Levi Strauss & Co.; p. 31: RoadTripAmerica.com for the adapted text from http://www.roadtripamerica.com. Copyright © RoadTripAmerica.com; p. 34: PageWise, Inc. for the text and listening exercise adapted from 'Grasse: perfume's French Centre' by Ruth Mark, http://www.pagewise.com. Copyright © 2005 by PageWise, Inc. Used with permission; p. 34: OsMoz.com for the text and listening exercise adapted from 'Manufacturing techniques', http://www.osmoz.com. Used by permission of OsMoz.com; p. 42: Palgrave Macmillan for the text adapted from 'Singapore Airlines, flying tiger' by Martin Roll, Asian Brand Strategy, published 2005, Palgrave Macmillan. Reproduced with permission of Palgrave Macmillan; p. 52: NI Syndication Limited for the text adapted from 'Cementing the bedrock of Anglo-French co-operation' by Susan MacDonald, The Times 02.04.04. Copyright © NI Syndication Limited; p. 55: Telegraph Media Group Limited for the text adapted from 'Netflix lets its staff take as much holiday as they want, whenever they want, and it works' by Daniel Pink, The Telegraph 14.08.10. Copyright © Telegraph Media Group Limited 2010; p. 57: Christopher Shevlin for the text adapted from 'Move out of range to think out of the box' by Christopher Shevlin, Financial Times 20.08.04. Copyright © Christopher Shevlin 2004; p. 63: Text adapted from 'Your commute is bad? Try 186 miles each way' by Gary Richards, Seattle Times, 04.05.06; pp. 96–97: Text adapted from 'Kalido', http://www.startups.co.uk. Copyright © Startups.co.uk. Reproduced with permission; p. 110: NI Syndication Limited for the text adapted from 'Football coaches train executives' by Matthew Goodman, The Sunday Times 12.09.04. Copyright © NI Syndication Limited; p. 111: Team Builders Plus, Inc for the listening exercise adapted from '360 degree feedback', http://www.360-degreefeedback.com. Copyright © Team Builders Plus, Inc.

Photo acknowledgements
p. 10 (T): Andrew Holt/Getty Images; p. 10 (Rosie): Thinkstock/Ron Chapple Studios; p. 10 (Sveta/Gamal/Daniel/Caroline): Thinkstock/iStockphoto; p. 10 (Ben): Shutterstock/Luis Santos; p. 10 (Alex): Thinkstock/George Doyle; p. 10 (Jan): Shutterstock/StockLite; p. 10 (Marcelo): Thinkstock/Ingram Publishing; p. 10 (John Paul): Thinkstock/Jupiterimages; p. 11: Citizen Stock/

Superstock; p. 12: Spencer Grant/Art Directors & TRIP; p. 14 (T): WestEnd61/Rex Features; p. 18 (T): AID/amanaimages/Corbis; p. 18 (a): Courtesy of Google Inc.; p. 18 (b): Samsung; p. 18 (c): Ford Motor Company; p. 18 (d): Courtesy of Sony; p. 18 (e): Virgin and the Virgin Signature logo are trade marks of Virgin Enterprises Limited; p. 18 (f): Image courtesy of Toyota (GB) PLC; p. 18 (B): cdsb/AP/Press Association Images; p. 20 (logo): Logo provided by Fresh Enterprises LLC; p. 21 (T): Helene Rogers/Art Directors & TRIP; p. 21 (B): Science Photo Library; p. 22 (T): Sam Edwards/Alamy; p. 22 (B): Thinkstock/Comstock; p. 24: Thinkstock/Hemera; p. 25: moodboard/Alamy; p. 27 (L): Photo by David & Judy Lomax/Rex Features; p. 27 (R): Courtesy of Levi Strauss & Co.; p. 28 (T): Tetra Images/Superstock; p. 28 (scanner): Ocean/Corbis; p. 28 (MP3 player): Helene Rogers/Art Directors & TRIP; p. 28 (lamp): Thinkstock/Hemera; p. 28 (camera): Thinkstock /iStockphoto; p. 28 (shredder): Ange/Alamy; p. 31: Courtesy of RoadTripAmerica.com; p. 32 (T): Thinkstock/Hemera; p. 32 Karhu logo used by permission Trak Sports USA and Karhu Sporting Goods Oy, Finland; p. 36 (TL): Thinkstock/Hemera; p. 36 (TR): Shutterstock/Péter Gudella; p. 36 (B): reppans/Alamy; p. 38: Shutterstock/Gary Blakeley; p. 39 (T): Thinkstock/Jupiterimages; p. 39 (B): Joe Luis Peleaz Inc./Getty Images; p. 40 (T): Chris Batson/Alamy; p. 40 (a, c, d, e): Helene Rogers/Art Directors & TRIP; p. 40 (b): Clynt Garnham Business/Alamy; p. 40 (f): Getty Images; p. 40 (g): Roger Bamber/Alamy; p. 42: Etienne de Malglaive /ABACAPRESS.COM/Press Association Images; p. 46 (T): Shutterstock/Stephen Coburn; p. 46 (planner): Sasco, courtesy of ACCO UK Ltd; p. 46 (tablet PC): Oleksiy Maksymenko/Alamy; p. 46 (diary): Helene Rogers/Art Directors & TRIP; p. 46 (phone): Fotolia/amorphis; p. 46 (BL) Thinkstock/Jupiterimages; p. 47 (T): Thinkstock/Purestock; p. 47 (B): SOMOS/Superstock; p. 50 (T): Vincenzo Lombardo/Getty Images; p. 50 (B): Gareth Brown/Corbis; p. 52: Micha Theiner/City AM/Rex Features; p. 54 (T): Fancy/Alamy; p. 54 (B): Larry Williams/Corbis; p. 55 (background): iStockphoto/Marcela Barsse; p. 57: Photograph of Claude Béglé. Copyright Geopost International, used with kind permission.; p. 58 (T): Rob Melnchuk/Getty Images; p. 58 (BL,BC): Thinkstock/iStockphoto; p. 58 (BR): Helene Rogers/Art Directors & TRIP; p. 60: Tetra Images/Superstock; p. 64 (T): Yuri Arcurs/Alamy; p. 64 (BL): Jiang Jin/Purestock/Superstock; p. 64 (BR): Shutterstock/AISPIX by Image Source; p. 68 (T): RunPhoto/Getty Images; p. 68 (B): Fancy/Alamy; p. 69: Helene Rogers/Art Directors & TRIP; p. 71: Thinkstock/Brand X Pictures; p. 72 (T): Thinkstock/Hemera; p. 72 (a): Courtesy of EML, Event Management & Logistics Ltd; p. 72 (b): Courtesy of Drum Café; p. 72 (c): Courtesy of MountainDeepMountainHigh.co.uk; p. 72 (d): Courtesy of My Chocolate, www.mychocolate.co.uk; p. 72 (e): Courtesy of Off Limits Corporate Events, www.actiondays.co.uk; p. 74: Thinkstock/George Doyle; p. 76 (T): Thinkstock/Hemera; p. 77: moodboard/Alamy; p. 79 (T): Thinkstock/iStockphoto; p. 79 (B): Thinkstock/Medioimages/Photodisc; p. 82 (T): Artbox/Superstock; p. 86 (T): Fotolia/merc67; p. 86 (BL): John Rowley/Getty Images; p. 86 (BR): Thinkstock/iStockphoto; p. 88: India Today Group/Getty Images; p. 90 (T): Shutterstock/zhu difeng; p. 90 (B): Action Press/Rex Features; p. 93: Corbis Flirt/Alamy; p. 94 (T): Kick Image/Getty Images; p. 94 (B): Thinkstock/Hemera; p. 95: African Leadership Academy; p. 96 (background): iStockphoto/Aleksander Velasevic; p. 97: iStockphoto/Aleksander Velasevic; p. 100 (T): Thinkstock/iStockphoto; p. 100 (B): Thinkstock/Jupiterimages; p. 103: Marcus Mok/Getty Images; p. 104 (T): NetPhotos Collection/Alamy; p. 104 (B): Thinkstock/Bananastock; p. 107: Thinkstock/iStockphoto; p. 108 (T): Eric Andras/Getty Images; p. 110 (pitch): iStockphoto/ © hudiemm; p. 110 (C): Back Page Images/Rex Features; p. 112 (T): Arcaid Images/Alamy; p. 112 (B): Thinkstock/Digital Vision; p. 114 (TL): Thinkstock/iStockphoto; p. 114 (TR): Corbis Super RF/Alamy; p. 114 (B): Thinkstock/Hemera; p. 115: Thinkstock/Fuse; p. 120: Photo courtesy of www.chokolit.co.uk.

Cover image by Shutterstock/Baloncici.

We are unable to trace the copyright holders of the photographs that appear on p. 66 and p. 87 and would appreciate any help to enable us to do so.

Illustrator acknowledgements
Simon Tegg for the illustrations on pp. 14, 29, 30 and the graphs pp. 82, 83, 84, 85, 119; Tim Oliver for the illustrations on pp. 34 and 51.

Audio acknowledgements
Studio: dsound Studios, London
Producer: James Richardson
Sound engineer: Dave Morritt

Text design and layout: Hart McLeod
Photo research: Kevin Brown
Project management: Jane Coates

The working day

Getting started

1 Read the introductions and write the correct first names on the organogram below.

My name's Sveta. I help to make sure the company is producing what people want to buy and promote our products.

My name's Caroline. My area of responsibility is finding and testing new products.

I'm John Paul. I lead the team who make our products and I'm responsible for their safety at work.

I'm Gamal. I do the bookkeeping and the payroll.

I'm Alex. I deal with our suppliers and make sure we buy equipment and materials at the best prices.

I'm Rosie. I'm responsible for recruitment and issues to do with staff welfare.

My name's Ben. I operate some of the equipment for making our products.

I'm Jan. I'm responsible for computer systems. I install hardware and software and fix any problems.

I'm Daniel. I meet possible new customers and give them information about our products.

I'm Marcelo. I unload deliveries, record stock and make sure it is stored correctly.

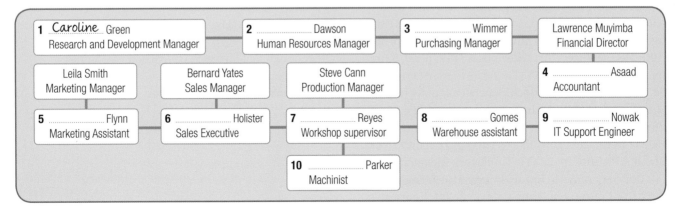

1 _Caroline_ Green
Research and Development Manager

2 .... Dawson
Human Resources Manager

3 .... Wimmer
Purchasing Manager

Lawrence Muyimba
Financial Director

Leila Smith
Marketing Manager

Bernard Yates
Sales Manager

Steve Cann
Production Manager

4 .... Asaad
Accountant

5 .... Flynn
Marketing Assistant

6 .... Holister
Sales Executive

7 .... Reyes
Workshop supervisor

8 .... Gomes
Warehouse assistant

9 .... Nowak
IT Support Engineer

10 .... Parker
Machinist

2   Do you know anyone who does any of the jobs in this organogram? Which do you think is the most difficult job to do?

Company departments

Vocabulary

Look at the list of company departments (a–h) and read situations (1–6). Decide which department each person should ask to speak to when phoning the company. There are two more departments than you need.

a   Personnel
b   Accounts
c   Technical support
d   ~~Quality Control~~
e   Sales
f   Marketing
g   Research and development
h   Production

1   Mr Mitchell is a marketing executive who has received several complaints from customers about faulty goods.   *d*

2   Mr Davies is a consultant who thinks he has not been paid for an invoice.   *b*

3   Mr Ivanov has just received the results of some laboratory tests on a possible new product.   *g*

4   Ms Santoro is a sales executive who is interested in working for the company.   *a*

5   Ms Evans works in the company as a secretary and she has a problem with her computer.   *c*

6   Mr Chen is a retailer who is interested in stocking the company's products.   *e*

Personal assistants

Listening

1   You are going to hear a conversation with a PA (personal assistant) who works for the director of a TV channel. Work in pairs and decide which of the following activities could be part of her job.

answering letters	☑	making coffee	☐
booking flights	☐	prioritising appointments	☑
booking train tickets	☐	taking notes in meetings	☑
co-ordinating special events	☑	taking phone calls	☐
looking up information	☑	welcoming visitors	☑

2   (1) 02 Listen to the first part of the interview. Which of the above activities does she mention?

3   (1) 02 Listen to the whole interview and complete the interviewer's questions:

1   So what ____do____ ____you____ ____do____ , Sally?
2   What ____does____ ____that____ ____involved?____
3   Do you ____enjoy____ your job?
4   ____What____ ____about____ the people you work with?

4   Complete the following statements with the correct adjective from the box.

~~busy~~   friendly   helpful   organised   reliable   stressful

1   Sally's workplace is always very ____busy____ .
2   According to Sally, it is important for a PA to be ____organised____
3   Sometimes the job can get ____stressful____ .
4   She thinks her colleagues are very ____friendly____ and ____helpful____ .
5   Sally's boss thinks she is ____reliable____ .

5   (1) 02 Listen to the interview again and check your answers.

Describing a job

Speaking

1 Make a list of the responsibilities that you have in your job. If you are not yet working, either think of another position you had (for example in a school club), or imagine you are doing a job from the organogram on page 10.

2 Work with a partner. Use some of the questions from the interview to ask your partner about his/her job. Tell your partner about your responsibilities. Use the useful language to help you.

> **Useful language**
> **Describing your job**
>
> I'm in charge of ....   I deal with ....
>
> It's my job to ....   I'm responsible for ....

Changing Places

Reading

Reality TV is where real people are filmed in different situations. Some reality TV programmes are set in the workplace, such as a hospital or a hotel.

1 **Discuss these questions in small groups.**

- Do you know any examples of reality TV shows which show people at work? Have you seen any of them?
- Read the quotes. Which opinion do you agree with? Why?

'Most people don't know what it's like to do another job. That's why reality shows like this are so interesting.'

'Shows like this give people the wrong idea because they only show the interesting parts of jobs. You can't know what a job is like from just one hour of TV.'

2 **Read the article quickly without using a dictionary to get a general understanding of what it is about. This is called *skimming* and it is very useful when you have a lot of text to read. If you are reading a text you may also be looking for key words or phrases. This is called *scanning*, and is useful if you are looking for specific information.**

When you have skim-read the text, scan it and write the paragraph numbers next to the names.

Paragraphs:
- Donald Eisner ...., ... • Alex Jennings ...., ...

3 Read the text again to see if the statements on page 13 are true or false. Begin by underlining a word or phrase in each statement you think you can find in the text. For example, in Statement 2, you can look for the word *pancakes*.

CHANGING **PLACES**

1 Many critics dislike reality TV shows, but one show which has received very favourable reviews is *Changing Places*. The main idea is simple. Take the Chief Executive Officer of a company and put him in the position of one of his own company's low-end workers.

2 Donald Eisner is the CEO of Absalon chain of hotels in Australia. His <u>family</u> have been hotel owners for three generations and are one of the <u>richest</u> in the Australian hotel industry. In the programme we see Donald Eisner working as a bellboy, cook and cleaner while supervisors monitor his performance, noting any mistakes. He has some triumphs, it is true. In the kitchen, he successfully cooks several pancakes, for example, and he makes the beds correctly. The rest of his housekeeping, however, is not a success as he fails to clean any rooms to the company's required standards. At the end of the programme we see his supervisor taking him from room to room, pointing out his mistakes.

3 Alex Jennings runs a highly successful chain of steak bars called Wayside Inn. He has a reputation for demanding quality from his staff, both in terms of food and service. However, when he changes places with some of them, we see him fail in a number of tasks in the restaurant. As a waiter, he continually forgets to ask customers how they want their steaks to be done, and mixes up the orders completely when he has to serve five tables at the same time. A few minutes later disaster strikes when his tie becomes caught under the drinks on a tray! The next day when he takes the place of the cook, the supervisor makes him redo several of the steaks.

Donald Eisner

4 Now that their experience is over, are the CEOs thinking of making any changes to their businesses? The answer is that they already have. 'We carried out several changes like sorting the knives, forks and spoons to make it easier for the person who washes the dishes,' says Mr Jennings. 'We're also redesigning the staff uniforms.' Mr Eisner found the experience even more of a shock. He is not only making changes in his hotels, like the policy on who orders new supplies of cleaning materials, but he also wants to create a *Changing Places* day at all Absalon hotels so that all senior management can go through a similar process to him.

Donald Eisner

1. He comes from a <u>rich family</u>. *T*
2. He can cook pancakes. *T*
3. He cleans the hotel rooms to the company's required standards. *F*
4. He is thinking of making a different person responsible for ordering the cleaning materials. *F* X True
5. He would not like other senior executives to work as cooks and cleaners. *F*

Alex Jennings

6. He believes quality is important in his restaurants. *T*
7. He has good skills as a waiter. *F*
8. He is making changes to the uniform that staff wear. *T*

4 Work with a partner. Discuss these questions.

1. What do you think of the idea of having a *Changing Places* day in your company or place of study?
2. Would it be a good idea? Why/Why not?

Grammar workshop

Present simple and present continuous

You use the **present simple** to talk about habits and things that are *always* or *usually* true.

Alex Jennings **runs** *a chain of steak bars.*
(He does this as part of everyday life.)
Question: **Does** *he* **run** *a chain of steak bars?*
Negative: *He* **doesn't run** *a chain of steak bars.*

You use the **present continuous** to talk about things which are true only at the moment, or a process which is not completed.

They **are redesigning** *the staff uniforms.*
(This is true only in this period of time.)
Question: **Are** *they* **redesigning** *the staff uniforms?*
Negative: *They* **aren't redesigning** *the staff uniforms.*

❯ **page 26** Present simple and present continuous

Note: Some verbs are not usually used in the continuous because they talk about states, not actions, e.g. *I know, he likes, it involves.* (NOT: ~~I am knowing, he is liking, it is involving~~, etc.)

1 Look at the time phrases in the box. Write present simple (PS) or present continuous (PC) next to the correct time phrase.

always *PS*	generally *PS*	this month *PS*
at the moment *PC*	now PC	today *PC*
currently *PC*	never *PS*	this week *PS*
every month *PS*	often *PS*	twice a month *PS*
each year *PS*	sometimes *PS*	usually PS

2 Write five sentences about things which happen or are happening at the moment in your company or place of study. Use a time phrase from the box in each sentence. Work in pairs and read them to your partner. Ask your partner a question about each of their sentences.

At the moment we're working on a big project.
What exactly are you doing?

We have a staff meeting every week.
What do you discuss in the meeting?

❯ **page 26** Position of time phrases

3 ⊙ Business English students sometimes wrongly use a state verb in a continuous tense. Read the following sentences. Decide which are incorrect and change them.

1. We ~~are needing~~ an audiosystem for the conference. **need**
2. Our staff are not understanding our financial position.
3. They are advertising for a new sales executive at the moment.
4. I can't employ him because he's ~~having~~ no references. *doesn't have*
5. Don't disturb Richard just now because he's doing the payroll.
6. I'm thinking this new system is a big mistake.
7. I'm thinking of going on holiday next week.
8. Some people are still ~~preferring~~ to use a flipchart instead of PowerPoint. *prefer to*

4 Which verb can be either a state verb or an action verb? What is the difference in meaning?

Online communication

Getting started

1 Read the following questions and note down your answers.

1 How much time do you spend on the computer for work or study? Is this amount of time increasing? Why/Why not?
2 Do you think you spend less or more time on the computer than your colleagues or friends?
3 Think what you have done on the computer over the past seven days. Draw a pie chart to show approximately what percentage of time you spent on the following activities:

- creating documents   *30*
- reading and answering emails *30*
- finding information on the Internet *15*
- visiting social networking sites like Facebook *5*
- playing games   —
- watching films or TV programmes —
- other

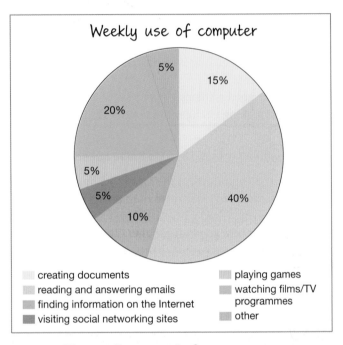

Weekly use of computer

5% 15% 20% 5% 5% 10% 40%

creating documents
reading and answering emails
finding information on the Internet
visiting social networking sites

playing games
watching films/TV programmes
other

Compare your answers with a partner. How similar is your use of time on the computer?

2 Match the computer icons (1–7) with the correct verb from the box.

attach copy cut highlight ~~paste~~ print save

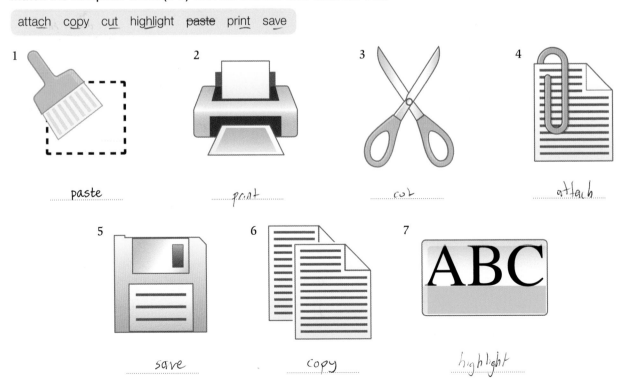

1 *paste*

2 *print*

3 *cut*

4 *attach*

5 *save*

6 *copy*

7 *highlight*

3 Complete the definitions with the correct verb.

~~browse~~ crash download drag log on post
restart upload

1 If you ___browse___ the Internet, you look around for information online.
2 If you ___download___ something, you move it from the Internet to your computer.
3 If you ___log on___, you start using a computer system, perhaps by typing in a password.
4 If you ___restart___ the computer, you switch everything off and start it again.
5 If computer systems ___crash___, they suddenly stop working.
6 If you click and ___drag___ a document, you move it to somewhere else on the system with the mouse.
7 If you ___post___ a message online, you put it on the Internet so other people can see it.
8 If you ___upload___ something, you move it from your computer to the Internet or a network.

4 Choose three things you did on the computer recently and tell a partner about them using three of the verbs in Exercise 3.

Digital media

Reading ⊬

1 With a partner, discuss what you think *word of mouth* means in advertising.

2 The title of the article below changes the phrase to *word of mouse*. What do you think this means? Discuss with a partner, then skim the article quickly to see if you are right.

3 Scan the article for each of the names in the box. Then match each name with the correct sentence (1–5) below. There is one name you do not need.

Adam Brimo   Dave Carroll   Hugh Bainbridge
~~the Nielsen Company~~   Paul Patterson   United Airlines

1 ___The Nielsen Company___ did research into different forms of marketing.
2 ___Dave Carroll___ possibly caused a company's share price to fall.
3 _____ believes that the rules for dealing with unhappy customers have not changed.
4 _____ made a chief executive aware of his grievances by writing about them on a website.
5 _____ suffered an unexpected crisis because of an online video.

THE POWER OF WORD OF MOUSE

People often say that the best form of promotion is by 'word of mouth'. After all, people normally trust a recommendation from someone they know. But in today's digital world, consumers don't just talk to friends and family members. By posting their opinions online, they can reach thousands of other consumers. What's more, this is a very good way of persuading people to buy things. A recent survey by the Nielsen Company revealed that 70 per cent of consumers trust opinions they find online, which is much higher than the figures for other advertising media, like TV and only slightly lower than opinions of friends.

The bad news for companies is that negative opinions can go online as well as good ones. When Adam Brimo, an Australian engineering graduate, was dissatisfied with his mobile phone provider, he decided to set up a website to talk about his experiences. It quickly filled up with posts from other dissatisfied customers. In the end, the company invited him to meet their chief executive, who then gave a public apology. When Dave Carroll, a US musician, took a flight with United Airlines, his guitar was broken during the trip. The airline company refused to pay for the damage, so he wrote three songs about it and uploaded them on YouTube. This was a public relations disaster for the airline, and possibly the reason why their share price dropped by 10 per cent that week.

Paul Patterson, a professor of marketing, agrees that companies now have less control over how the public view them but points out that the way to deal with dissatisfied customers is the same as always. Companies just need to react faster in case a customer decides to contact other customers online. Some analysts worry that a company's image could be damaged by a small number of dissatisfied customers. But Hugh Bainbridge from the Australian School of Business says consumers do not believe everything they see online, and that brands are only damaged when a large number of customers are clearly unhappy. Instead of seeing it as a threat, companies should treat this new medium as a useful source of customers' opinions.

Perhaps the biggest success story comes from Coca-Cola. In 2008, Dusty Sorg couldn't find a Coke fan page he could join on Facebook, so he downloaded a picture of a Coke can and created his own. Unexpectedly, it was a big hit with other fans. When Coca-Cola found out about it, they didn't try to get control over the page. Instead, they flew Dusty to Atlanta to meet their management team and told him to carry on the good work, with help from a few senior executives from the company. The result was a Facebook page run by a passionate fan and a good PR story for Coca-Cola. That really is a smart use of 'word of mouse'.

4 Choose the correct answer, A, B or C. Before you answer each question, use the underlined name to decide where to look in the text.

1 According to the <u>Nielsen Company's</u> research, which is most likely to make someone buy a product?
   (A) a recommendation from a friend
   B a recommendation posted online
   C a TV advertisement

2 According to <u>Paul Patterson</u>, in the digital age, companies need to
   A use different media to advertise products
   B respond more quickly to customer complaints
   C put satisfied customers in contact with each other

3 What does <u>Hugh Bainbridge</u> feel about the effect of online opinions?
   A They give too much importance to a small number of complaints.
   B They allow customers to spread wrong information about brands.
   C They do not harm brands if there is no good cause for complaint.

4 What point does the story about <u>Coca-Cola</u> illustrate?
   A Companies have lost most of their control over their brands.
   B Companies can use consumers to create online content for them.
   C Companies need to monitor online content very carefully.

5 Discuss with a partner.

1 Do you know any websites where people post opinions online? Have you ever posted an opinion online?

2 Do you look at online opinions before making a purchase (for example, before booking a hotel)? How much do they influence you?

3 Do you visit any product or service fan pages (for example on Facebook)?

Emails

Vocabulary

1 Match each symbol from a website address (1–6) with its name (a–f)

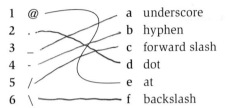

1 @
2 .
3 _
4 -
5 /
6 \

a underscore
b hyphen
c forward slash
d dot
e at
f backslash

2 🎧 03 Listen to the following parts of some common email addresses. Which are said as words and which as separate letters?

| com | uk | org | biz | us | ac | co | net |

3 🎧 04 Listen to these email addresses. Circle S if the spoken and written addresses are the same and D if they are different.

1 gbrent_39@gmail.com — S/(D)
2 sales@taylormills.co.es — (S)/D
3 bendmurphy@hotmail.com — S/(D)
4 natalieomar@blogspot.com — (S)/D
5 www.glf.com\products — S/(D)
6 Mary-Ann.Perkins@copeland.org.uk — (S)/D
7 www.gaskelltraining.biz — S/(D)
8 s.denham@dur.ac.uk — S/(D)

4 Computer technology means there are some differences between the language used in emails and letters. Read the following sentences. Put *E* if the sentence could only be in an email, *L* if it could only be in a letter and *B* if it could be in both.

1 Nice to hear from you. __B__
2 I attach a copy of the relevant form. _____
3 I enclose a copy of the relevant form. _____
4 Your request was forwarded to me. _____
5 I'm afraid I couldn't open the document. _____
6 I am sorry for the delay in replying. _____
7 I am copying James in on this message. _____
8 Thank you for your message. I will be out of the office from 26 to 28 May inclusive. _____
9 I am also sending a hard copy. _____
10 I look forward to your reply. _____

Writing

Emails can be written in a formal or an informal style. Usually they are shorter and more like spoken English than letters.

1 Match the verbs (1–10) with the more formal verb (a–j) with the same meaning.

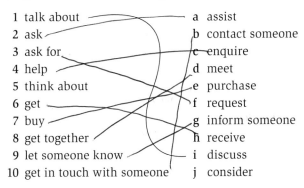

1 talk about
2 ask
3 ask for
4 help
5 think about
6 get
7 buy
8 get together
9 let someone know
10 get in touch with someone

a assist
b contact someone
c enquire
d meet
e purchase
f request
g inform someone
h receive
i discuss
j consider

2 Look at the following ways to begin and end emails. Number each list in order of how formal you think the beginnings and endings are. (1 = most formal; 5 = least formal).

Beginnings
Dear John   2
Dear Mr Green 1
Hi John   3
John   5
Hello John 4

Endings
Yours sincerely 1
Best wishes   3
All the best   4
Bye for now   5
Kind regards   2

3 Number these two lists from 1–4, depending on how formal you think the expressions are. (1 = most formal; 4 = least formal).

Requests
Could you ...   3
Can you ...   4
I would be grateful if you could ... 1
Please could you ...   2

Apologies
We are sorry about ...   3
Sorry about ...   4
We would like to offer our sincere apologies for ...   1
Please accept our apologies for ...   2

4 Below are a list of phrases from two emails about the same meeting. Write the formal and informal phrases with the same meaning in the table in the order they appear in the email.

~~to discuss the schedule for training day~~
~~Looking forward to your reply~~
~~Hi Andy~~
~~but I could manage the week after~~
~~Can we get together sometime~~
~~Susan Jackson~~
~~to talk about the schedule for training day~~
~~but perhaps you could suggest a suitable time for the week after~~
~~let me know~~
~~Dear Mr Morris,~~
~~I'm pretty booked up next week~~
~~Sue~~
~~I would like to arrange a meeting~~
~~My diary is very full for next week~~

Formal	Informal
Dear Mr Morris,	Hi Andy
Can we get together sometime	to talk about the schedule for training day
I would like to arrange a meeting	I'm pretty booked up next week
to discuss the schedule for training day	but I could manage the week after
My diary is very full for next week	let me know
but perhaps you could suggest a suitable time for the week after	
Looking forward to your reply	
Susan Jackson	Sue

5 You have arranged a meeting with a member of staff from another department. Unfortunately you cannot now attend. Write an email to your colleague.

- explaining why you cannot meet
- apologising for the change of plan
- suggesting an alternative day and time

You have not worked with this person before so keep the tone friendly but formal. Write 30–40 words.

Company growth

Getting started

How do you think these international companies began? Now match each company with a sentence. Then compare your answers with a partner.

a

b

c

d **SONY**

e

f **TOYOTA**

1 *Samsung* began as a food trading company near the South Korean city of Daegu.

2 *toyota* began when a Japanese company that made weaving machines decided to set up an automobile department.

3 *Google* began as a research project by two students at Stanford University, California.

4 *Sony* began just after World War II when two engineers came together and started Tokyo Tsushin Kogyo. Its first commercialised product was a 'power megaphone'.

5 *Ford* began in 1901 as a reorganisation of the Detroit Automobile Company.

6 *Virgin* began when an entrepreneur started buying discounted records and selling them to stores in London.

Which company do you think is the most successful today? Why?

Haier

Reading

1 Make sentences about a Chinese company called Haier by matching the beginning of a sentence(1–7) with the correct ending (a–g).

1 Haier is a Chinese company ...*c*...
2 It began in the 1920s ...*e*...
3 In the 1950s it became ...*g*...
4 For the next thirty years ...*b*...
5 Then in 1984, the local government appointed ...*d*...
6 Mr Zhang was a keen student ...*a*...
7 He planned to turn the company around ...*f*...

a of management theory and management techniques.
b it did not experience very high growth.
c which manufactures electrical appliances.
d a new young manager, Mr Zhang Ruimin.
e as a simple refrigerator factory.
f and make it a success.
g a state-owned enterprise.

2 Now read the article, which is about what happened after Mr Zhang arrived at Haier.

Mr Zhang soon realised that one of the problems was the company did not pay enough attention to quality control. In 1985, on his orders, the manufacturing team carried 76 substandard fridges onto the factory floor. Mr Zhang then handed out hammers to the workers and told them to smash the fridges. Some workers did not want to because the fridges were so expensive, but Mr Zhang insisted. One of the hammers is still on display today to remind employees of the importance of maintaining quality.

Under Mr Zhang's leadership, the company grew rapidly and over the next fifteen years, they broadened their product range to include other electrical goods like air conditioners and televisions. It also acquired a number of other companies. In 2008, Haier overtook Whirlpool as the world's top producer of fridges.

3 Look at Exercises 1 and 2 and find words with the following meanings.

1 pieces of equipment for the home *appliances*
2 a company or business ....
3 very interested in something ....
4 not of acceptable quality ....
5 break into many pieces ....
6 increased, or included more things in ....
7 obtained something (often another company)
....

4 The following statements are false. Look at Exercise 2 again and correct them.

1 Quality control was good at Haier in the early 1980s.
No, it wasn't very good / it was poor.
2 The manufacturing team decided to carry 76 fridges onto the factory floor. *No, team didn't decide it*
3 The staff accidentally smashed the fridges.
4 In the 1990s, Haier only sold fridges. *No, In 1990s they sold other appliances*
5 In 2008, Whirlpool produced more fridges than Haier. *No, Haier produced more than whirlpool in 2008*

Grammar workshop 1

Past simple

Most of the verbs in the article are in the **past simple** tense.

1 Decide which TWO of the following statements about the past simple are correct. Look at the article again to help you if you are not sure.

1 You use the past simple for a finished action in the past. ✓
2 You use the past simple for an action which is not yet finished. ✗
3 You use the past simple if you say when the action happened. ✗

2 Regular verbs in the past simple are made by adding -ed, but the spelling of some regular past simple verbs can be a problem. Answer the following questions. Look back at the verbs in the text if you are not sure.

• What happens if:
  1 the verb already ends in e (e.g. *realise*)? *add "d"*
  2 the verb ends in *consonant* + y (e.g. *carry*)? *ied*
  3 the verb has one syllable and ends in one vowel and one consonant (e.g. *plan*)? *double n + ed*
  4 the verb ends in one vowel and one consonant, but has two or more syllables and the last syllable is not stressed (e.g. *broaden*)? *not double consonant*

3 Look again at Exercises 1 and 2 and find five irregular verbs (apart from the verb *to be*).

4 ⊙ Business English students often make mistakes with the spelling of irregular verbs in the past simple. Correct the mistakes in the following sentences.

1 They ~~spended~~ over 5 thousand pounds on that project. *spent*
2 I ~~beared~~ the news about the merger yesterday. *heard*
3 I think we ~~payed~~ too much for that new equipment. *paid*
4 He ~~red~~ business studies at university. *read*
5 He ~~toke~~ a taxi across town to visit the factory. *took*
6 He ~~choosed~~ not to go into the family business. *chose*

Past simple questions

We form questions in the past simple with *did* plus the base form.
When **did** the company **begin**?
It began in the 1920s.

We form past simple questions with *was/were* by inverting the verb and subject.
Why **was the company** a success?
The company was a success because ...

⟩ page 27 Past simple and past continuous

5 Read the statements about another Chinese company. Write questions for statements (1–6).

1 Midea started up in 1968.
When did Midea start up?
2 It made plastic tops for bottles.
What *did the do* ?
3 The founder only had 5,000 renmimbi at the time.
How much *money the founder have* ?
4 It employed just 28 people at first.
How many *employees did employed have* ?
5 Their first electrical products were fans.
What *kind of product did they produce* ?
6 They acquired an air conditioning company in 1998.
When *did they acquire an air condo company?*

Growing pains

Listening

1 (1) 05 You will hear an interview with a business consultant about a chain of sandwich bars called *Spectrum*. Listen to the first part of the interview and choose the correct newspaper headline (A–C).

Ⓐ SANDWICH BAR CHAIN FACES COLLAPSE

B **RECORD PROFITS AT SPECTRUM**

C **SANDWICH BAR CHAIN OPENS NEW BRANCH**

> **Task tip**
>
> In a business situation, you often don't have time to look up all the words you don't know. If you are not sure of your answer to Exercise 1, choose one word in the headlines to look up in your dictionary before you listen.

2 Work with a partner and think of some possible reasons for the current situation at Spectrum. Work with another pair. Did you think of the same reasons?

3 (1) 06 Now listen to the whole interview and decide if the following statements (1–6) are true or false. Write T or F.

1 Profits at Spectrum began to fall one year ago. F
2 Spectrum needs to find a buyer quickly. T
3 One of their main selling points was their cheap prices. F
4 Spectrum have a total of twenty branches. F
5 They tried to enter a very competitive market. T
6 They never used frozen ingredients in their products. F

4 (1) 07 Listen to the last part of the interview again and complete Adrian's advice.

1 It's best for a company to expand *slowly and carefully*.
2 Don't try to enter a new market without doing *proper Mkt research*
3 Don't open a new branch before the existing ones are *profitable*.
4 Remember what makes your company *what make your company special*

5 Which of Adrian's advice in Exercise 4 do you think is the most important?

Speaking

1 Work in pairs. You are going to read about a food company called Baja Fresh.

Student A: look at the information below.
Student B: look at the information on page 118.

Ask your partner questions in the past simple, using the question words in brackets, to complete the missing information.

BAJA FRESH   *BAJA FRESH.*

Student A

Baja Fresh is a chain of restaurants which serves fresh food with a Mexican theme. The company began in 1990 when a husband and wife team opened the first restaurant in .... (*where?*). They paid for it by taking out a mortgage on their house.

Their selling point was .... (*what?*) and they refused to use microwaves and freezers in their kitchens. The restaurant was very successful and they gradually opened more. In 1997, they had .... outlets (*how many?*).

Then in 2002 Wendy's, the international fast food restaurant, acquired Baja Fresh. They paid .... (*how much?*) for it. They wanted to make Baja Fresh into a big international chain but unfortunately this didn't work out. They tried to expand very quickly but they didn't pay enough attention to the original business model. .... (*when?*) sales began to decline and in 2004, they fell by 6.4 %. Faced with these figures, in .... (*when?*) Wendy's sold Baja Fresh for just $31 million to a group of private investors.

After the sale, Baja Fresh .... (*what?*) and tried to recreate the original brand. Now the restaurant is doing well again. In 2010, they opened a new branch in .... (*where?*) and in 2011, David Kim, the Chief Executive, appeared on the TV programme Undercover Boss.

2 What is the main message of this case study? Discuss with a partner and choose the best sentence: A, B or C.

A Private investors often understand their companies better than big corporations.
Ⓑ It's more important to look after your brand than to expand quickly.
C Large international companies have different priorities from smaller, local ones.

Business ideas

Reading

1   Read the article about how to come up with good business ideas. Skim it quickly to get a general idea of the content.

HOW TO FIND A GREAT IDEA

Every successful business starts with a good idea. But how can you think of one? We can all learn to think more creatively. Here are three tips to increase the chance of coming up with that great money-making idea.

1   .... The frozen food industry began when its founder, Clarence Birdseye, was working on a government project in the Arctic. One day he went fishing with some Inuits. He noticed that when they pulled a fish out of the water, it froze almost immediately. Later, when the time came to eat the fish, he also noticed it tasted almost the same as a fresh one. His observations led to the invention of the process for freezing food, and in time to the whole Birds Eye frozen food empire.

2   .... The most famous example of this is the story of Archimedes, the ancient Greek mathematician who needed to find out whether the king's crown was pure gold or not. The answer came to him while he was taking a bath. Many successful business people will also tell you that their best idea came to them as they were doing something unrelated to their work. So, if you are stuck on a problem, leave it and do something completely different. Your unconscious mind will continue to search for a solution and eventually you may get that flash of insight.

3   .... Think about successful ideas and how you could improve them or combine them with something else. For example, a fax machine was a telephone line combined with a photocopier, and YouTube a combination of a website and videos.

2   Match each paragraph in the text to the correct advice.

A   Most good ideas develop out of one or more things that existed before.   **3**

B   Good ideas often come from looking carefully at the world around you.   **1**

C   The best ideas often come to people when they are not expecting it.   **2**

3   Find words and phrases with the following meanings in the article.

1   pieces of advice ...... *tips* ......
2   someone who starts a business ..... *founder* .....
3   a group of businesses controlled by one person or organisation ..... *corporation /empire* .....
4   unable to progress with ..... *stuck* .....
5   join to something else ..... *combine* .....

Grammar workshop 2

Past continuous

The text contains verbs in the past simple tense and the **past continuous**. (*was/were + -ing* form)

1   Match the past simple and past continuous rules with the correct example from the text, A, B or C.

1   We use the past simple when one event happened after another in the past.

2   We use the past simple and past continuous together to show an action that happened in the middle of another activity.

3   We use the past continuous to describe the background and the past simple for the events of a story.

A   The answer came to him while he was taking a bath.   **2**

B   When they pulled a fish out of the water, it froze almost immediately.   **1**

C   He was working on a government project in the Arctic. One day he went fishing with some Inuits.   **3**

2   We can use words like *as* to join an action in the past simple with an action in the past continuous. Find two similar words in sentences A–C.

3   Read the story and put the verbs in brackets in the correct form, past simple or past continuous.

ANNA DICKSON: MUMMY MITTS

Anna Dickson **1** _came_ (come) up with the idea of Mummy Mitts while she **2** _pushing_ (push) her daughter's pram. It was a cold day and so she **3** _wearing_ (wear) gloves. Every time her mobile **4** _rang_ (ring) or she **5** _needed_ (need) to attend to her daughter, she **6** _had_ (have) to take off the gloves and find somewhere to put them. Then the idea **7** _hit_ (hit) her. Why not attach the gloves to the handle of the pram? That was the beginning of Mummy Mitts. She **8** _launched_ (launch) the product in 2006 and now they are on sale across Europe.

❯ page 27 Past simple and past continuous

Corporate culture

Getting started

What makes a company a good place to work?
Number the following in order of importance for you
(1 = the most important).

- 2 a good relationship with your boss
- 4 friendly colleagues
- 5 a variety of different things to do
- a fixed routine
- 1 good opportunities for promotion
- 3 flexible hours

Compare your list with a partner. Try to agree on the
three most important things.

Company culture

Reading

1 Read the following dictionary definition.

> **Company culture** *n*. the values, beliefs and traditions
> in a company which influence the behaviour of its
> staff. It is important for jobseekers to know about
> the culture of an organisation before accepting a
> job.

2 What kind of company culture is best for you?
Do the quiz to find out. Circle A for *agree* or D for
disagree.

What kind of company culture would suit you?

SECTION A

1 I like taking time to have a chat with colleagues even
   if this means spending more time at work. Ⓐ/D

2 It's nice when people at work celebrate birthdays or
   special occasions. Ⓐ/D

3 I prefer people to fix a time to meet me rather than
   come to my office or my desk at any time. A/Ⓓ

4 I don't like working in an open space with everyone's
   desk in the same area. I work better in an office of
   my own. Ⓐ/D

5 I like to put photos and personal objects in my
   workplace. Ⓐ/D

SECTION B

6 If I disagree with my boss, I should be able to tell
   him/her. Ⓐ/D

7 I prefer to receive a formal report about my work,
   not just casual comments. A/Ⓓ

8 When my boss gives me something to do, I like to
   get detailed instructions that I can follow. A/Ⓓ

9 It's important for me to feel I am involved in the
   decision-making process at work. Ⓐ/D

10 A company should have standard procedures and
   policies that everyone must follow, not ones which
   change with people's situations or personalities.
   Ⓐ/D

SECTION C

11 A company must keep up with the times. Ⓐ/D

12 I need to take on challenges to make my job
   interesting. Ⓐ/D

13 When planning a strategy, it is useful to look at what
   has worked well in the past. Ⓐ/D

14 A company should be proud of its traditions Ⓐ/D

15 Finally, which of these proverbs do you prefer?
   a Better safe than sorry
   ⓑ Nothing ventured, nothing gained

---

3 Add up your scores for sections A, B and C.

SCORES

Section A

1 A=1 D=0	**4** A=0 D=1
2 A=1 D=0	**5** A=1 D=0
3 A=0 D=1	

Questions 1–5 are about your relationship with colleagues. A score of higher than 2 suggests that you like to work for a company where employees are friends and can talk about personal matters. A score of 2 or less means that you prefer to keep your work life separate from your personal life.

Section B

6 A=1 D=0	**9** A=1 D=0
7 A=0 D=1	**10** A=0 D=1
8 A=0 D=1	

Questions 6 to 10 are about your relationship with your managers. A score of higher than 2 suggests you like to work in a company where roles between managers and staff are flexible. A score of 2 or less means that you like to work in a company where people have clearly defined roles and there is more distance between staff and managers.

Section C

11 A=1 D=0	**14** A=0 D=1
12 A=1 D=0	**15** a=0 b=1
13 A=0 D=1	

Questions 11 to 15 are about your attitude to tradition. A score of higher than 2 means you like to work in a company which values new ideas and takes serious risks. A score of 2 or less means you prefer the security of a company with strong traditions.

4 Compare your scores with a partner to see if you would like to work in the same sort of organisation.

Vocabulary

When recording vocabulary it is useful to record words which are often used together. These are called *collocations.* Usually the words are from different parts of speech.

verb–noun collocations like these are very useful.
run a business   launch a product

1 Look at the questions in the corporate culture quiz again. Find verb–noun collocations with these meanings.

1 talk informally _have a chat_
2 make an appointment _fix a time_
3 change things to be more modern _keep up with the times_
4 agree to do something difficult _take on challenges_
5 decide the way to do something in the future _planning a strategy_

There are other types of collocations like these:

adjective–noun
We offer a ***wide range*** of services.
This seems an ***effective solution***.

noun–verb
Sales increase in the summer.
The ***market is expanding*** quickly.

verb–adverb
They have ***invested heavily*** in new technology.
I have to ***work closely*** with my colleagues.

2 Find adjective–noun collocations in the quiz with these meanings.

1 the normal ways of doing something _standard procedures_
2 *(in the scores analysis)* big danger _takes serious risks_

It can also be useful to record the verbs that often go before adjective–noun collocations, for example, the collocation **wide range** is often preceded by the verbs **offer** or **provide**.

What verbs would commonly come before the two adjective–noun collocations you found for questions 1 and 2 above? Look back to the quiz to find out.

3 Which words and expressions in the box can form collocations with the verbs below? You can use some of the words and expressions more than once.

> a meeting   your needs   a good relationship
> prices   the risk   a deadline   a system
> a business   costs   your confidence

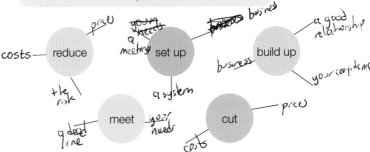

4 Read the following company profiles from a networking site for professionals, and circle the correct words. Use the vocabulary information and the collocations in Exercise 3 to help you.

Geniolink provides software and IT support for small businesses. We specialise in **1** *meeting*/ *touching* the needs of customers in local markets. We work **2** *tightly*/ *closely* with each of our clients to **3** *build up*/ *set up* good relationships, look at how technology can provide **4** *capable*/ *effective* solutions to their problems and help them to **5** *take on*/ *keep up* new challenges. Communicating with us is easy. We provide our clients with just one number to call for all their IT needs, so they can **6** *run*/ *make* their businesses while our local experts manage the systems.

IV Software is a global technology company which deals with clients in over 150 countries. We offer a **7** *tall*/ *wide* range of technology and consulting services and each year we invest **8** *heavily*/ *deeply* in research and development. We aim to bring benefits to all the countries we work in. With our cutting edge technology, we promote growth, encourage investment and **9** *reduce*/ *cut* risks. Our work includes helping governments to **10** *build up*/ *set up* systems which will increase the availability of clean water and improve the health and safety of populations. We hope to make the world a better place for everyone.

5 Look at the profiles again and choose three more useful collocations to record in your vocabulary notes.

6 ⊙ Business English students often confuse collocations with *make*, *do* and *have*. Choose the correct collocation with *make*, *do* or *have* in the following sentences.

1 For my visit, please *do*/ *make*/ *have* a reservation at the Station Hotel.
2 You need to *make*/ *do*/ *have* all the arrangements as soon as possible.
3 I am looking forward to *making*/ *doing*/ *having* business with you.
4 I want to *do*/ *make*/ *have* a meeting with all staff.
5 Our employee *did*/ *made*/ *had* a mistake with the sending date.
6 Could you come and *make*/ *do*/ *have* a product demonstration in our office?
7 I need to *make*/ *do*/ *have* changes to the product.

7 Write three questions using the *make*/*do*/*have* collocations above. Then ask and answer the questions in pairs.

When did you last make a hotel reservation?
Last month when I went to New York.

Describing changes

Listening

1 🔘 **1 08** A company's culture often changes over the years. Listen to a telephone conversation in which one person is asking another about the company culture at his place of work. In which order do they talk about the following things?

- possibilities for promotion
- staff benefits
- the company culture

2 **1 08** Listen to the conversation again. Make notes on what Adam says about:

1 the company when he joined
2 the company now

3 Compare your notes with a partner. Did you write down the same points?

4 Adam says the change in the company happened after a merger. What other events do you think could change the culture of a company? Discuss your ideas with your partner.

Writing

1 You are the staff representative in a company. The management are proposing some changes to your working hours. You decide to call a meeting with staff to discuss the changes with them. Plan an email to all staff:

- saying what the changes to the working hours will involve
- giving the time and day of the meeting
- explaining why the meeting is important

2 Match the sentence beginnings with the possible continuations on the next page.

1	The management are planning to make
2	The management want to introduce
3	I would like to set up
4	Could we have
5	I think we need to

a   let them know our opinions …
b   a meeting …
c   make our feelings clear …
d   some changes …

3   Now choose three of the sentences to complete and put them in the right order to create your email. Write 30–40 words.

Asking for information

Speaking

1   Look at the list of questions below. Find five pairs of questions which have the same meaning and write them next to each other in the table below. You will be left with four questions which do not form a pair.

~~What's the name of your company?~~
What's your job?
What are you studying?
What do you hope to do in the future?
What do you enjoy about your job/studies?
What time do you start and finish work?
Do you do many different things in your work/studies?

Do you travel much in your job?
What exactly do you do?
What are your plans for the future?
What are your working hours?
~~Who do you work for?~~
What does your job involve?
What do you do?

Question A	Question B
What's the name of your company?	Who do you work for?

2   Work in pairs. Choose three of the questions from Exercise 1 to ask your partner.
When your partner answers, ask another question of your own.

Student A: What are your plans for the future?
Student B: I want to work for my father's company.
Student A: Oh. Where is that based?

3   Work in a different pair. Read through the list of questions (1–6) and the list of reasons (a–f). Take it in turns to ask and answer questions. When answering, choose a reason from the box and add either another reason or more detail of your own.

• Is it important for a company to:
   1   offer flexible hours? ....c....
   2   give employees their own workspace? ....
   3   provide laptops for their employees? ....
   4   offer training to their employees? ....

5   have a workforce with different types of people? ....
6   have rules about what their employees can wear? ....

a   this is part of the company's image
b   different people can bring different ideas
c   some staff have family commitments
d   staff need a place to leave unfinished work
e   staff need to feel they can develop
f   staff can work when they are travelling

Student A: Is it important for a company to offer flexible hours?
Student B: Yes, because some staff have family commitments. It can be a good thing for working parents who need to organise childcare.

Grammar workshop 1

Units 1–4

Present simple and present continuous

1 **Complete the email by putting the verbs in brackets in the correct form, either present simple or present continuous.**

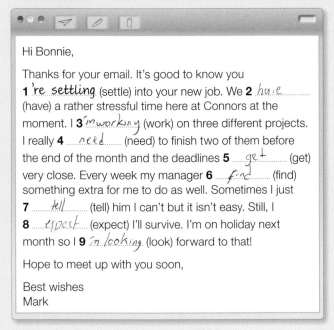

Hi Bonnie,

Thanks for your email. It's good to know you
1 're settling (settle) into your new job. We **2** have
(have) a rather stressful time here at Connors at the
moment. I **3** 'm working (work) on three different projects.
I really **4** need (need) to finish two of them before
the end of the month and the deadlines **5** get (get)
very close. Every week my manager **6** find (find)
something extra for me to do as well. Sometimes I just
7 tell (tell) him I can't but it isn't easy. Still, I
8 expect (expect) I'll survive. I'm on holiday next
month so I **9** 'm looking (look) forward to that!

Hope to meet up with you soon,

Best wishes
Mark

- Usually the verb **have** is a state verb.
  *Our company **has** (= possesses) three offices in Scotland (NOT 'is having').*
  (In an informal style, we can also use *have/has got* in this case.)
- In expressions where it does not mean 'possess', we can use it in the continuous.
  *The manager **is having** lunch at the moment.*

---

2 ⊙ **Business English students sometimes confuse these two uses. Choose the correct form of *have* in the following sentences.**

1 'Where are your colleagues?' 'They *have /* ~~are having~~ a drink in the bar.'
2 We ~~have~~/ *are having* a number of products which might interest you.

3 You can't come in now because the department *have /* ~~are having~~ a meeting.
4 We ~~have~~/ *are having* a really good new designer in our department.
5 We ~~have~~/ *are having* a big meeting room with an electronic whiteboard and computer.
6 'Why is the training room empty?' 'The team *all have /* ~~are all having~~ coffee in the canteen.'
7 I can't do that today because I ~~have~~ */ am having* too much other work to do.
8 My colleague *has /* ~~is having~~ a really interesting time at the trade fair.

Position of time phrases

- Short time adverbs of frequency like *sometimes* usually go after the verb *to be* but before another main verb.
  *We **always** meet at 9 o'clock.*
  *He is **sometimes** late.*
- Frequency expressions like *every day* usually go at the end of the phrase.
  *We speak on the phone **every day**.*
  *The manager is having lunch **at the moment**.*

Put the words in brackets in the correct position in these sentences.

1 I check my emails from home. (sometimes)
  I sometimes check my emails from home.
2 She is in the office on Mondays. (never)
3 They promote people from within the company. (often)
4 We have a shareholders meeting. (twice a year)
5 My PA doesn't deal with matters like this. (usually)
6 He comes to the board meeting. (every week)
7 They use artificial flavourings in their products. (never)
8 Those suppliers aren't very reliable. (always)
9 The hotel is fully booked in July. (often)
10 We are reviewing a number of our policies. (currently)

Past simple and past continuous

1 Read the text and then write questions in the past simple for the given answers.

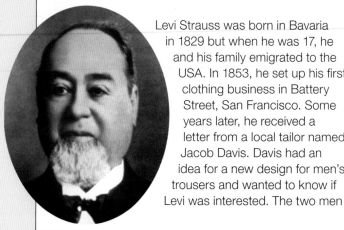

Levi Strauss was born in Bavaria in 1829 but when he was 17, he and his family emigrated to the USA. In 1853, he set up his first clothing business in Battery Street, San Francisco. Some years later, he received a letter from a local tailor named Jacob Davis. Davis had an idea for a new design for men's trousers and wanted to know if Levi was interested. The two men went into partnership and production began in 1873. At that time the trousers were called 'overalls'. Later, in 1960, they stopped using this name and started calling the trousers 'jeans' instead.

The company always ran strong advertising campaigns for their products. At first they used posters and billboards, but later advertised on the radio and made their first TV commercial in 1966. Their strong advertising is probably one reason why the company grew so rapidly.

1 When did Levi Strauss' family emigrate to the USA?
   When he was seventeen.
2 *where did he start the bsness*
   In Battery Street, San Francisco.
3 *When the prodction was started?*
   In 1873.
4 *When he changed the company name?*
   In 1960.
5 *When the 1st TV commersial was made*
   In 1966.
6 *why the company is so strong?*
   Probably because of their strong advertising.

2 Put the verbs in brackets in the correct form, either past simple or past continuous. Use each tense once in each sentence.

1 I ___was taking___ (take) out my phone when your message ___came___ (come) through.
2 When I ___went___ (go) into the boardroom, the CEO ___was sitting___ (sit) at the head of the table.
3 They ___were wearing___ (wear) visitors badges so I ___knew___ (know) they didn't work there.
4 He ___was living___ (live) in the USA when he ___met___ (meet) his business partner.
5 I ___was writing___ (write) an email to our suppliers when the computer screen ___freezed___ (freeze).
6 I ___didn't send___ (not send) the document because the scanner ___didn't work___ (not work).

3 ☺ Business English students sometimes try to use the past continuous too much instead of the past simple. Correct the following sentences by replacing the past continuous with the past simple. TWO of the sentences are correct.

1 I was on holiday for three weeks and I ~~was just coming~~ back yesterday. *just came*
2 I am writing with regard to your advertisement which I ~~was reading~~ in *Business Chronicle*. *read*
3 The refreshments arrived while he was giving the presentation.
4 I couldn't print the document because the printer ~~was falling~~ *fell* on the floor.
5 They ~~were locking~~ *locked* up when the manager phoned to say she was still in the building.
6 I ~~was working~~ *worked* in the same department for six years so after that I was ready for a change.

4 ☺ Business English students sometimes spell -ing forms and past tenses wrongly. Correct the following wrong spellings made by candidates in Cambridge business exams. TWO of the sentences are correct.

1 He is ~~studing~~ business administration at Harvard. *studying*
2 I am writting to confirm the conference room booking.
3 We stopped making that model two years ago.
4 Profits droped in the second half of the year.
5 Two new clients are comming this afternoon.
6 You can get the information by refering to the website.
7 Our company is ~~planing~~ *planning* to make a video.
8 They delivered the order this morning.

Describing equipment

Getting started

Label the parts of the objects (1–11) with the correct words from the box (a–k), using your dictionary if necessary.

a buttons
b blade
c cable/lead
d cover
e lens
f touch screen
g stand/base
h bulb
i switch
j plug
k headphones

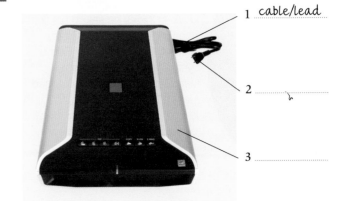

1 cable/lead
2 *h*
3

4
5 tuch screen
6 bulb
7 base
8 button / switnc
9 buttons
10 lens
11 blade

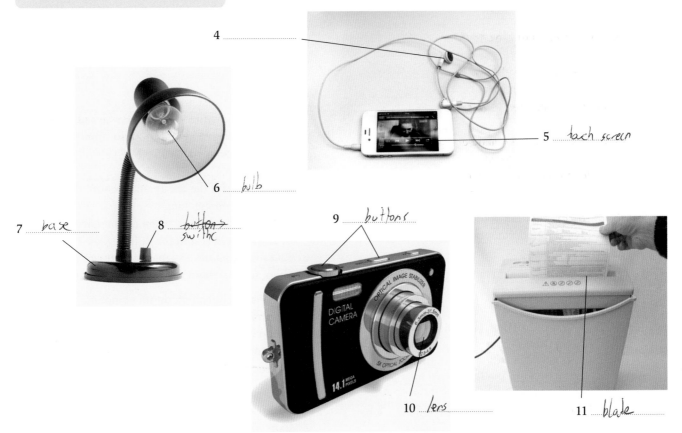

Describing objects

Vocabulary

1 Think of the desk you use in your workplace or at home. What objects are on it at the moment? Make a list. Compare your list with a partner. Do you have anything personal on your desk like photos?

2 Look at the objects (a–h) in the box and match each one with its correct description (1–8).

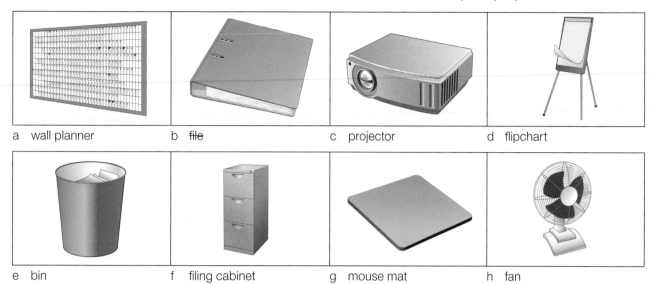

| a | wall planner | b | ~~file~~ | c | projector | d | flipchart |

| e | bin | f | filing cabinet | g | mouse mat | h | fan |

1 It's usually made up of three rectangular pieces of cardboard and inside there are two steel rings. You use it to keep documents in. __b__

2 It's a large rectangular piece of paper which you put on the wall. You use it to record your appointments and deadlines. __a__

3 It's made up of a stand at the bottom and some blades at the top. You use it to keep the office cool. __h__

4 It's a container usually made of plastic. You put some types of rubbish in it. __e__

5 It's made of plastic, or glass and metal and it works by electricity. It makes an image appear on a screen by using light through a lens. __c__

6 It's a rectangular piece of furniture with two or three drawers. You use it to keep documents in. __f__

7 It's made up of a piece of plastic on a stand. You use it to hold large pieces of paper when you give a talk. __d__

8 It can be rectangular, square or circular. The base is made of rubber. You use it when you work on the computer. __g__

3 Read the descriptions again and write six more materials and three shape adjectives in the table.

Materials	Shape adjectives
cardboard	

4 Add four materials and four shape adjectives to the table. Use a dictionary if necessary. Then compare your answers with a partner.

Dimensions

Listening

1 **(1) 09** Listen to a conversation between people who are choosing display equipment for their shop. Do they agree about what to buy?

2 Unscramble the letters in the box to make words to complete the questions in column B.

phetd   nethgl   tehihg   itdhw   ~~ezsi~~

A	B
How + *adjective* + is it?	What's the + *noun*?
How big is it?	= What's the _size_ ?
How wide is it	= What's the 1 _width_ ?
How deep is it?	= What's the 2 _p_ ?
How high is it?	= What's the 3 _highet_ ?
How long is it?	= What's the 4 _lenght_ ?

We use *long* and *wide* for two-dimensional areas like the space in a room.

We usually use *wide*, *high* (from top to bottom) and *deep* (from front to back) for three-dimensional objects.

Notice the word order in the answer:
How long is it?
It's three metres long (NOT: ~~It's long three metres.~~)

3 (1 09) Listen again and label the equipment with the correct measurements.

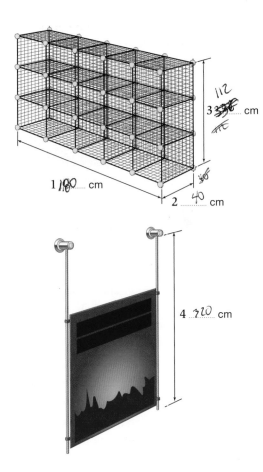

3 3~~36~~ 112 cm
1 1~~00~~ 80 cm
2 40 cm
4 2~~10~~ cm

4 (1 10) You will hear another conversation about an order for some storage boxes. Listen and fill in the missing information.

Product: tool storage box
1 Customer's name: Routledge
2 Size: 480 mm × 800 mm × 500 mm
Model number: JNV90
3 Colour: Black
4 Price: 96 → 340
5 Delivery: week beginning 19th July

Speaking

1 If you don't know the English word for something you need, you can describe it. There are several ways you can do this.

1 Describe the parts of the object:
   It has/ it's made up of a small screen and several buttons.
2 Describe the shape and material:
   It's rectangular. It's made of plastic and metal.
3 Describe the dimensions:
   It's quite small, about 10 cm long and 4 cm wide.
4 Describe what you use it for:
   You use it to call people or send messages.

2 Work in pairs. What is the object described above? Take it in turns to choose an office object or a tool that is used in your company. Describe it to your partner without naming it or saying what you use it for. Your partner must guess what it is.

Problems with equipment

Vocabulary

Match the pictures (a–e) with the problems below (1–5).

1 The system keeps crashing.
2 The paper keeps running out.
3 The battery needs charging.
4 The paper keeps jamming.
5 The toner needs changing.

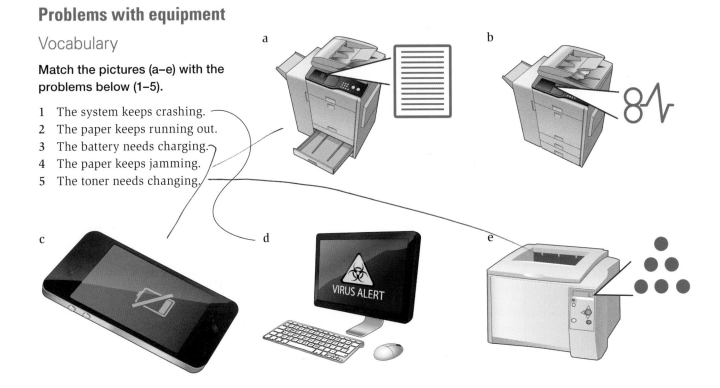

Reading

At work, you sometimes have to use two texts to find different pieces of information so that you can put them together in another document, like a form or a report. The following exercise gives you practice in extracting this sort of key information.

1 Read the headings in the repairs request form below. Then answer the following question.

In which space(s) would you expect to write:
a   the name of an object?   b   a place?
c   the name of a person?

REPAIRS REQUEST FORM

For the attention of   **1** (Department) _technical support_
                        2 (Name) ....

Equipment: **3** ....
Location: **4** ....
Problem: **5** ....
Noted by: **6** ....
Date noted: **7** ....

2 Now read the two emails below and complete the repairs request form.

To: Maria Hawkins
From: Richard Parker
Sent: 10 April
Subject: Training session

Dear Maria

I'm afraid my training session today was a bit of a disaster. We were moved from seminar room 1 to seminar room 2 because of the last-minute boardroom meeting but space was a real problem. There were three desks missing. However, the worst thing was the PowerPoint presentation as the projector bulb needs changing. Who should I report this to?

Richard

INBOX   File | Edit | View | Favourites | Tools | Actions | Help   ☒

To: Richard Parker
From: Maria Hawkins
Sent: 11 April
Subject: Re: training session

Dear Richard,

Sorry about that! Broken equipment should be reported on a repairs request form so please could you fill one in and give it to technical support? Robert Beale, the equipment technician is away, but you can give it to Murat Yuzgun who's helping out at the moment. I know the room is smaller but it is supposed to have the same number of desks so I don't know why you didn't have enough. Did you find three spare desks from anywhere?

Hope this helps
Maria

The gizmo game

Listening

1 You can use the word *gizmo* to describe a gadget whose name you cannot remember. Work with a partner. Look at the object below and discuss what you think it is used for.

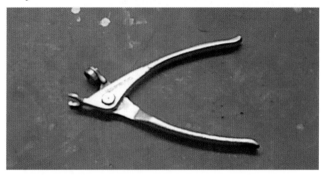

2 Complete the description of the object using the words in the box. Check your answers in pairs.

handles   pliers   ring   round   scissors   ~~screw~~

This tool is made up of two pieces of metal, joined in the middle with a **1** _screw_ or rivet, rather like a pair of **2** _scissors_ or **3** _pliers_ . I imagine they form **4** _handles_ that you can hold in your two hands. At the top of one of the pieces, there is a small semicircular piece of metal like a **5** _ring_ with a piece missing. At the top of the other piece, there is another **6** _round_ solid piece of metal.

3 The following verbs describe actions that you might do with different tools. Match the verbs (1–6) with the definitions (a–f).

1   assemble   a   attach something so it cannot move
2   dismantle   b   put the parts of something together
3   fit   c   take something to pieces
4   fasten   d   change something slightly
5   adjust   e   take something away
6   remove   f   put something into a small place designed for it

4 ①11 **Listen to Speakers 1–3 describe what the tool above is used for. One speaker is telling the truth about its use and the other two are lying. Note down the use each speaker gives for the tool. When you have completed your notes, compare your answers with a partner.**

Women ✓
Man ✗
Women2 ✗

5 ①11 **Listen to the recording again and write down more details about what each speaker says. Work with your partner and decide which speaker is telling the truth. Check your answer with your teacher.**

Processes and procedures

Getting started

1 Complete the two definitions by choosing the correct word:

2 Complete the diagrams with the past participles in the box below.

> The ¹*life cycle / lifespan* of a product refers to the different stages that it goes through, from when it is produced to when it is thrown away, or from when it is put on the market by a company to when it is withdrawn. The ²*life cycle / lifespan* of a product is the average length of time that it can be used.

assembled
cut
dismantled
distributed
~~printed~~
purchased
put
recycled
removed
shredded
thrown away

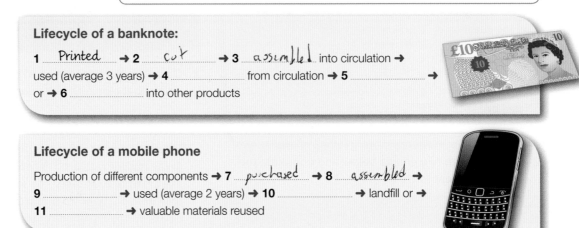

Lifecycle of a banknote:

1 _Printed_ → 2 _cut_ → 3 _assembled_ into circulation → used (average 3 years) → 4 _____ from circulation → 5 _____ → or → 6 _____ into other products

Lifecycle of a mobile phone

Production of different components → 7 _purchased_ → 8 _assembled_ → 9 _____ → used (average 2 years) → 10 _____ → landfill or → 11 _____ → valuable materials reused

3 Look at the diagrams and decide if the following are true (T) or false (F).

1 Old banknotes are sometimes recycled into other products. _T_
2 The average lifespan of a banknote is 2 years. _F_
3 At the end of its life cycle, the materials from mobile phones are always recycled. _F_
4 After banknotes are removed from circulation, they are shredded. _T_

Grammar workshop

The passive

Company background
Karhu is a Finnish brand of sports equipment. The brand began in 1916 and appeared on their skis. Now it is licensed to a number of different manufacturers, but Karhu skis are still produced by the original company. The word 'Karhu' is Finnish for 'bear' and the picture of a bear is used as a logo on many of their products.

KARHU®

1 Read the information about Karhu in the box above and underline all the verbs.

2 Three of the verbs are written in the passive. Compare the passive sentences in bold with the active sentences with the same meaning in the table below. For each sentence (1–4) write S next to the subject, O next to the object and V next to the verb. Not all sentences require an object.

Note: in the passive sentences, the object of the active sentence becomes the subject.

1 The original company _S_	still produces _V_	Karhu skis. _O_	
2 Karhu skis ____	**are still produced** ____	**by the original company** ____	**on their**
3 They ____	use ____	the picture of a bear ____	**products.**
4 The picture of a bear ____	**is used** ____		

3   Look at Sentences 2 and 4 in the table again and complete the rules below.

1   You form the passive with _to be_ + _past participle_

2   When you use the passive, what or who does the action is usually not very important. When you do want to say what or who does the action, you use the preposition ....

4   Change these active sentences into passive sentences.

1   They test each ski in the factory.
    Each ski _are tested_ in the factory.
2   People use Karhu skis in many different countries.
    Karhu skis _are used_ in many different countries.
3   They take new products to the mountains for testing.
    New products _are taken_ to the mountains for testing.

5   Complete this paragraph with more information about Karhu by putting the verbs in brackets in the passive. Some of the verbs are irregular.

> Karhu skis 1 _are produced_ (produce) in their factory in Kitee, Finland, and also in Russia. The company is proud of the quality of their products. The skis 2 _are built_ (build) by many different technicians and each one 3 _is tested_ (test) in the factory. Over 200,000 pairs of Karhu skis 4 _are sold_ (sell) in Finland each year and they 5 _are exported_ (export) to a number of other countries. They 6 _are bought_ (buy) by many champion skiers.

6   ⊘ Business English students sometimes have problems with the correct forms of past participles. Correct the mistakes made by candidates of Cambridge business exams in the following sentences. ONE of the sentences has no mistake.

1   The design is ~~choosen~~ by the marketing team.
    chosen
2   Staff do not feel that they are ~~payed~~ _paid_ enough.
3   Meetings are always ~~hold~~ _held_ in the production department.
4   Invoices are always ~~send~~ _sent_ with the order.
5   Protective gloves are always worn in the workshop. ✓ _correct_
6   Some of the money is ~~spend~~ _spent_ on staff travel.

Speaking

1   Work in pairs.

Student A: look at the sentences below.
Student B: look at the sentences on page 118.

One in every three sentences is false. Read the sentences to each other and in each case try to identify the one which is not true, and say why.

Example: A: _Hyundai cars are made in South Korea._
             They are sold in over 150 different
             countries.
             They are used by a lot of Formula One
             drivers.
          B: _No. I don't think they're used by Formula_
             One drivers, because …

> **Student A**
>
> **Lamborghini:**
> Lamborghini cars are produced in Italy.
> They are only sold in Europe. (**FALSE**: They are sold all over the world.)
> They are aimed at the top end of the market.
>
> **Gouda cheese:**
> Gouda cheese is made in Switzerland. (**FALSE**: It is made in the Netherlands.)
> It is made from cow's milk.
> It is exported all over Europe.

2   Choose a product that you know and write three sentences for each using the passive. One of the sentences must be false. Then work in pairs and read the sentences to each other. Your partner must identify the false sentence.

❯ page 44 Passive forms

Chanel No. 5

Vocabulary

The flow chart below shows the process used to extract the scent from flowers used to make Chanel No. 5.

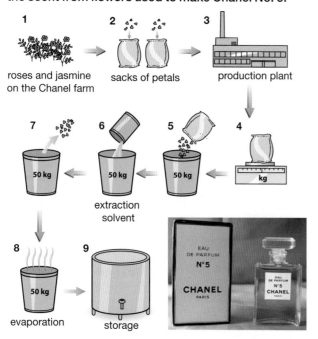

1 roses and jasmine on the Chanel farm

2 sacks of petals

3 production plant

7 50 kg

6 50 kg

5 50 kg

4 kg

extraction solvent

8 50 kg evaporation

9 storage

EAU DE PARFUM N°5 CHANEL PARIS

N°5 CHANEL PARIS

Study the flow chart and then complete the description with the verbs in the box in the passive form.

Chanel No. 5 is the world's best-selling perfume. Its main ingredients are roses, jasmine and musk. On the Chanel farm, the flowers **1** _are picked_ and the petals **2** _are put_ into sacks. Then, within half an hour, they **3** _transport_ to the production plant. At the plant, the petals **4** _are add_ , and then they **5** _loa_ into 50 kg vats. Next, an extraction solvent **6** _evaporate_. The petals **7** .... three times in this solution.

Eventually, the flowers **8** .... from the vats and the remaining solvent **9** .... This leaves a solid material known as the 'concrete', which can be stored for several years until the perfume **10** ....

add   evaporate   load   pick   put   remove
require   transport   wash   weigh

Listening

1 **(1) 12** Listen to an interview with a Chanel employee describing the production process for Chanel No. 5. Close your book and make notes on the main points as you listen.

2 Work with a partner. Take it in turns to describe the production process, using your notes.

Outsourcing

Reading

1 Instead of *outsourcing* the production of their raw materials, Chanel have their own farm where they produce them. Work in pairs and discuss what you understand by *outsourcing*. Then read the definition to see if you were right.

> **Outsourcing** *n.* handing over a business process like accounting or a production process to another provider.

2 Work with a partner. Try to think of two advantages and two disadvantages of outsourcing a production process.

3 You are going to read an article about a clothing company based in Australia. Skim the article and write the paragraph numbers in the boxes below to show where you read about the following.

a   outsourcing production within Sydney | 4 |
b   in-house production | 2 |
c   outsourcing production to companies overseas | |

Waratah

1 Ruth and Eileen Miller grew up in a family where their mother regularly made clothes for herself and her two daughters. The two girls were able to design and make their own outfits by the time they were teenagers. Now they run 'Waratah', a clothing company based in Sydney.

2 The Waratah label started to establish itself in the mid-1990s. At first, the Miller sisters used a number of outside manufacturers in Sydney to produce their clothes. After a few years, however, they decided to bring the production in-house. 'We found the outside suppliers very difficult to manage' says Eileen. 'They were often unreliable and we always had problems getting clothes to our customers on time. We needed more control so we decided to do the manufacturing ourselves.'

3 In fact the switch to in-house production led to its own set of problems. It was hard to find new staff and labour costs were rising. Because of this, the Miller sisters found it impossible to raise productivity beyond a certain level.

4 After five years of in-house production, the sisters decided to adopt a different system and closed down the manufacturing section of the business. Now, designing and making up samples takes place in Sydney, but the company outsources all of its production to other countries. At first they used manufacturers in India but now they also outsource to China where they are developing new production methods. 'We still do all the main work in Sydney,' says Eileen, 'but moving the production abroad has brought down our staff costs. It can be complicated but the quality is excellent.'

4 Read the paragraphs in Exercise 3 in more detail and complete the table with the phrases from the box below. You do not need to use everything in the box.

Disadvantages of outsourcing	⌐ acess to new techniques
Disadvantages of in-house production	recruitment └ not meeting deadlines disagreements on staff
Advantages of outsourcing to companies abroad	low staff cost promotion brand

access to new techniques
difficulties with recruitment
disagreements between management and staff
promotion of the brand overseas
suppliers not meeting deadlines

high staff costs
low staff costs
poor quality sewing

Short texts

Reading

1 In texts like notices, newspaper headlines and short notes, people often don't include the verb *to be* in passive tenses as the message can be understood without it. In the texts below, the verb *to be* is missing. Add it in the correct form in each sentence.

1
PROTECTIVE CLOTHING KEPT IN STORE CUPBOARD.

2
Counterfeit banknotes believed to be in circulation

3
➜ candidates given first interview ➜ selection ➜ successful candidates interviewed again ➜

2 Match one of the sentences (1–6) to the texts (a–i). There are three texts you will not use.

1 Employees receive their travel expenses each month. __c__
2 The meeting will take place later than the original time. __i__
3 A bank is guilty of poor financial control. __f__
4 The goods will arrive late as a result of industrial action. __a__
5 You cannot enter if you don't have a security pass. __e__
6 The company can claim insurance if the goods do not arrive. __b__

a
John from Wilton's phoned. Goods held up because of transport strike.

b
Heard from suppliers. They confirmed goods insured against all forms of loss or damage.

c
Travel expenses paid on monthly basis. Please submit all expenses before 30 Nov.

d
ENTRANCE LOCKED AT 8 PM. AFTER THIS TIME, PLEASE CONTACT SECURITY.

e
Access only permitted on production of a valid pass.

f
Billions of dollars lost through corruption each year, says World Bank

g
AUDIT FAILURES FOUND AT HIGH STREET BANK

h
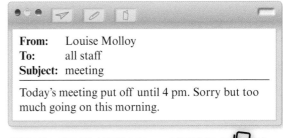
From: Louise Molloy
To: all staff
Subject: meeting

Today's meeting put off until 4 pm. Sorry but too much going on this morning.

i
From: Ahmed Sayed
To: Howard Wilson
Subject: Meeting

Notes from meeting attached. Talk later. A.

Writing

You see this notice in your place of work:

TRAINING FOR NEW CLIENT RECORD SYSTEM 9AM NEXT MONDAY. ALL STAFF EXPECTED TO ATTEND.

You cannot attend the training because you will not be in the office on that day. Write an email to your manager, Bettina. In your email:

- apologise for not attending
- explain why you will be out of the office
- suggest another way you could receive the training

Use the following structure. Write 30–40 words.

INBOX   File | Edit | View | Favourites | Tools | Actions | Help

Dear Bettina,
I (*apologise*) .... because (*explain why*) ....
Could .... (*make your suggestion*) ....
Yours,

Distribution and delivery

Getting started

1 Look at the photo. What kind of business do you think this person runs? Do you think this is a good way of making money?

2 You have decided to set up a courier business (a business which is paid to deliver documents or packages). Work in pairs and make a list of everything you think you need to start the business. Think about:

- equipment
- record keeping
- legal requirements

3 Now read the advice below from a business website. Is there anything in it you didn't think of?

Thinking of starting a courier business?

In these days of online shopping, there is an increased need for courier services. You can also set up a courier business with relatively little money. But in most towns and cities there is tough competition, so you **shouldn't** expect things to be easy at first.

- Firstly, of course, you will need a vehicle. This will probably be your biggest expense but you **don't have to** own it. Many courier businesses start by just leasing a car or van. Some also use motorbikes, but this will limit your customer base, because you **can't** carry large parcels on a bike.

- If you use your own car, check your insurance. You will probably find you **have to** pay more if you're using it for business purposes.

- You will also need a mobile phone so customers **can** contact you on the road. If possible, you **should** give a landline number as well because this makes the business seem more professional.

- Of course, you **must** provide customers with receipts and keep financial records, so you will also need access to a computer and the right computer software.

- You **must** also have enough money to cover your expenses, like petrol, until you start receiving your first payments.

Grammar workshop

Modal verbs of obligation

1 Look at the verbs in bold in the text and complete the following table.

Verb is used to say that	Example
1 an action is necessary (an obligation)	have to / must
2 an action is a good idea (advice)	should
3 an action is not a good idea (advice not to do something)	shouldn't
4 an action is possible	can
5 an action is not possible (because it is against the rules or for another reason)	can't
6 an action is not necessary (there is no obligation	→ don't have to

2 Using the examples in the table on page 36 to help you, complete these grammar notes about describing rules.

must and **1** have to	*mustn't* and *don't have to*	**5** _____
These have similar meanings.	These have different meanings.	This is used for an action which is not possible for you (because it is against the rules or for another reason).
Both refer to something which is necessary.	**Mustn't** is used about something which is wrong to do.	
You must switch off your phone in the board meeting.	*You* **3** _____ *smoke in the workshop.*	*We* **6** _____ *deliver the goods before Friday.*
You **2** _____ *switch off your phone in the board meeting.*	**Don't have to** means that something is **4** _____ necessary. You can do it if you want, but there is no rule.	
Have to is more common when talking about the law or company rules.	*You* **don't have to** *put a stamp on the letter. Postage is free.*	

3 Use a suitable verb from the table in Exercise 1 to complete the additional information below about running a courier business. More than one verb is sometimes possible.

1 Another advantage of using a van instead of a motorbike is that you _don't have to_ wear protective clothing in bad weather.

2 Any vehicle will do, but if possible you _should_ try to get one that looks good, because this will create a better impression.

3 Of course, as in all other businesses, you _must_ pay tax on your earnings.

✗ 4 You _shouldn't_ buy a Sat Nav if you just want to work in your own town, but it's probably essential for travelling from city to city.
   don't have to → don't need

5 It goes without saying that you _can't / mustn't_ employ anyone as a driver without checking they have a valid licence.

6 The best form of advertisement is word of mouth from satisfied clients, so you _should_ always be polite and friendly.

7 When you start making a profit, you _should_ think about investing in some new vehicles.

❯ **page 44** Modal verbs

4 Read these workplace signs and notices. Choose the sentence which correctly explains the meaning of each sign: A, B or C.

1 **NO** ADMITTANCE WITHOUT YOUR HELMET

A You can wear your helmet.
Ⓑ You must wear your helmet.
C You shouldn't wear your helmet.

2 **! PLEASE DO NOT DISTURB. MEETING IN PROGRESS.**

Ⓐ You mustn't interrupt the meeting.
Ⓑ You don't have to interrupt the meeting.
C You should interrupt the meeting.

3 **Delivery is FREE. There is no charge for postage and packing.**

A You mustn't pay delivery charges.
Ⓑ You don't have to pay delivery charges.
C You can't pay delivery charges.

4 **THIS IS A NO-SMOKING BUILDING**

A You can smoke in this building.
B You don't have to smoke in this building.
Ⓒ You can't smoke in this building.

5 **Cheques without a banker's card definitely not accepted.**

Ⓐ We can't accept cheques without a banker's card.
B We don't have to accept cheques without a banker's card.
C We can accept cheques without a banker's card.

Selling overseas

Reading

1 What do you need to think about if you want to sell a product abroad? Complete the diagram by putting the words and phrases from the box with the correct headings.

airfreight   customs   distributor
embassy   IP protection   insurance
label   lorry/truck   ~~packaging~~   patent
price   sales agent   ship

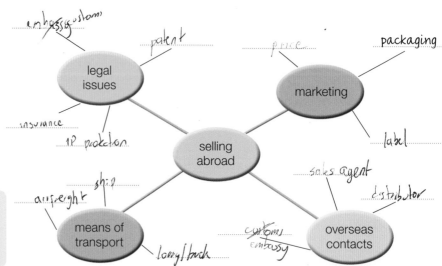

[Diagram — central node: "selling abroad" connecting to: "legal issues" (patent, insurance, IP protection, embassy/custom); "marketing" (price, packaging, label); "means of transport" (airfreight, ship, lorry/truck); "overseas contacts" (sales agent, distributor, customs, embassy)]

2 Skim the following text about selling overseas. In which order does it deal with the four areas on the diagram?

Thinking of selling your product abroad?

1 In today's global marketplace, selling your product overseas is not just something for big corporates. Many small businesses decide to target overseas markets too. But it still needs careful research and a number of key decisions to be made first.

2 First of all, you need to carry out research into your target market. You shouldn't assume that a product which sells well at home will sell well overseas. There may be no demand for it, or you may have to change it in some way. It may be that customers in your target country can't afford the prices you charge in the domestic market, so you will need to lower them. Or you may have to change the product in some way (for example, the packaging) to suit the local culture. At the very least, you will need to present the product in the language of the new country, although this can usually be done with a stick-on label in the new language at first.

3 You also have to decide how to organise your sales. You may be able to sell over the Internet or face to face at trade fairs, but in general, it is a good idea to look for a partner who understands the local market. This may be a sales agent who will sell the product for you, or a distributor who will buy your product and then sell it locally. Your embassy in the target country may help you identify possible clients and there are also a number of websites that contain directories of foreign buyers.

4 Another key decision is what mode of transport to use. Often you will need more than one; for example, you may need to send goods to a port by lorry and then overseas by ship. You need to have a written contract which says who is responsible for transport and insurance using 'Incoterms' (the international trade terms for sales). Usually you must take responsibility for your country's customs procedures, and your customers look after the customs procedures in their country. A lot of paperwork is needed so you should consider using a freight forwarding specialist because then you don't have to deal with it all yourself.

5 Intellectual property (IP) protection is another important issue. Patents and trademarks are only protected in their country of origin so you will have to get trademark protection in the country where you want to sell.

3 In which paragraph of the text do you find the ideas (a–h)? You can use a paragraph more than once. ONE of the ideas is not in the text.

a You can hire an expert to help you with transportation documents. ___4___

b It may be necessary to sell your product more cheaply. ___2___

c You should ask your customers how they want you to send the goods. ___1___

d You have to take action to stop people copying your product. ___5___

e You can find information online about possible customers. ___3___

f There are ways of making direct contact with overseas customers. ___3___

g Nowadays small businesses don't only deal with local customers. ___1___

h You don't have to spend a lot of money on translation. ___2___

4 Work with a partner and discuss these questions.

• What famous products are exported from your country?

• Does your country produce anything which you think would not sell well overseas? Why not?

Telephoning

Listening 1

(1) 13 **Listen to some short phone conversations or messages. For each recording, choose the correct answer, A, B or C.**

1 How will the company send the order?
   A by air
   B by rail
   C̲ by road

2 When will the company deliver the projectors?
   Ⓐ today
   B tomorrow
   C next week

3 Which item has the company not received?
   Ⓐ ink cartridges
   B envelopes
   Ⓒ address labels

4 Why is the woman phoning the company?
   A to complain about damaged goods
   Ⓑ to report a problem with paperwork
   C to make changes to an order

Role-play

Work in pairs.
Student A: look at the role card below.
Student B: look at the role card on page 118.

Prepare what you are going to say. When you are ready, Student B begins.

Student A

You are a **customer services manager** for Roco, a company that produces leather goods. A customer phones with a problem about an order they have received. Take the call and note down the details.

Order:
Order number: CO43724
Customer's name: Multizalli
Problem: 220 Jacket   40 S   40 S
                         40 M   20 M
                         40 L   0

Apologise to the customer and say you will contact the warehouse immediately about the problem. You will be able to deliver the large jackets next Thursday and your courier will take back the extra medium ones then.

Chasing an order

Listening 2

1 You are going to listen to a telephone conversation between a customer who is enquiring about an order for industrial paint and their supplier. Look at the supplier's notes and decide which answers (1–7) you expect to be numbers and which the speaker will need to spell out.

Name of company:	1 Khalil
Account reference number:	2 25431
Goods ordered:	3 industrial paint A535
Date on order form:	4 3 wk ago 18 Apr
Date goods will arrive:	5 Next week 18 Apr – 20 May
Contact's extension number:	6 375 / 398
Contact's name:	7 Selina Macphine

2 **(1) 14** **Listen to the conversation and complete the notes.**

Advertising and marketing

Getting started

1 Work in pairs. Choose one of the advertising methods in the photos (a–g) and make a list of its advantages and disadvantages. Try to think of three advantages and three disadvantages.

2 With your partner discuss what you think an *advertising agency* does.

a

b

c

d

e

f

g

3 Read these paragraphs from a book about advertising. Decide which paragraph (1–4) describes each type of advertising (a–g). There are more pictures than you need.

1 This form of advertising can reach a large number of homes. Consumers can take their time reading the message so it can contain details like phone numbers or website addresses. However, adverts here have a short lifespan as most people throw them away after one day.

2 With this marketing technique, you can direct your message to the people who are most likely to buy your product or service. You can focus on a particular area of a city or on previous customers. However, it can be difficult to get your audience's attention as some people throw these away without even looking at them.

3 This medium allows you to reach a large number of people in a short space of time. Perhaps its main advantage is that you can get your message across with both visual images and sound. The problem for many businesses is that it is expensive. You need to have plenty of money to pay for the cost of producing the ad and to pay for a suitable time to show it.

4 This type of advertising certainly reaches its audience because people can't switch it off or throw it away. However, consumers are usually moving at the time, so they only see the ad for about two or three seconds. It is normally used to remind consumers of messages which other media have already communicated to them.

Marketing

Advertising is one part of marketing. The marketing department of a business deals with the way a product is sold generally (for example, where it is available, etc.)

Vocabulary

1 Read the following dictionary definitions (1–7) and then unscramble the letters at the start of each to make six terms connected with marketing. Write the correct word next to each definition.

1 *brand*   **nadbr** name used to identify a particular product or service.

2 *logo*   **gool** symbol used by a company to advertise its products.

3 *slagan*   **nsogal** a short phrase that is easy to remember and which is used to advertise a product.

4 *Campaign*   **pimagnca** advertising of a product or service during a particular period of time.

5 *market share*   **kamtre rahes** the percentage of sales that a company has for a type of product compared with its competitors.

6 *market leader*   **kamtre raleed** a company which sells more products than its competitors.

7 *sponsor*   **ronpsso** a person or business who pays money to support an event in order to advertise their product, or to support an event in this way

2 Look at the chapter titles from a book about marketing. Match each title (1–6) with the correct summary (a–f) on the right.

1 **Channels of distribution**

2 **Sales forecasting**

3 **Market research**

4 **Product life cycles**

5 **Pricing**

6 **Public relations**

a How to get information about consumer preferences and the demand for new products.

b How to make decisions about what to charge for a product or service.

c Ways in which products and services get to their intended markets.

d How the sales of a product increase when more people want it and then decrease when other products become more popular.

e How to keep the high opinion of the people that the company comes in contact with.

f How to estimate the future demand for products.

Speaking

1 ① 15 Listen to someone talking about a famous product. Can you identify it from the description?

2 ① 15 Listen again and complete these extracts from the description. Write one word in each gap.

1 It *targets* young people in particular.
2 It's .... with being young and active.
3 The company .... a lot of sports events.
4 I think they always .... the Olympic Games.
5 Its .... is very famous.
6 They've used a lot of different .... over the years.

3 Work in groups of three or four. Choose another famous product and describe it to your group who must guess what it is. Use the language in Exercise 2 to help you.

Singapore Airlines

Reading

1 You are going to read an article about a famous brand in the air travel industry. Skim the first two paragraphs and tick the boxes if the following aspects of the brand (1–4) are mentioned.

1 logo ☐ 3 colour scheme ☐
2 staff uniform ☑ 4 slogan ☑

SINGAPORE **AIRLINES**

Singapore Airlines is one of the most successful airlines in the world. The main reason for this is its strong brand management. Because the airline has no domestic flights, it had to compete for international routes straight away. This difficult start led to a strong emphasis on branding. In order to stand out from the other major airlines, Singapore Airlines invested heavily in research and development. They aimed to offer the best technology and excellent customer service.

One of the most important aspects of the brand was the cabin crew. When the airline was launched in 1972, it employed the French designer, Pierre Balmain, to design the uniform. He created a special version of the Malaysian sarong. The image of the Singapore Airline flight stewardess in her sarong became one of the best known in the air travel industry. It illustrated the brand values of hospitality and customer care. Singapore Airlines ran a very detailed training programme for the cabin crew to make sure that the brand was always fully delivered. Their slogan 'a great way to fly' also emphasised the high quality of the brand.

2 Texts which describe marketing plans or strategies often talk about causes and effects, or results. Identifying the link between causes and effects in a text will help you to understand its general meaning, even if it contains words you don't know.

Read the first paragraph again and identify the causes for the two effects in the table below. Write no more than three words for each cause.

Cause	Effect
1 *strong brand mngt*	one of the most successful airlines
2 *No domestic flights*	competed immediately for international airspace

3 The second part of the paragraph talks about an *action* and the *reason* for it. Write the phrase used to introduce the reason into the text below.

Action: Singapore Airlines invested greatly in research and development
Reason: .... stand out from the other major airlines

4 Match each of the causes (1–4) with the correct effect (a–d).

1 Many low cost airlines have started up recently.
2 Major airlines want to compete with these low-cost carriers.
3 Major airlines earn less from airfares than they used to.
4 Customers see them as more like low cost airlines.

a Some of them have lowered their prices.
b They lose their brand identity.
c They have to save money by cutting customer services.
d Air travel is more competitive nowadays.

5 Read the following sentences to check your answers and put a word or phrase from the box into each one.

> as a result   ~~because~~   so   This means that

1 _Because_ there are many low cost airlines now, air travel is more competitive.

2 Some traditional airlines want to compete with low cost carriers and _so_ they have reduced their prices.

3 Some airlines earn less from passenger fares now. _as a result_ they have to cut customer services.

4 They appear more like low cost airlines and, _This means that_ they lose their brand identity.

❯ **page 45** *because* and *so*

6 Now read the final paragraph. Some words are missing. Decide in which gap(s) you need to put the following types of words. Write the gap numbers (1–7) next to each item (a–d).

a a possessive adjective (*my, his,* etc.)   _3, 7_
b a relative pronoun (*who, which* or *that*) _1, 5_
c a preposition (*at, on,* etc.)   _2, 6_
d an article (*a, an* or *the*)   _4_

Singapore Airlines has tried to avoid this problem. In 2003, together with two other investors, it founded a new carrier, Tiger Airways, **1** _which_ is used for shorter, local flights. This competes **2** _with_ other low-cost airlines in South East Asia. Then in 2011, the company announced plans to launch **3** _his_ second low-cost airline, New Aviation. Hopefully, this will address **4** _the_ growing demand for budget travel, while the core brand, Singapore Airlines, keeps its brand identity. There will always be customers **5** _who_ are willing to spend money **6** _for_ a quality product and Singapore Airlines plans to keep **7** _his_ promise to deliver high quality customer service.

7 Choose the correct word from the box below to put in each gap. There are more words than you need.

> at   for   her   his   its   on   to   a   the   an   who
> ~~which~~   with   your

A promotional letter
Writing

1 Work in pairs. Imagine you work for a company which is planning to launch a new product. If you are working, this can be your own company; if not, you can invent one.

Decide together:
- what the new product is
- who your target customers are
- when it will be available
- where it will be available (online, your shop, retailers …?)
- something extra you can do to attract customers (e.g. discounted price for a short period, free samples, a competition …?)

2 You need to tell your customers that the product is new. Advertisements often put other adjectives in front of *new* to make the product sound attractive. Which of the words in the box often go in front of *new*?

> brand   bright   brilliant   exciting   fabulous   great   pretty

Apart from *new*, think of two other adjectives you want customers to associate with your product.

3 Work together to write a letter to your customers about the new product, which will appear on the company website. Begin:

To our customers,

We're writing to give you some news …

Write 60–80 words.

4 Swap letters with another pair. Does their letter make you want to buy the product? Why?/Why not?

5 Think of one improvement you could make to the letter you have just read. Then tell the other pair your ideas. Listen to their ideas and make any changes you want to your letter.

Grammar workshop 2

Units 5–8

Passive forms

1 **Change the following sentences to the passive. Do not use *by*.**

1 We train our staff to deal with difficult customers.
Our staff are trained to deal with difficult customers.

2 We keep the invoices in the filing cabinet.
The invoices _____ .

3 They sell most of their products over the Internet.
Most of their products _____ .

4 The company teach their staff basic accounting skills.
Their staff _____ .

5 We don't allow staff to smoke in here.
Staff _____ .

- Modal verbs like *must* can be followed by a passive infinitive.
  *The budget manager **must sign** the purchase order.*
  *The purchase order **must be signed** by the budget manager.*

---

2 **Change the following sentences to the passive. This time, use *by*.**

6 Two members of staff should check the figures.
The figures should be checked by two members of staff.

7 An American company may acquire Simsons.
Simsons _____ .

8 The secretary can't authorise the purchase.
The purchase *can't be authorsed by the screlay.*

9 Your friend should not write your CV.
Your CV _____ .

10 Your company must meet these expenses.
These expenses _____ .

3 ⊙ **Business English students sometimes confuse the active and passive forms of the verb. Choose the correct form, either active or passive, in the following sentences.**

1 He *accepts* / is accepted the invitation to attend the conference.

2 Most of our coffee imports / *is imported* from Brazil.

3 We *agree* / are agreed with your suggestion.

4 We *apologise* / are apologised for the mistake.

5 The conference will hold / *be held* on 17 March.

6 My talk will *concentrate* / be concentrated on our company structure.

7 The travel expenses must reduce / *be reduced* next year.

8 The meeting schedules / *is scheduled* for next week.

9 The report *explains* / is explained why we chose those advertising methods.

- In passive sentences, one word adverbs of frequency go after the verb *to be*.
  *The work surface is **always** cleaned at the end of the day.*
- If there is a modal verb, they go after the modal.
  *Cars should **never** be left in front of the exit.*

---

4 **Write the following sentences with the words in the correct order.**

1 rail goods usually transported by the are
The goods are usually transported by rail.

2 courier sent never are by payments

3 are the boardroom held meeting always in

4 in never the left be should deliveries corridor

5 signed claim forms must manager be by the always

6 are orders discounts offered usually large on

Modal verbs

1 **Read the signs and choose the best modal verb to complete each sentence.**

1
FIRE DOOR. KEEP CLOSED.

You *mustn't* / can / don't have to leave this door open.

2 REFRESHMENTS PROVIDED.

You *have to / don't have to/ mustn't* bring food.

3 **HAND WASH STATION ONLY**

You *can/ don't have to/ shouldn't* wash your coffee cup here.

4 **SCRAP PAPER. HELP YOURSELVES**

You *can / must / mustn't* take some of this paper.

5 **Stop before you leave the building!**
HAVE YOU SWITCHED OFF THE LIGHTS?

You *must / mustn't / don't have to* forget to turn off the lights.

6 **BAGS CAN BE LEFT AT RECEPTION.**

You *don't have to / can't / mustn't* keep your bag with you.

7 **PARKING AREA: CYCLES AND MOTORCYCLES ONLY**

You *can / can't/ don't have to* park your car here.

8 *A tidy desk means a tidy mind.*

You *should/ can't / don't have to* keep your desk tidy.

2 ⊙ Business English students sometimes make mistakes with verb forms in sentences with modal verbs. Correct the mistakes in the following sentences. ONE sentence is correct.

1 We can ~~doing~~ the report later this week. *do*
2 I think we should ~~to~~ have at least a 10 per cent discount.
3 The successful candidate must ~~has~~ *have* good computer skills.
4 Everyone at the conference will must wear a name badge.
5 All staff have to have a parking permit.
6 I am afraid the company cannot ~~sent~~ *send* payment until next week.

■ In language like contracts or formal instructions we often avoid modal verbs. We can express the same ideas using passive verbs.
Staff **are required** to give three months' notice (= Staff **have to give** three months' notice).
Guests **are advised** to avoid this area of the city (= Guests **should avoid** this area of the city).

3 In each of the following sentences, complete the second sentence with a modal verb so it has the same meaning as the first. Sometimes more than one answer is possible.

1 Employees are required to obtain a sicknote from their doctor.
Employees _must/have to_ obtain a sicknote from their doctor.
2 Mobile phones are not permitted in the room.
You _are not allowed to_ take mobile phones into the room.
3 You are advised to discuss holiday plans with your manager.
You _should_ discuss holiday plans with your manager.
4 Photos are not required for the application form.
You ~~may not~~ include a photo on the application form. _don't have to_
5 Smoking is only permitted in the designated areas.
You _should_ only smoke in the designated areas.
6 Employees are not allowed to take part in the competition.
Employees _can't_ take part in the competition.

because and so

■ We can use both *because* and *so* to join a cause and an effect in the same sentence.
The product didn't sell well (effect) **because** *the price was too high (cause).*
The price was too high (cause) **so** *the product didn't sell well (effect).*
■ Sometimes we put **because** at the beginning of the sentence. In this case, we need a comma in the middle.
Because *the price was too high, the product didn't sell well.*

⊙ Business English students sometimes wrongly use *because* and *so* in sentences. Make the following pairs of sentences into one by adding *because* or *so* at the sign ^. Change the punctuation as necessary.

1 Please call me today. ^ I need to discuss this with you.
Please call me today because I need to discuss this with you.
2 I was off sick. ^ I couldn't send you the information last week. *so*
3 The sales manager is coming. ^ He wants to check the figures. *because*
4 ^ *Because* The service was so unsatisfactory, We do not intend to use your company again.
5 Interviews are taking place in our usual room, *so* We will have to meet in room 10.

Making arrangements

Getting started

Work with a partner and discuss the following questions.

1 Which of the following methods (a–e) do you use to help you remember the dates and times of appointments?
   a wall planner
   b traditional paper diary or organiser
   c palm-held electronic diary or organiser
   d electronic diary on your computer
   e smartphone

2 What do you think of the above methods of organising your time? Which do you think is the best method? Why? Use these adjectives to help you.

> compact   complicated
> convenient   old fashioned
> stylish   user-friendly

A company visit

Listening

Mr Gavino represents a food service equipment manufacturer called Cibos. He has arranged to visit Interexpress, his Australian distributor, and a programme of business events and entertainment has been planned for his visit.

1 16 The evening before his arrival, Jeannette Smith, PA to Paul Price at Interexpress, receives a message on her voicemail. Listen to the message and complete Jeannette's notes.

Mr G. missed connection from
1 ....

Now arriving on 2 .... March,
flight number 3 .... Book taxi.

Re-book restaurant for day after
tomorrow at 4 ....

Grammar workshop 1

Present continuous for future arrangements

1 ①16 **Listen again and complete the sentences with the correct words.**

1 He .... not .... tomorrow after all.
2 He .... on the 14th at 6.20 am.
3 .... still .... him tomorrow morning?

> This is the **present continuous** (see Unit 1, page 13) and it is often used with a date or time to talk about fixed arrangements in the future.

2 Now read Mr Gavino's revised programme.

Tues 14:	6.20:	arrive Melbourne
	11.30:	Mr Gavino demonstrates new products/equipment
	19.30:	dinner at 'White Carnation'
Wed 15:	10.00:	meeting with reps from Park Hotels
	19.30:	dinner at Park Hotel, Melbourne
Thurs 16:	10.00:	presentation of new products to restaurant reps
	14.30:	visit to 'Quality Catering' to present new equipment
		evening free
Fri 17:	10.20:	flight home

3 Complete the following sentences about the programme. Use the correct verb from the box in the present continuous.

> do   fly   ~~give~~   have   meet   present   visit

1 On Tuesday morning he *is giving* a demonstration of new products.
2 He .... dinner at the 'White Carnation' on Monday any more because Jeannette has re-booked it for Tuesday.
3 On Wednesday morning he .... representatives from Park Hotels.
4 On Thursday morning he .... the new equipment to restaurant representatives.
5 Later that day, he .... a catering company.
6 On Thursday evening he .... anything.
7 On Friday morning he .... back to Hong Kong.

Making an appointment

Listening 1

Carmen Vanegas, a sales representative for a medical supplies company, telephones one of her clients, Stefano Cigada, to arrange a meeting.

1 ①17 **Cover the dialogue below, listen to their conversation and write down what day and time they arrange to meet.**

Day: ....   Time: ....

2 ①17 **Listen to the conversation again and fill in the missing words below.**

Carmen: Hello, this is Carmen Vanegas from Medica. I was wondering if we could **1** *fix* a time to meet next week?

Stefano: Yes of course. What time would **2** .... you?

Carmen: Well I was wondering if you could **3** .... Tuesday afternoon?

Stefano: Sorry, I'm not **4** .... at any time on Tuesday as I've **5** .... to be at our other branch all day.

Carmen: How about Wednesday afternoon?

Stefano: I'm **6** .... Wednesday afternoon as well, but I could **7** .... Wednesday morning, or I'm free all day on Thursday.

Carmen: Could you **8** .... Thursday at two o'clock?

Stefano: That would be fine, yes.

Carmen: OK. So let's confirm that then, Thursday at two o'clock.

3 **Look at the sentences (1–4) which are similar to the dialogue. Choose the alternative, A, B or C, which is NOT possible.**

1 Could we *fix* a time to meet?
   A arrange   B appoint   C organise
2 Would this Thursday *suit* you?
   A be suitable for
   B be convenient for
   C fit
3 Sorry, I'm *not available* then.
   A not free   B booked up   C engaged
4 Could you *make* 4.00?
   A take   B manage   C do

Role-play

Work in pairs.

Student A: look at the role card below.
Student B: look at the role card on page 119.

Prepare some of the language you want to use before you speak.

Student A

You are Stefano Cigada, Carmen Vanegas' client in the Listening exercise on page 47. You realise that you cannot make the meeting with her at 2 o'clock on Thursday after all. You telephone Carmen to arrange a meeting for the following week. Here is an extract from your diary for that week. Apologise for the change, and arrange a new time for the meeting when you are both free.

Monday	AM	
	PM	management meeting
Tuesday	AM	financial review
	PM	interview candidates for new post
Wednesday	AM	
	PM	

Listening 2

Task tip

In many conversations, you do not need to understand every word. It is often enough to understand the important information, like the correct date or time or who is doing what. If the speakers are making a decision about something, you may also need to pick out the thing that they finally decide from a number of different suggestions.

①18 Listen to these short recordings about future plans and arrangements. For each recording (1–4), circle the correct answer, A, B or C.

1 What time is the flight that the woman wants to take?
   A 11.30
   B 4.20
   C 6.30
2 How is Miss Casale going to get to the office?
   A by car
   B by taxi
   C on foot
3 What is the correct spelling of the visitor's name?
   A Bulkiewicz
   B Bulkeiwicz
   C Bulkiewisz
4 What is going to happen to Mr Jonsson?
   A He is going to retire.
   B He is going to become chief executive.
   C He is going to become chief financial officer.

Grammar workshop 2

will and *going to* future forms

The **present continuous** is just one way to talk about the future in English. If something is not a fixed arrangement, you use different future forms.

1 **①19 Listen to the beginnings of four more short conversations about the future and decide which of the following functions (a–d) describes each conversation. Write the correct number (1–4) in the boxes.**

a a prediction based on an opinion ☐
b an offer or request for instructions ☐1
c a decision made *at* the moment of speaking ☐
d a decision made *before* the moment of speaking ☐

2 (1 19) **Listen again and write the missing words in the sentences (1–4) below.**

1 A I need to get to the airport by 6.30.
   B Shall I book you a taxi?
2 A What are you doing with those files, Roger?
   B I .... sales figures for Mr Durand.
3 The Bank of Canada have announced that economic growth .... relatively slow this year.
4 A I've tried to set up the room for the presentation but the microphone isn't working.
   B .... the technician. I've got the number somewhere here.

3 **Which future form is used in each case? Complete these rules about the future by putting the functions (a–d) from Exercise 1 in the correct gap.**

> You use the **will future** for .... and ....
> You use the **going to future** for ....
> You use **shall** for ....

▶ **page 62** Future forms

4 (1 20) **Now listen to the rest of each conversation and circle the correct answer, A, B or C, for each question (1–4).**

1 What time does the man book the taxi for?
   (A) 5.30
   B 5.45
   C 6.30
2 What is Roger going to do first?
   A send the documents
   B finish the report
   C type up the figures
3 According to the Bank of Canada, what will be the percentage growth for this year?
   A 2%
   B 2.4%
   C 2.8%
4 What does the man want the woman to do?
   A phone the technician
   B fix the microphone
   C find the hand-held microphone

5 **Underline the correct future forms in these sentences (1–6). More than one answer is sometimes possible.**

1 Do you have any plans for this evening?
   Yes, I *will read* / *I'm going to read* / *I'm reading* all those reports for tomorrow's meeting.
2 The phone's ringing.
   I'll answer / *I'm going to answer* / *I'm answering* it.

3 Oh dear, I don't seem to have the agenda for this meeting.
   Am I making / *Shall I make* / *Am I going to make* you a copy?
4 It is forecast that China's gross domestic product (the total value of goods and services produced) *is going to grow* / *is growing* / *will grow* by 6 per cent next year.
5 I'd like to keep in touch.
   OK, *I'm going to give* / *I'm giving* / *I'll give* you my card.
6 Have you made an appointment to see the bank manager?
   Yes. *I'm seeing* / *I'll see* / *I shall see* him tomorrow morning.

Role-play

Work in groups of four or five. Read the following role card and follow the instructions.

You are **members of the sales team** of a company which produces soft drinks.

You have recently developed a new product which is aimed at sportspeople or young adults who are interested in keeping fit. You want to organise a series of events to launch the product. Decide:

- what kinds of events to use (*presentation, roadshow*, etc.)
- who to invite (*retailers, distributors, famous people*, etc.)

Decide in your team what each person should do to prepare for the event. Then report your plans back to the class.

Remember: Use *will* for decisions made at the time of speaking and for predictions:
I'll send out an email to some retailers.
I'm sure it will be a success.

Use *shall* for offers or suggestions:
Shall we invite …?
Shall I send an invitation to …?

Use *going to* to report your plans to the class:
We're going to organise a roadshow.
We're going to invite …

Transport

Getting started

Work with a partner and discuss these questions.

1 Which of the following is most important to you when choosing which airline to fly with to go on holiday?
 • cost
 • comfort
 • service

2 Would your choice be different when travelling on business? Why/why not?

3 What are the advantages and disadvantages of flying and travelling by train for business trips? Try to think of two advantages and two disadvantages for each method of transport.

Air travel

Vocabulary

Compound nouns are formed from *two nouns* or *an adjective + noun*. There are many compound nouns connected with transport, for example *railway station*.

1 **Complete the following story by putting a compound noun from the box into each gap.**

> boarding card/pass   ~~check-in desk~~
> departure lounge   duty free shop   hold luggage
> information desk   passport control

> The last time I came to this airport, I lost my passport. I was nice and early, so there were no queues at the **1** *check-in desk* . I checked in my **2** _____, got my **3** _____ and went through **4** _____ all very quickly. Then, just because I had so much time, instead of just sitting in the **5** _____, I decided to do some shopping. I wanted to get a present, so I was trying all the different perfumes in the **6** _____ . I don't know how it happened but I must have dropped my passport there. I went to the gate to board the plane and then I realised that I couldn't find my passport. At that moment, they called me over the loudspeaker. 'Will passenger Martinez travelling to Madrid please contact the **7** _____ .' I felt so embarrassed.

2 **(1)(21)** **Listen to the story and check your answers to Exercise 1.**

3 **Match the words (1–6) with (a–f) to make six more compound nouns for items which are found on a plane.**

1 aisle   a belt
2 seat   b locker
3 window   c attendant
4 flight   d seat
5 overhead   e exit
6 emergency   f seat

4 **Now match these verbs (1–12) and nouns (a–d) to make collocations. Several collocations are possible.**

1 catch	a	a flight
2 miss		
3 get off	b	a plane
4 board		
5 get on	c	seats
6 pass through		
7 book	d	customs
8 swap		
9 cancel		
10 reschedule		
11 go through		
12 reserve		

5 Work with a partner. Take it in turns to tell each other about a plane or train journey you remember well, using the vocabulary in Exercises 1–4.

Reading

When travelling by air or train, it is important to understand notices and messages about problems, delays, changes in arrangements, etc.

Read these messages about travel arrangements. For each message (1–5), circle the correct summary, A, B or C.

1

> Dear Jeff
> Hope to meet up with you on Sun evening, but if our flight is delayed, will call you before the meeting on Mon.
> Sarah

Ⓐ Sarah would like to see Jeff on Sunday.

B Sarah is going to catch a later flight than originally planned.

C Sarah wants to put off the meeting until Monday.

2

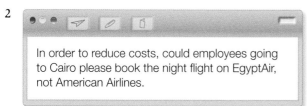

In order to reduce costs, could employees going to Cairo please book the night flight on EgyptAir, not American Airlines.

A Staff will arrive in Cairo at night.

B The American Airlines flight to Cairo has been cancelled.

C Staff should take a cheaper flight than the American Airlines one.

3

> **DELAYS EXPECTED ON THIS LINE DUE TO SIGNALLING PROBLEMS.**

A No trains are running on this line.

B Your journey on this line may take longer than usual.

C The signalling problems on this line have been fixed.

4

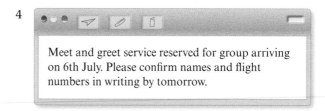

Meet and greet service reserved for group arriving on 6th July. Please confirm names and flight numbers in writing by tomorrow.

A You must confirm with the 'meet and greet' service that the group will arrive tomorrow.

B You must write to the 'meet and greet' service to confirm exactly who is arriving.

C You must call the 'meet and greet' service to let them know how many people are coming.

5

Flight cancelled due to fog. Arriving tomorrow same time. Pls call this evening. Jamie.

REPLY

A Jamie cannot fly today because of the weather conditions.

B Jamie will call the receiver of this message this evening.

C Jamie does not know when he will arrive.

Train travel

Reading

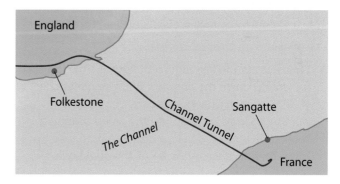

Eurostar is the train service which runs between Britain and France under the Channel.

1 Work with a partner. Guess the correct answer to the following questions (1–3). Circle A, B or C.

1 In which year did the Eurostar service begin?
   A 1986   B 1994   C 1996

2 How long does it take to travel between London and Paris on the Eurostar?
   A 1 hour 45 minutes
   B 2 hours 15 minutes
   C 3 hours

3 How many passengers travelled on the Eurostar in the first year?
   A 3 million   B 7 million   C 15 million

2 Now scan the text to find out if you were right.

Eurostar

Building a railway under the Channel is probably the greatest act of Franco-British co-operation in recent history. Tunnel schemes were first proposed in 1882, so the idea was not new. However, it was only in 1986 that the British and French prime ministers announced that the scheme would go ahead. Now the carriages of the Eurostar trains are a common venue for business meetings as British and French people travel to meet clients on the other side of the Channel.

The Channel Tunnel opened in 1994 with trains travelling the 50 kilometres of track at an average depth of 40 metres below the seabed. In the first ten years, 7 million trucks, 22 million cars, 55 million passengers, 21 tonnes of rail freight and 50 thousand dogs and cats passed through it. The shortest of Eurostar's journeys is a trip to Lille, a beautiful old city, now just 1 hour 20 minutes away from London. The journey between London and Paris now takes 2 hours 15 minutes and London to Brussels is just under two hours. It now takes less time to make the London-Paris journey by rail than by air. Although there are of course occasional setbacks, Eurostar trains are also much more punctual than most air routes.

The passenger figures may look good but they fall far short of what was expected. The original prediction was for 15 million passengers in the first year but the actual figure was only around 3 million. Forecasts for later years were also too optimistic. At the same time, despite these initial disappointments, Eurostar's chief executive remained upbeat. Passenger numbers have in fact grown steadily each year and the company now has a larger market share for London-Paris travel than any airline. One reason for this is the introduction of budget price tickets. In the first year of business, the cheapest return fare on Eurostar was £99 whereas now it is much less than that. Eurostar have also targeted business travellers by introducing Business Premier tickets, which offer faster check-in times and meals served at your seat. According to the chief executive, there is also still plenty of opportunity for growth and expansion through investment in new trains, and the introduction of services like London to Amsterdam.

3 Now extract the key facts and figures from the text by writing down the answers to these questions (1–8). For each question decide what *type* of number to look for, then use the same scanning technique you used in Exercise 2. Aim to take no more than three minutes for all the questions.

1 How many million cars used the tunnel in the first ten years? *22 million*
2 How long does it take to travel from London to Lille? ....
3 In which year was the suggestion for a tunnel first made? ....
4 What was the original forecast for the number of passengers in the first year? ....
5 What is the average distance between the bottom of the sea and the tunnel? ....
6 What was the cheapest price of a return ticket on Eurostar in the first year? ....
7 In what year did the British and French governments approve the plan for a tunnel? ....
8 How long is the tunnel? ....

4 Look at these sentences from the text with the contrast words underlined. They contrast the idea in the first part of the sentence with the idea in the second part.

1 The passenger figures may look good <u>but</u> they fall far short of what was expected.
2 <u>Although</u> there are of course occasional setbacks, Eurostar trains are also much more punctual than most air routes.

5 Now read these sentences from the text and underline the contrast words.

1 Tunnel schemes were first proposed in 1882. However, it was not until 1986 that the British and French prime ministers announced that the scheme would go ahead.
2 In 1994, the cheapest return fare on Eurostar was £99 whereas now it is much less than that.
3 Despite these initial disappointments, Eurostar's chief executive remained upbeat.

6 Work with a partner and answer the following questions about the words in Exercises 4 and 5.

1 Which word usually contrasts *two separate sentences* instead of *two ideas in the same sentence*?

2 Which word is followed by a phrase without a verb in it?

3 Which words can be put at the *beginning of the sentence* and be replaced with a *comma* in the middle?

7 ◉ Business English students sometimes use the wrong punctuation with contrast words. Correct the punctuation in the following extracts (1–6). ONE extract is correct.

1 The talk on time management didn't tell me anything new. Although the second one on work flows was interesting.

The talk on time management didn't tell me anything new although the second one on work flows was interesting.

2 We will be happy to give the session at your premises. But the maximum number of trainees is sixteen.

3 That airline is usually rather expensive, however the customer service is better.

4 The training day was very well organised. Although the breaks were too short.

5 Driving to work can be very stressful, whereas the train journey is much more relaxing.

6 We hoped our TV advertisement would increase sales, however. The results have been disappointing.

❯ page 62 Contrast words

Bicycle share schemes

Writing

1 Read the information below about bicycle share schemes and discuss the questions with a partner.

> Bike shares are schemes where a number of bicycles are made publicly available for people to use within a city. There are schemes in all parts of the world, in cities as far apart as London, Mexico City and Beijing. You pay a small fee to unlock and use a bicycle for a given time from a 'cycle station', and then return it to another cycle station when you are finished. They are often popular with people who want to help the environment or avoid sitting in traffic jams, and tourists. The schemes are sometimes sponsored by particular companies; for example, the London scheme is sponsored by a bank.

1 Is there a scheme like this in your city? If there is, do you think it's a good idea? If not, could it work in your city?

2 What do you think are the main problems with setting up a scheme like this? How could you solve them?

2 Your company has decided to sponsor a new bike share scheme. You are the PA to Mr Groves, the Chief Executive, and you receive this email:

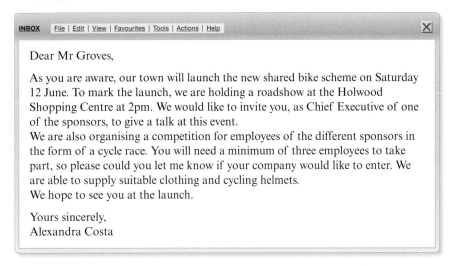

INBOX   File | Edit | View | Favourites | Tools | Actions | Help ✕

Dear Mr Groves,

As you are aware, our town will launch the new shared bike scheme on Saturday 12 June. To mark the launch, we are holding a roadshow at the Holwood Shopping Centre at 2pm. We would like to invite you, as Chief Executive of one of the sponsors, to give a talk at this event.

We are also organising a competition for employees of the different sponsors in the form of a cycle race. You will need a minimum of three employees to take part, so please could you let me know if your company would like to enter. We are able to supply suitable clothing and cycling helmets.

We hope to see you at the launch.

Yours sincerely,
Alexandra Costa

3 You need to write a reply to Alexandra Costa. Write the phrases in the box below in the right order to create your reply. Divide the letter into two paragraphs.

> Many thanks   to attend and give a short talk.   how long this should be.
> we have three employees   Yours sincerely,   their own cycling clothes.
> for your invitation to the roadshow.   However, all three are keen cyclists
> Please could you let us know   I can also confirm
> seeing you at the roadshow.   who will take part in the race.
> and so they would prefer to wear   1 Dear Ms Costa,
> We look forward to   Mr Groves will be very happy

4 Now swap your answer with a partner. Are they the same? If not, discuss any differences and decide which order is best.

Working holidays

Getting started

Work in pairs and discuss the following questions.

1 How many public holidays are there in your country? Can you name them all?
2 Imagine you could create an extra public holiday in your country. What day do you think it should be and why?

Half holidays

Listening

1 ⓵ 22 **You will hear a conversation between two colleagues about holiday time. Listen and answer the following questions.**

1 According to the woman, what are the problems with taking a complete break from work?
2 What does she mean by 'half holidays'? What advantages do they have?
3 Do you agree with her ideas?

2 ⓵ 22 **Listen to the conversation again and write the missing words in sentences (1–7).**

1 It was _much better_ in the past when people didn't have BlackBerries.
2 The last two or three days before you go are .... normal.
3 Coming back to work is ....
4 Organising three weeks away is a .... staying in the office.
5 I actually think that's ....
6 It certainly makes your last day ....
7 The half holidays could be .... the holidays people take now.

Grammar workshop 1

Comparatives

1 **Answer the questions below on how to form comparatives. Use the sentences you have just completed to help you.**

1 How do one syllable adjectives like *long* form the comparative?
 They add –er at the end: longer
2 How do adjectives of three or more syllables like *relaxing* form the comparative?
 ....
3 What happens to the spelling with two syllable adjectives ending in *-y* like *busy*? ....
4 What happens to the spelling of one syllable adjectives ending in one vowel and one consonant like *big*?
 ....
5 In comparatives, what word is used for the opposite of *more*? ....
6 What word is used after a comparative to introduce the second thing in the comparison? ....
7 What words can we put before comparatives to mean *very*?
 ....
8 What are the comparative forms of *good* and *bad*? ....

2 **Write the comparative forms of the following adjectives.**

1 cheap   _cheaper_
2 tidy   ....
3 expensive ....
4 large   ....
5 hot   ....
6 important ....
7 far   ....

3 Look at the holiday entitlements offered by two different companies and complete sentences (1–7) using the comparative forms of the adjectives in the box.

COMPANY A

Staff are entitled to 20 days annual paid leave. A maximum of 12 can be taken in a block.

Requests for leave must be made at least three months in advance.

Only six members of staff can take leave at New Year or during the month of August.

COMPANY B

Staff are entitled to 25 days annual paid leave, which can be taken at different times or in a block.

In addition staff can buy or sell up to five of these 25 days.

Requests for leave must be made 10 weeks in advance.

Only 10 members of staff can take their leave in the summer (July and August).

easy   far   flexible   ~~generous~~   good   long   small

1 Company B is more generous with its holiday entitlements.
2 In company B, you can take a .... period of time on leave.
3 In company A, a .... number of staff can take their holiday in August.
4 Company B is .... in its holiday arrangements.
5 In company A, you have to book your holiday .... in advance.
6 I think staff-management relationships are probably .... in company A/B (you choose).
7 Personally, I would find it .... to arrange my holidays in company A/B (you choose).

Netflix

Reading

1 You are going to read an article about Netflix, a company which has an unusual policy on staff holidays. Skim the article quickly to find out what the policy is.

NETFLIX®

CHANGING HOLIDAY POLICIES: NETFLIX

Netflix is a US company that offers movies and TV shows to subscribers over the Internet or on DVDs. When it first began, the company had a traditional policy for holidays. Staff had a certain number of days a year and they either took them or were paid for the ones they didn't take.

But soon some employees realised that this arrangement didn't fit in with how they really did their jobs. After all, they were answering emails at weekends and solving problems online at home at night. The company didn't track how many hours they did each day or each week. Logically, the employees argued, this meant that tracking how many holidays people took was just as old fashioned as asking them to work a strict nine-to-five day.

The management agreed. Now at Netflix, employees can take as much time off as they like, at any time they like. No one monitors annual leave at all. It may sound like complete chaos, but in fact it hasn't harmed the company in any way. They have continued to grow rapidly and have now expanded into a number of other countries.

The fact is that in many workplaces today, monitoring the time people spend at work is not as important as it was in the past. If someone worked on an assembly line, then there was a clear connection between the time they worked and the amount they produced. By contrast, in a great many workplaces today, the important things are innovation and problem solving. This means that the link between the time you spend and the results you produce is not so clear. If people produce good results, why is it important to know exactly how long it took to achieve them?

2 Find words and phrases in the article with the following meanings:
1 people who pay money for a service subscribers
2 record and carefully watch (two verbs)
   .... / ....
3 a system for producing things where each worker makes a different component ....
4 the process of introducing new ideas and methods ....

3 The following statements are false. Look at the article again and correct them.

1 Netflix never had a traditional policy on staff holidays.
   They had a traditional policy on staff holidays when they first started.
2 Employees at Netflix don't work at home.
3 Now at Netflix, employees track their own annual leave.
4 Netflix only operates in the US.
5 Monitoring the time employees spend at work has become more important.

4 Discuss the following questions in pairs.

• Do you agree with the writer of the article that monitoring time at work is less important nowadays?
• If you are working, do you think a policy of 'no policy' on staff holidays could be a success in your place of work?

Grammar workshop 2

as … as structures

1 Look at the following sentences from the article and choose the correct alternatives to answer the grammar questions below.

> *Tracking how many holidays people took was just **as** old fashioned **as** asking them to work a strict nine-to-five day.*
> *Monitoring the time people spend at work is not **as** important **as** it was in the past.*

1 We use *as … as* if we want to say that two things are
   a the same   b different
2 *It is not as important as it was in the past …* means that now it is
   a more important   b less important

2 For sentences (1–5), use *not as … as* to complete the second sentence so it means the same as the first. Use the adjectives in the box to help you.

~~big~~ early easy expensive fast

1 The third conference room is smaller than the others.
   The third conference room *is not as big as* the others.

2 The local train is slower than the Express.
   The local train .... the Express.
3 Finding a PA is more difficult than I expected.
   Finding a PA .... I expected.
4 Their products are cheaper than I thought.
   Their products .... I thought.
5 My flight arrives later than yours.
   My flight .... arrive .... yours.

3 We often use expressions with *as … as* to talk about possibilities. Study the expressions in the box and then choose one to complete sentences (1–6). More than one answer is often possible.

as soon as as close as	possible I/you … can
as much as as long as	possible I/you … like/can
	I/you … want/like
as far as	I/you … can go

1 That report is urgent so please type it up *as soon as you can* .
2 We are not paying for the food so you can eat ....
3 We probably won't finish this before the deadline but we must do ....
4 No one else is using the room today so you can stay in here ....
5 We must make the two parts exactly the same size or ....
6 I can increase the discount to 8 per cent but that's ....

Offsite meetings

Reading

Sometimes companies decide to take people away from the office for a short period to work on a project or make key decisions. These are often called *away days* or *offsite meetings*.

1 Work in pairs and think of three advantages of working away from the office.

2 Working with a partner, look at the title of the article opposite and discuss what you think it means. Then scan the article and answer the following questions.

1 Where did they spend the four days?
2 What did they do when they got there?

THINKING OUTSIDE THE BOX

An invitation to attend the annual summer meeting of Geopost, a France-based transport company, was sent to the top 40 executives along with some extra advice: bring a warm jumper.

Claude Béglé, then Geopost's chief executive, was already starting to spread rumours that Copenhagen was not the real location. Nobody, however, suspected the truth: that the 40 managers would find themselves aboard a small boat in the Arctic Circle in almost continual daylight and with no methods of contacting the outside world apart from the ship's radio. It sounds like a completely crazy way of running a company but Mr Béglé believed it was the right thing to do. At the time, Geopost needed to make some key decisions about the group's structure and bring together what was a diverse group of companies.

Geopost was created in 1999 by La Poste, the French postal service. It grew rapidly by acquiring other companies and now covers over 40 countries throughout the world. At the time of the Arctic trip, it was made up of companies from France, Germany, Spain, the Netherlands and the UK, all operating under their own brand names. But why were the managers taking key decisions in the Arctic Ocean instead of at the smart Hyatt Hotel in Copenhagen?

The answer is that Mr Béglé wanted to be sure that the decisions they made were based on the interests of Geopost as a whole and not on office politics. The Arctic Ocean is one of the few places in the world where you cannot get a mobile phone signal. The managers were forced to work on their relationships with one another, rather than keeping in touch with their company headquarters back home. As Mr Béglé said, 'You cannot sleep because it is always light and you cannot get out of the boat. So what happens? You fight, you make friends again, you argue again, you discuss business. Four days later we had a structure. I've never seen it in the management books but it worked.'

It is certainly not in the management books. Usually when a company is acquired by another company, it is not allowed to keep its own brands. Geopost took a different approach. Acquired companies could keep their own brands and identities and could also make many of their own decisions about things such as which technology to use. To balance this local autonomy, Geopost needed a strong common culture, which is why it decided to spend a lot of time on team building activities on the trip. As Mr Béglé said, for the company to stay together, it needed to do something crazy.

3 Read the following statements (1–7) about the information in the text. If the text agrees, circle A. If it disagrees, circle B. If the information is not given in the text, circle C for doesn't say.

1 Claude Béglé made an original booking in Copenhagen.
 A right   B wrong   C doesn't say

2 Managers could not call their branch of the company from the boat.
 A right   B wrong   C doesn't say

3 At the time of the trip, Geopost was the largest parcel company in Europe.
 A right   B wrong   C doesn't say

4 Companies acquired by Geopost were not allowed to keep their own brands.
 A right   B wrong   C doesn't say

5 Claude Béglé got the idea of the Arctic trip from a management book.
 A right   B wrong   C doesn't say

6 Companies acquired by Geopost did not have to use the same technology.
 A right   B wrong   C doesn't say

7 Claude Béglé believes that Geopost's management style should be adopted by other companies.
 A right   B wrong   C doesn't say

Making decisions

Speaking

Work with a partner. Imagine you need to make some key decisions about something (e.g. your studies, or your future career). Which of the following do you think would be the best way to come to a decision about it? Why?

- Go away to a different place (even if not the Arctic Circle!) to think about it alone.
- Go away to a different place with one or two friends to talk about it.
- Stay in the same place and ask as many friends and family members as possible about it.
- Not think about it and hope the answer will come to you when you are not expecting it.

Conferences

Getting started

1 Why do business people attend conferences? Think of three reasons, then compare your ideas with a partner.

2 Read this conference programme and match the words in italics (1–8) with the correct definition (a–h).

a Meetings in which people discuss a particular subject.   *7 seminars*

b A talk on a particular subject. ....

c The place where an event, like a conference, takes place. ....

d People who attend a conference as representatives of their organisation. ....

e A session where all the people at a conference come together. ....

f The audience of a particular session. ....

g Research which deals with the development of a particular organisation over a period of time. ....

h Online meetings where people discuss a particular topic. ....

3 Which two of the sessions on the programme would you most like to attend? Compare your answers with a partner.

HUMAN RESOURCES CONFERENCE

This year's conference will be the biggest in the event's five year history, with attendance up 15 per cent on last year. A big thank you to all speakers and **1** *delegates* who have made it a success and we hope you enjoy our new **2** *venue* at the Grand Hotel. Don't forget to pick up a programme for our series of free **3** *webinars* beginning next autumn.

CONFERENCE PROGRAMME

9.00 Opening speech by Dr Rania Walshe

9.30 Towards a first class workforce at Acrira
Dr Richard Carr, London Business School
In this **4** *lecture*, Dr Carr presents a **5** *case study* of insurance company Acrira and how their HR policies helped to promote company growth.

11.00 Talent management
Specialists from Executive Solutions International will present a number of techniques for talent management. In the second half, participants will have the chance to create their own strategic plan for managing their workforce and there will be time for questions from the **6** *floor*.

LUNCH

2.00–3.30 7 *Seminars:*
A: Improving staff retention: Techniques for employee engagement
B: Staff training: Integrating personal and company goals
C: The work-life balance: Family friendly HR policies
D: Supporting new staff: That important first month

4.00–5.00 Recruitment Challenges for the 21st century
8 *Plenary* session led by Dr Richard Carr

Choosing a venue for a conference

Listening

1 ①23 Listen to two work colleagues talking about three possible venues for a conference and read the information below about the three centres.

AVILON HOTEL
Situated only a short drive from the airport, the Avilon hotel offers the highest standards of service and dining and a fully equipped business and conference centre.
Distance from airport: 2 kms
Largest conference room capacity: 40
Number of seminar rooms: 3

FLAMENCO HOTEL
The Flamenco Hotel is in the heart of the city, with easy access to shopping and restaurants. The conference centre has a capacity which few other venues can match.
Distance from airport: 25 kms
Largest conference room capacity: 450
Number of seminar rooms: 6

RYDES VALE
Rydes Vale's stunning countryside location and beautiful lake makes it one of the best out-of-town venues for conferences in our region.
Distance from airport: 40 kms
Largest conference room capacity: 350
Number of seminar rooms: 12

2 Complete the conversation about the three hotels by writing one of the words or phrases from the box in the gaps (1–8).

> best   larger   biggest (x2)   least suitable   further   ~~most convenient~~   smaller

A: The **1** _most convenient_ is the Avilon. It's only two kilometres from the airport.

B: But it's too small. The **2** .... conference room only holds 40 people. I think the **3** .... place is the Flamenco.

A: It certainly has a **4** .... conference room than the Avilon. But actually our rooms don't need to be as big as that.

B: But that's just the room with the **5** .... capacity. I expect they have some **6** .... rooms as well. The only thing is it's 25 kilometres from the airport.

A: Rydes Vale sounds nice.

B: But I think that's the **7** .... of the three. It's even **8** .... from the airport than the Flamenco. We don't want to be right out in the countryside.

3 ①23 Listen to the conversation again and check your answers.

Grammar workshop

Superlatives

> **Comparatives** compare one item with another.
> *The Flamenco has a bigger conference room than the Avilon.*
>
> **Superlatives** compare one item with all the others in a group of two or more.
> *The biggest conference room holds 40 people.*

1 Answer the following questions about how to form the superlative. Use the conversation in Exercise 2 to help you.

1 How do one syllable adjectives like *big* form the superlative? _They add –est_

2 How do adjectives of three or more syllables form the superlative? ....

3 What word is used before a superlative form?

....

4 What are the superlative forms of *good* and *bad*?

....

5 What is the superlative form of *less*? ....

To avoid spending money on travel and accommodation, some businesses today prefer to do web conferencing, where people attend an online conference via an internet link.

2 Look at the table from a website which gives details of software packages for web conferencing. Write six sentences about the software packages using the superlative forms of the phrases in the box.

	Telepresent	Onlyconnect	Roco Webinars
price	$79 per month/ 40 cents per minute/ 25 cents per minute per participant	$59 per month	$50 per month
payment methods	monthly rate /rate per minute/ fee per participant	monthly rate only	monthly rate only
speaker capacity	40 speakers	15 speakers	20 speakers
number of features	excellent	lacks instant messaging	lacks instant messaging
easy to use	✓✓✓	✓✓✓✓	✓✓
secure	✓✓✓✓	✓✓✓✓	✓✓✓✓✓

> cheap   difficult to use   easy to use   expensive   ~~flexible payment system~~   high speaker capacity   number of features   secure

Example: Telepresent has _the most flexible payment system._

▶ **page 63** Comparatives and superlatives

A welcome speech

Listening

You will hear the chairman of a conference giving a welcome speech to a group of delegates.

1 24 **Listen to the chairman's speech and complete these notes on the main points by writing one to three words in each gap (1–7).**

Theme of conference: **1** *social media*

Mr Pineda's session will be replaced by a session about **2** .... advertising.

Mr Shi's talk will be held in the **3** ....

The discussion panel will be held in the **4** ....

Feedback forms should be placed in the container next to the **5** ....

Delegates will receive a free **6** .... as a souvenir.

Title of book to be published: **7** ....

Feedback comments

Reading

Read the following extracts from feedback forms that were given in at the end of the conference. For each extract, circle the correct summary, A, B or C.

1

> Venue a big improvement on last year but I really think you need to make better catering arrangements next time.

A Both the venue and the catering arrangements were better than last year.

B The caterers arranged for food to arrive at the wrong time.

Ⓒ The venue was better but the catering arrangements were unsatisfactory.

2

> I was looking forward to Tim Shi's talk but in the event found it disappointing, lacking in new information.

A Tim Shi's talk did not meet the writer's expectations.

B The writer found Tim Shi's talk more useful than he expected.

C The writer had difficulty finding the location for Tim Shi's talk.

3

> Interesting lectures and discussion panel but more time was needed for comments and questions from the floor.

A The discussion panel was less interesting than the lectures.

B The audience did not have enough opportunity to participate in the sessions.

C The sessions were scheduled at an inconvenient time.

4

Please indicate your overall satisfaction with the following aspects of the conference:

	satisfied	somewhat satisfied	neutral	somewhat dissatisfied	dissatisfied
Content		✗			
Registration				✗	
Venue	✗				
Food					✗

A The least satisfactory aspect of the conference was the registration process.

B The actual sessions given were not as impressive as the venue.

C Of the four aspects, the catering and refreshments were the most appreciated.

5

> The format of the conference brochure should be revised, as it has a very dated feel to it.

A The conference brochure needed to look more modern.

B The revised dates in the conference brochure were not clear.

C The conference brochure needed to be available earlier.

6

> The organisers have concentrated too much on lectures. How about more seminar/workshop style sessions?

A It was easier to concentrate in the lectures than in the seminars.

B Future conferences should contain fewer lecture style sessions.

C The lectures contained more useful content than the workshops.

Booking a venue

Role-play

Work in pairs.

Student A: look at the role card below.
Student B: look at the role card on page 119.

Prepare some of the language you want to use before you speak.

Student A

You need to find and book a venue for a one-day conference for about 100 people on 4 March. The text below is from the website of a possible venue.

Walfords Conference Centre is a high quality venue, ideal for conferences and corporate events. We offer two large lecture halls and a number of fully equipped seminar rooms.

For further details and bookings, please telephone 0207 6744493 or email sales@walfordsconference.co.uk

Telephone the conference centre and ask for some information. Find out about:

the size of the lecture hall	car parking facilities
what equipment is available	how you can book
the centre's availability on 4 March	

grateful and *pleased*

Writing

1 ☉ Business English students sometimes confuse the words *grateful* and *pleased*. Both can be used in formal written communications.

Grateful is how we feel when someone does something for us. It is often used to make requests.
I would be grateful if you could...

Pleased is how we feel when we are happy to do something.

We say *pleased with/about* or *pleased to do* something.

We say *grateful for* something.

Only people can be grateful or pleased. We cannot say ~~It would be grateful~~ or ~~It would be pleased~~.

2 Complete the following sentences with either *grateful* or *pleased*. If you cannot use either word, put an X.

1 I am ..pleased.. to introduce our new designer, Mary Watts.
2 I would be .... if you could book a single room for me.
3 I am very .... to accept your invitation.
4 It would be .... if you could arrange a taxi from the airport.
5 We would be .... if you could send us a temporary secretary.
6 It would be .... to have a company car.
7 I am very .... for the information that you sent me.
8 It would be .... if you could let me know when the deadline is.

3 Look at the sentences in 1 where you put X. Talk with a partner and decide on an adjective that could fit these sentences.

4 Read the email that you received after your telephone call to Walfords Conference Centre.

Further to your telephone call, please find attached our brochure which gives further details about Walfords Conference Centre. I will be pleased to provide any further information you may require.

I would be grateful if you could fill in the form on the website as soon as possible in order to confirm your booking.

Yours sincerely

Vasileios Kospanos

Conference Centre Manager

5 Unscramble the following phrases to form the beginnings for three sentences.

1 be could grateful very if I would you
2 prefer we If would possible
3 tell Please you me could

6 Now write your email to Mr Kospanos:

- confirming you have completed the online booking form
- enquiring how to book catering arrangements
- giving your preference for the type of lunch you want
- asking for a time when you can visit the centre before the event

Use the beginnings of the sentences in Exercise 5 to help you. Write 60–80 words.

Grammar workshop 3

Units 9–12

Future forms

Choose the correct future forms in the following sentences.

1 'Where are you taking those brochures?' *'I'll leave / I'm going to leave* some copies at reception.'
2 'Mr Johnson needs to leave an hour early.' 'OK, *I'll call / I'm going to call* him a taxi.'
3 I can't possibly come to the meeting. *I'll leave / I'm leaving* for Canada that day.
4 *Shall we / Will we* discuss the contract over lunch?
5 *'Will you ask / Are you going to ask* for unpaid leave next month?' 'No, I've decided not to bother.'
6 'I need to find a hotel for the 19th.' *'Shall I see / Am I going to see* if I can book one online?
7 'Have you fixed a time to meet James?' 'Yes, *he'll come / he's coming* to see me tomorrow morning.'
8 According to the latest report, house prices *will fall / are falling* by 10 per cent over the next year.

Contrast words

1 ⊙ **Business English students sometimes confuse the use of different contrast words. Choose the correct contrast words from the two alternatives.**

1 Sales were disappointing at first *but*/*however* they slowly began to pick up.
2 *Despite/Although* they have offered a discount, I still feel the price is too high.
3 The train costs 80 euros *whereas/instead* the coach is much cheaper.
4 I imagine they offer an after-sales service *despite/although* their brochure says nothing about it.
5 *However/Despite* the economic situation, sales continued to increase.
6 I can drive to Heathrow Airport in an hour *whereas/however* it takes much longer to reach Gatwick.
7 *Despite /Although* all these benefits, the product has a number of disadvantages.
8 Passenger numbers remained the same in the first four months. *However,/Although* they showed a big increase over the summer.

2 ⊙ **Business English students sometimes use unnecessary link words in sentences. Correct the following sentences by deleting a link word. Write the unnecessary word at the end. ONE of the sentences is correct.**

1 We can supply you with your first order but ~~and~~ not the second. *and*
2 We need a hotel with a good business centre but and if possible Wi-Fi access in the rooms.
3 I am afraid but we cannot offer you a discount.
4 Although the hotel prices are low now but they will start to go up next month.
5 I am sorry but I cannot agree to your request.
6 She is a good manager however, but she has little experience of this field.
7 Although the plane left on time, despite the bad weather.
8 Although the talk was interesting, and it didn't relate to my area of work.

Comparatives and superlatives

1 The following table gives details about three models of business travel case. Using the information in the table, complete sentences (1–8) with the comparative or superlative form of the adjectives in brackets.

	Travel case A	Travel case B	Travel case C
Material	nylon	nylon	leather
Colours	black, brown	black, brown, grey, red	black
Capacity	25 litres	28.5 litres	23.5 litres
Weight	3.3 kg	3.5 kg	4.09 kg
Cost	£279	£299	£510

1 Travel case C is the *most expensive* (expensive).
2 Travel case A is .... (cheap) than travel case B.
3 Travel case B is available in the .... (wide) range of colours.
4 Travel case A has a .... (great) capacity than travel case C.
5 Travel case A is .... (light) than travel case B.
6 Travel case C is the .... (heavy) of the three.
7 The leather case is probably .... (attractive) than the nylon ones.
8 Which of the three cases do you think is the .... (good) value for money?

2 ☉ Business English students sometimes make spelling mistakes with comparative and superlative sentences at this level. Correct the following sentences which contain spelling mistakes made by candidates in Cambridge business exams. TWO of the sentences are correct.

1 The new software will be installed two days ~~latter~~ than originally planned. *later*
2 I was wondering if you could start the job a week earlyer than we planned.
3 Of all the hotels, the Marquis has the bigest conference room.
4 Your desk is looking tidier than I ever remember.
5 We need one large conference room and another smaler room.
6 We need to find a fairer way of giving bonus payments.
7 This is one of the busyest airports in the world.

Text completion

1 Complete the following text by writing ONE suitable word in each gap.

David Givens, **1** *an* engineer at Cisco Systems, may hold the record for the man with **2** .... longest journey to work. Every weekday he drives 186 miles across California to his workplace in San José **3** .... another 186 miles back to his home in Mariposa in the evening. The journey **4** .... three and a half hours each way and he spends more **5** .... $800 a month on petrol. With the radio to keep him company, he claims that it's not **6** .... bad as some people might think. One of the most obvious advantages **7** .... that this way he can have a big house in the beautiful Yosemite mountains and a **8** .... better quality of life at weekends. One year, he came first in a competition to find 'America's Longest Commute', **9** .... he claims that he was surprised to win. 'I thought for sure someone else would have a **10** .... commute,' he says.

2 In each of the following sentences (1–9) one word is missing. Insert it in the correct place.

1 That was definitely ^*the* most interesting lecture I've been to.
2 We going to organise a training day next month.
3 We must send in our report soon as possible.
4 I would be very grateful your advice in this matter.
5 We are pleased confirm your booking for the conference centre.
6 You may have to leave some parts blank, but complete as much of the form you can.
7 I would be grateful if you send me some information.
8 I was looking forward to the talk but I found disappointing.
9 Please complete the form in order confirm your booking.

New places, new people

Getting started

1 Work with a partner and make a list of some possible reasons why someone might decide to change jobs. Compare your list with another pair.

2 Imagine you are going to start a job for a new company. Which two of the following options do you think would be the best way to learn about your new role?

- Read a manual about the company.
- Attend training sessions in the first two weeks of your employment.
- Attend a training day before you start the job.

- Be paired up with a 'buddy', another employee who can explain things to you and help you with any difficulties for the first few months.
- Just be thrown in at the deep end (start the job without any help or preparation so you have to learn as you go along).

Compare your choices with a partner. Did you choose the same options? Can you agree on the best two together?

The career doctor

Reading 1

1 The following text is taken from a website called *The Career Doctor*. People write in for advice on their careers or work problems. Read the letter and the career doctor's answer. Do you agree with the advice?

I work as a secretary. It's a secure job and the salary is reasonable. But I've done it for five years now. I feel that I've learnt everything I can from the job. I'm quite bored. I've always liked the idea of working in sales but I don't have any experience.

1 *I've just seen an advertisement online* for a course in selling skills. Do you think I should apply? Or is there anything else I could do to persuade an employer that I would be a good sales rep, even though **2 *I've never done the job before***?

Angela

Dear Angela,

In the past, people usually did the same job all their lives. These days people often change careers and there is nothing unusual about applying for a different type of job, even if **3 *you haven't had any experience in that field yet***.

Before spending money on a course, you should think about what you do in your present job. Sales reps need excellent interpersonal and communication skills. As a secretary, **4 *you've probably already developed these***. Look again at your current job description and rewrite it to emphasise the people skills. The most important skill for a sales rep is persuasion. **5 *Have you ever needed to persuade someone to change their mind about something***, or to do something for your boss? You'll probably come up with lots of examples, so rewrite your CV so it reflects all the experience you've had of dealing with people, and then start applying for sales jobs. Good luck!

2 Read the following statements (1–8) about the information in the text. If the text agrees, circle A. If it disagrees, circle B. If the information is not given in the text, circle C for doesn't say.

1 Angela is afraid that she will lose her job soon.
   A right   Ⓑ wrong   C doesn't say

2 Angela feels that she is not paid enough.
   A right   B wrong   C doesn't say

3 Angela would like to have a more interesting job.
   A right   B wrong   C doesn't say

4 According to the career doctor, most sales reps have worked in other fields first.
   A right   B wrong   C doesn't say

5 The career doctor feels that the selling skills course is not suitable for Angela.
   A right   B wrong   C doesn't say

6 The career doctor feels that Angela has already acquired many useful skills.
   A right   B wrong   C doesn't say

7 Angela's main duty in her current job is to schedule meetings.
   A right   B wrong   C doesn't say

8 The career doctor believes that Angela already has experience of persuading people to do things.
   A right   B wrong   C doesn't say

Grammar workshop 1

Present perfect

> We form the **present perfect** with *have/has* + the past participle.
>
> We use the present perfect when we are thinking about both the past and the present, especially when the past action has a result now.
>
> *I've learnt everything I can* = I know everything now, but I didn't in the past.
> *The job market has changed* = It is different now to how it was in the past.

1 Match each of the following uses of the present perfect (a–d) to the phrases in bold (1–5) in Reading 1.

a We use the present perfect with *just* to say that something happened very recently.

b We use the present perfect with *already* to say something has happened, often earlier than you expected.

c We use the present perfect with *yet* in questions and negative sentences when we expect something to happen.

d We use the present perfect with *ever/never* when we mean 'at any time up to now'.

2 In what position in sentences do we put *just/already/ever* and *never*? How is *yet* different?

3 Complete the following sentences with the present perfect form of the verbs in brackets.

1 I _have_ already _written_ the letter. (write)
2 .... you ever .... Mr Miyasaki? (meet)
3 I .... him the news yet. (not tell)
4 She .... never .... to New York. (be)
5 We've just .... of that model. (sell out)
6 I'm afraid I .... the telephone number. (forget)
7 He .... already .... the report. (read)
8 The share price .... recently. (fall)

4 For each of the sentences in Exercise 3, think of a sentence in the present with a similar meaning.

1 _The letter is ready._

Reading 2

1 Now read a second letter written to the career doctor.

> I worked for six years in a company where I had a good job. Then three months ago, I left to take a promotion with one of the leading companies in my field. Unfortunately, since then I've felt more and more disappointed. I don't like the way the new place is managed and my new colleagues are cold and unfriendly. Last week, an ex-colleague told me that my previous boss wants me to come back. I'm wondering if I should contact him, but I don't want to make any hasty decisions. What do you think I should do?

What advice would you give this person? Discuss with a partner.

2 Now read the career doctor's answer. Was your advice the same?

> It's true that sometimes career moves turn out to be a mistake. However, I am concerned that you've only worked in the new place for three months. That isn't really long enough to settle in, and it will take time for your colleagues to accept you.
> If your ex-boss knows that you aren't happy in the new job, it is possible he will contact you. If he does, you'll be in a good position to negotiate a higher salary. In the meantime, give the new place a chance by making a big effort to be as friendly as possible to your colleagues. You may find you start to get on better with them and that the new place isn't so bad after all.

3 Find words and phrases with the following meanings in the letter and answer.

1 a higher level job in the same company *promotion*
2 area of work ....
3 too quick, without careful thought ....
4 to be shown or found to be true (*verb and preposition*) ....
5 worried ....
6 feel comfortable in a new place (*verb and preposition*) ....
7 have a good relationship with someone (*three words*) ....

Grammar workshop 2

Present perfect and past simple

1 Read the rules about the use of the present perfect and past simple and complete the examples with sentences from Reading 2.

1 We use the present perfect with *for* to talk about something which started in the past and is still continuing now.
.... *only* .... *in the new place for three months.*

2 We use the past simple with *for* when the time finished before the present.
.... *for six years in a company where* .... *a good job.*

3 We use the present perfect with *since* to refer to the beginning of a period which continues until now.
Since then .... *more and more disappointed.*

4 We use the past simple with *ago* or any other finished time.
Three months ago, ...
Last week an ex-colleague .... *me that my previous boss wants me back.*

2 Look at the time phrases in the table and decide which of them can be used to complete sentences (1–6). There are two or three possibilities for most of them. Write one possibility in each sentence.

Present perfect	Past simple
already	as soon as I left school
before	last month
for the last 5 years	in 2010
just	three years ago
recently	when I was eighteen
since 2010	
yet	

1 I've worked for Samsung *since 2010* .
2 We've .... opened a new branch in Hull.
3 Export sales showed a strong performance ....
4 I started working for Santander ....
5 She hasn't sent in the sales report ....
6 Have you stayed in this hotel ....?

❯ **page 80** Present perfect and past simple

A career change

Listening

1 You will hear an interview with Matthew Beale. He now works for Fortbridge, a company which deals with investor relations for mining companies, but started his working life as an opera singer.

Look at the expressions in italics in the following sentences and use the context to decide what they mean. Compare your ideas with a partner.

1 You can't always please people in this job. Sometimes you just need to *put your foot down* and say 'No, this can't happen.'

2 Setting up your own business can be very exciting. *The reverse side of the coin* is that it's quite risky and you can lose a lot of money.

3 The finance department have been on *a very steep learning curve*, as we have just introduced new accounting software.

4 That field of work was new for me so I had to *jump in at the deep end* and learn about it while I was doing the job.

2 Match each expression in Exercise 1 with the correct definition (a–d).

a an opposite way of thinking about something
b a process in which you have to learn a lot very quickly
c to do something difficult without preparing for it first
d say very definitely that someone must or mustn't do something

3 (1) 25 Listen to the first part of the interview with Matthew and answer the questions.

1 When did Matthew start his singing career?
2 How long did he work as an opera singer?
3 What two things did he enjoy about working as an opera singer?
4 What did he dislike about it?
5 What skills does he bring from singing to working at Fortbridge?

4 (1) 26 Listen to the final part of the interview and write in the missing verbs.

> **I:** And has the job changed at all since you started?
> **M:** The job 1 *has changed* enormously simply because I 2 .... what the job involves. This 3 .... part of the fun of the whole thing in that I jumped in, and had to learn jumping in the deep end and whilst I've been on the job, I 4 .... what's important, what I need to concentrate on and what I 5 .... a bit of time on.

5 Answer the questions.

1 What tense is used in Exercise 3, questions (1–4)?
2 What tense is used in Exercise 4, gaps (1–5)?
3 Why is there this difference in the tenses used?

Role-play

1 You are someone who, like Matthew, has made a big career change in your working life. Look at the lists of jobs and choose a previous and a current job for yourself. Then think about:

- how long you worked in the previous job
- how long you have worked in your current one
- what skills you have been able to use from your previous job
- what new skills you have had to learn

Previous jobs	**Current jobs**
actor	university lecturer
accountant	accountant
police officer	web designer
lawyer	children's entertainer
flight attendant	chef
a job of your choice	a job of your choice

2 Work in pairs and each take one of the roles.

Student A

You are going to be interviewed about your job change for an article in the local newspaper. Use the information from 1 to help you answer the questions the journalist asks you.

Student B

You are a journalist on a local newspaper. You are going to interview someone who has made an unusual job change. Ask:

- how long they worked in the previous job
- how long they have worked in the current job
- why they decided to change jobs
- what they liked/disliked about their previous job
- what they like and dislike about the current one
- if they bring any skills from their previous job to the new one

Carry out the interview. Then swap roles so that Student A interviews Student B.

3 Tell the rest of the class about the two job changes and if they were a good career move or not.

Corporate gift-giving

Getting started

1 If you go on a business trip, it is often a good idea to take a present for your host. Which of the following verbs (1–8) do not collocate with *a gift* or *a present*?

1	give	5	close
2	receive	6	wrap
3	accept	7	unwrap
4	open	8	fasten

2 Read the following email written by a sales representative to her manager asking for advice about taking presents to clients on her next sales trip.

I often have very little space in my luggage and I don't want to carry a gift from my country as well. Couldn't I just buy my clients some flowers when I arrive?

Now read the beginning of her line manager's reply.

INBOX   File | Edit | View | Favourites | Tools | Actions | Help

It's doubtful whether flowers make a good gift generally for a business client....

Work in pairs and discuss why you think flowers might not make a good present for business clients.

3 Read the rest of the line manager's reply to see if your ideas are mentioned. Are there any reasons different from the ones you thought of?

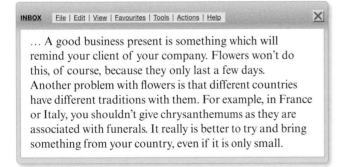

INBOX   File | Edit | View | Favourites | Tools | Actions | Help

... A good business present is something which will remind your client of your company. Flowers won't do this, of course, because they only last a few days. Another problem with flowers is that different countries have different traditions with them. For example, in France or Italy, you shouldn't give chrysanthemums as they are associated with funerals. It really is better to try and bring something from your country, even if it is only small.

4 Discuss the following questions with a partner.

1 Is there anything that you shouldn't normally give as a present to a business partner in your country? Why?

2 In some jobs or companies, employees are not allowed to accept gifts. Why do you think this is?

Promotional gifts

Reading

1 What kinds of free promotional items have you received from companies? (Think about clothing, writing equipment, small everyday objects ...) Make a list and compare it with a partner. Did any of them encourage you to buy products from the company?

2 Now scan the article on promotional gifts. Are any of the items you and your partner discussed mentioned in the text? If so, which ones?

Top promotional items

At some point, nearly all businesses give free promotional **items** to their customers, and some of them can spend a lot of **time** deciding on the best thing to give. But in this matter at least, it seems that thinking out of the box is not always a good **idea**. I've carried out a small **survey** among friends and colleagues and it seems that the best promotional gifts are often the most obvious ones. Here are my top three.

1 The promotional bag with your company name and logo on it. This is probably the most common item and still the best. If it's well made and nicely produced, **people** will use it to carry their **stuff** in the street, on the train and into their office, which is a great way to advertise your company.

2 The memory stick. Everyone needs to back up their **documents**, so a memory stick will almost certainly be kept and used, and the **cover** can easily be customised. The disadvantage from the company's point of view is that not many other people will see it.

3 The umbrella. Again a useful promotional gift, with lots of **room** for your company's branding. Like the promotional bag, if you live in a country where there's lots of **rain**, an umbrella will give people plenty of opportunities to see your company's name around town.

So if these are the top three, what are the ones to avoid? **Consumables** like **stationery** don't make good promotional

items because they are soon used and forgotten. The same goes for **food** items like **chocolate**. You should also avoid sports **equipment** (not everyone will use it) and **goods** which can break easily like **glassware**. But my **prize** for the worst promotional item goes to the stress ball. These little pieces of **rubber** are nearly always left at the back of drawers of cupboards and then thrown away after a few months. Have you ever seen anyone using one?

3 **Which of the following ideas about promotional gifts are mentioned in the article?**

a They should last a long time.
b They should be something that most people use.
c They should relate to the company's activity.
d They should be unusual.
e They should be visible in public places.
f They should be well made.
g They should look more expensive than they are.

Grammar workshop 1

Countable and uncountable nouns

> **Countable nouns** must have *a*, *an* or *the* in front of them in the singular and can be used in the plural (e.g. *a bag*, *the bag*, (*some*) *bags*).
>
> **Uncountable nouns** do not have *a/an* in front of them in the singular and have no plural forms. We use *some* (or *any* in questions and negatives) to refer to uncountable nouns.

1 **Look at the words in bold in the article and write them in the correct column in the table below.**

Countable (singular)	Countable (plural)	Uncountable
	items	

2 **Work in pairs to answer the following questions.**

1 Which of the words in Column 2 have no singular form? Which is an irregular plural?
2 Sometimes the same word can be countable or uncountable but with a change of meaning. For example:
rubber (uncountable) = the material
a rubber (countable) = something for removing pencil marks
3 Which other three words in Column 3 can be both countable and uncountable?

3 **Complete the following sentences by writing *a/an* or *some* in each gap.**

1 I saw ___some___ very interesting new equipment at the trade fair.
2 I would be grateful if you could send me _____ information.
3 I have _____ suggestion that might be useful.
4 He gave us _____ good advice about bookkeeping.
5 Could we rearrange the office to make _____ room for the new desks?
6 I am writing to complain about _____ item of clothing I purchased from your store.
7 I hope we can fix _____ time to meet soon.
8 Our department has just invested in _____ new software.

4 ⊘ Business English students sometimes try to use uncountable nouns in the plural. Decide if the plurals in the following sentences are correct. If not, change them and make any other necessary changes to the grammar.

1 The ~~informations~~ *information* that you sent about the product ~~were~~ *was* not all correct.
2 Members of staff will be happy to answer your questions and to give advices on products.
3 I am afraid that your ideas were not accepted by the board.
4 Please can you confirm that the equipments we requested are available.
5 All electrical devices need to be checked regularly.
6 The company spent a lot of money on travels last year.
7 We have managed to save the business but I'm afraid the works have only just begun.
8 We can provide transports to and from the airport.
9 What are your responsibilities in the new job?
10 It's only a weekend trip so I don't need to take many luggages.

❯ page 80 *a/an* and *some*

Cultural awareness

Listening

1 You are going to listen to an interview about gift-giving with Tara Brandon, who runs a consultancy which gives training on cultural awareness. Which of the following do you think would be good gifts to take to new business partners in another country?

a something that your hosts can't usually find in their country
b something obviously expensive
c something with your company logo on it
d a present especially for your contact person
e identical items for everyone in the company

2 ①27 Listen to the first part of the interview. Which of the ideas above does the consultant agree with?

3 ①27 Listen again and note down why she agrees or disagrees with each idea (a–e). Then compare your ideas with a partner.

4 ①28 In the second part of the interview, the consultant talks about giving gifts in Japan. Listen and write one or two words in each gap in the notes.

The main times of the year for giving gifts in Japan are in 1 December and 2 _____ .

Tara recommends goods from a well-known 3 _____ as a present, or possibly good quality 4 _____ .

Don't wrap gifts in 5 _____ .

Traditionally, gifts are not opened immediately. This is done 6 _____ .

Give and receive gifts with 7 _____ .

Don't give four pieces of anything because the word for 'four' sounds like 8 _____ in Japanese.

5 Imagine you are going on a business trip from your country to visit a Japanese company. You need to take one special gift for the CEO and six gifts for the rest of the team. What items from your country could make good presents? Decide with a partner what you would take, then compare your ideas with another pair.

Grammar workshop 2

Articles

1 Look at extracts (a–f) from the listening and complete the grammar rules (1–6) about articles by underlining the correct alternative and matching it to the correct extract.

a *It sounds like the word for **death**.*

b *You need to take **a present** for your hosts.*

c *If your host suggests you open the present, you mustn't just tear **the paper (= the paper around the present)**.*

d *This is when **companies** might give **presents** to **good customers**.*
Light blue paper is the best choice.

e *Presents **in Japan** are always wrapped.*
*You mustn't just tear the paper like we might do **in Europe**.*
In Japanese the word for four sounds like ...

f *It can be a problem if you're bringing **a present** through customs, so it's often best to wrap **the present** while you're there.*

1 When we are talking in general, we use *a or an/the/no article* with uncountable nouns and plurals.

    d *This is when **companies** might give **presents** to **good customers**.*
      ***Light blue paper** is the best choice.*

2 When we are talking in general, we use *a or an/the/no article* with singular countable nouns.

3 We use *a or an/the/no article* when the person we are speaking to knows which thing we are talking about. Often this is because it is the second time we have mentioned it.

4 We also use *a or an/the/no article* when a particular thing that has not been mentioned before can be understood from something we have said previously.

5 We use *a or an/the/no article* in front of most countries, continents and languages (plural countries like *the United States* are the exception).

6 We use *a or an/the/no article* with some general words like *life, society,* etc.

2 Complete the following text by putting *a/an*, *the* or (–) *no article* into each gap.

1 __–__ people often think that 2 _____ gift will be more appreciated if it is expensive. However, 3 _____ studies have found that this is not necessarily true. For example, it seems that most fiancées feel just as grateful for 4 _____ modestly priced engagement ring as for 5 _____ expensive one. Likewise, in 6 _____ business, 7 _____ same researchers have found that 8 _____ companies don't need to give their staff 9 _____ expensive rewards. 10 _____ small gift or token will be just as effective if you want to show 11 _____ appreciation. It seems that 12 _____ words of 13 _____ old Beatles' song are true: 14 _____ money can't buy you 15 _____ love.

❯ page 80 Articles

Saying thank you
Writing

Helmut Schulz works for a German engineering company which produces irrigation equipment. He has just returned from a business trip to Qatar, where he demonstrated some of his company's products.

1 Complete Mr Schulz's thank you letter to his Qatari hosts by putting a phrase from the box (a–i) in the correct gap (1–9).

a Finally thank you once again
b ~~I am writing to thank you~~
c I especially enjoyed
d I look forward to hearing from you
e I was also very interested
f I was most impressed
g In the meantime I enclose
h It was very interesting
i Please extend a special thanks

Dear Mr Amin,

1 __b__ for a most enjoyable visit to Doha. 2 _____ to see the city and 3 _____ the meal in your beautiful restaurant along the Corniche. All of your staff were extremely courteous and 4 _____ with their knowledge of irrigation technology.

5 _____ to see the desalination plant. 6 _____ to Mr Ashraf Zanaty for taking so much time to guide me round.

7 _____ in due course regarding your decision on our irrigation equipment. 8 _____ a few small promotional items from my company which I hope you will find useful. 9 _____ for making my stay in Qatar such a pleasant experience.

Kind regards

Helmut Schulz

2 Imagine you have just returned from a business trip to (a city of your choice) to look at some possible new products. Write a thank you letter to your host similar to the one in Exercise 1. In the letter:

- thank your host for their hospitality and a meal or any other entertainment they provided
- say how useful the visit was
- say when you will be in touch with a decision about the products

Write 60–80 words.

Teamwork

Getting started

1 Think of a team that you have been a member of (a work, study or sports team). Then make notes on the following questions.

  1 What was the team's aim and how successful were you?
  2 Did the people in the team have specific roles?
  3 How similar or different were the people in the team? (Think about experience, age and personality.)
  4 Were there disagreements between different team members at any point? How did you solve them?

2 Work with a partner and take it in turns to tell each other about your team and what it achieved.

Team-building

Reading

Sometimes companies arrange team-building events for their staff especially if a group of people have not worked together before. In the text, you will find the details of five different team-building events.

1 Scan the text to find the titles of each event and match it to the correct picture (a–e).

a   3   b   c   d   e

TEAM-BUILDING EVENTS

1 CHOCOLATE WORKSHOP
This event is designed for groups of 8 to 50 people. After a short introduction on the history of the topic, participants are split into groups to make and decorate their own chocolates. The decorating is bound to bring out your creative talent and getting messy together is a great way to break down barriers. Hats and protective clothing are provided. At the end of the session everyone takes home an average of 25 chocolates in a gift-wrapped box.

2 BLIND DRIVING
This is an excellent exercise if you want to see an improvement in your team's communication skills. Participants work in pairs. One person is blindfolded and has to drive a car around our special course with only his partner's instructions to guide him. The winning pair is the one who can complete the course in the shortest time, but without knocking over any of the plastic walls

and trees we use as obstacles. Completing a successful circuit together is a real achievement. See if you can beat the present record of 10 minutes, 15 seconds.

3 TREASURE HUNT
Treasure hunt adventures are based on the Scandinavian sport of orienteering where participants use a map to find their way through a forest. The object of a treasure hunt is to find clues which are shown on a map and discover the location of the mysterious treasure chest. Normally a treasure hunt lasts about 3 hours. To see how the group has to work together, watch our film of a recent event, the first day for 900 new students at a business school, with a total of 70 teams. Nearly all participants agreed that the event was a wonderful way of forming new friendships.

4 DRUM CIRCLE
This is a musical event where participants sit in a circle playing drums, bells or shakers. Our representative leads

2 Read questions (1–10), then scan the text quickly and write the answer next to each question.

1 During which months can you book the raft building event? *April to September*

2 What is the fastest time for completing the blind driving course? ....

3 What is the maximum number of people who can attend the chocolate workshop? ....

4 How long does a treasure hunt usually last?

....

5 Apart from drums, what instruments can you play in a drum circle? ....

6 What do people wear for the chocolate workshop?

....

7 Which hotel can people stay at for the raft building event? ....

8 Which part of Europe does the sport *orienteering* come from? ....

9 What obstacles are there on the blind driving course? ....

10 How many teams took part in the film of the treasure hunt? ....

3 Scan the whole text to find out which event would be best for skills (a–d). Write the event number.

a improving communication skills *2*

b encouraging a large team to all co-operate ......, ...

c getting a group to solve practical problems with equipment ....

d encouraging creativity ....

the circle and helps them to reach their full potential as an orchestra. This activity is recommended for any group who need to come together in a co-operative way instead of competing with each other. It is one of the few interactive exercises you can use with a large group. You can't beat it as a way to break the ice between new colleagues.

5 RAFT BUILDING
This is for the company manager who wants to take his staff out of the familiarity of their office. It takes place in a beautiful mountain setting and can be booked from April to September. Block booking for large groups can be made at the famous Scheuble Hotel, subject to availability. Each team is given 100 tokens which they use to buy raft-making equipment from the instructor. Groups have to use their problem solving skills and all their practical knowledge about how things work to produce the best design. At the end of the day, there is a race on a nearby lake.

4 Find two expressions in the text with the verb *break* which both mean *get to know someone better*.

1 .... 2 ....

5 Work with a partner and discuss the following questions.

1 Which team-building event would you most enjoy?

2 Which event do you think would benefit the staff in your company or your fellow students most? Why?

Suffixes

Vocabulary

1 Suffixes usually change the type of a word (e.g. from a verb to a noun). Which of the following suffixes are used to form nouns and which are used to form adjectives? Write noun (N) or adjective (A) next to the suffix.

-al -ful -ity -ive -ment -ous -tion **N** -y

2 Now think of an example word for each suffix.

Example: -tion   direct (verb)   direction (noun)

3 Write the noun forms of the following words, then check your answers in the reading text.

1 introduce *introduction*
2 improve ....
3 equip ....
4 achieve ....
5 instruct ....
6 familiar ....
7 available ....

Which suffixes are usually added to verbs? Which to adjectives?

4 Write the adjective forms of the following words, then check your answers in the reading text again.

1 help *helpful*   7 mess ....
2 success .... 8 practice ....
3 fame ....   9 protect ....
4 music ....   10 interact ....
5 wonder .... 11 create ....
6 mystery .... 12 co-operate ....

Which suffixes are usually added to nouns? Which to verbs?

❯ **page 81** Word types

Speaking

1 **Work in groups. You want to organise a team-building event for one of the following groups:**

- 15 employees in an engineering company who are soon going to start a major new project
- a management consultancy which has recently taken on 40 new members of staff
- employees in your own workplace or college

2 **Choose a group and then decide which of the skills in Reading Exercise 3 you want to develop through one of the following activities:**

- a quiz or games night, based on a TV quiz or game show you know
- a competition involving cooking or making food
- a sports day held somewhere in the countryside
- a scavenger hunt (teams have to collect specific items from around your city in a given time)
- a team-building activity of your choice

Decide together:
- what exactly teams will have to do
- where and when it will take place
- how many people will be involved and how many teams
- what you will give as a prize
- what you want the outcome to be in terms of skills development

3 **Report back to the rest of the group about what you have decided to do and why. Who designed the best event?**

> **Useful language**
> **Aims and intentions**
>
> Our aim is to break down barriers
> between ....
> We want to encourage creativity/
> cooperation/interaction ....
> We're going to organise ....
> at ....

Teamwork

Listening

1 **Before you listen, read the statements about teamwork (1–5) and decide if they are true or false. Write T for true or F for false in the *You* column of the table. Talk with a partner and compare your ideas.**

	You	Speaker
1 A team leader should be the most intelligent person in the team.		
2 In a good team, you need lots of creative people with original ideas.		
3 The best teams are the ones where team members have similar personalities.		
4 There are some people who cannot work well in a team.		
5 Poor team players do not reach high positions in business.		

2 🔊 1 29 **Listen to the presentation. According to the speaker, which of the statements on the left are true and which are false? Write T or F in the *Speaker* column of the table.**

3 🔊 1 29 **Listen again and make notes on the details of what the speaker says about each point in the table. Then work with a partner and discuss the following questions.**

1 What do you think about the speaker's ideas for building successful teams?
2 Would you follow her suggestions for choosing a new member of your team?

Kaizen

Reading

1 You are going to read an article about a system for improving companies with its origin in Japan. Work with a partner. Read the list of questions (a–g) and decide which are likely to be the headings of the *first* and *last* paragraphs. Write 1 in the box next to the first paragraph and 7 in the box next to the last paragraph.

a When does it take place? ☐

b How can employees put forward their ideas? ☐

c How important is *kaizen* for the future? ☐

d What does *kaizen* mean? ☐

e Who takes part? ☐

f Are the suggestions acted on? ☐

g What kind of improvements are made? ☐

2 Skim the first and last paragraphs to find out if you were right.

3 Skim the rest of the paragraphs (2–6) and match each with headings (a–g) in Exercise 1. Write the correct paragraph number in the box next to each heading.

4 Read paragraphs 2, 3, 4 and 6 again and put phrases (a–e) into gaps (i–v).

a rather than dealing with major changes

b in many companies the attitude is 'if it isn't broken, don't fix it' whereas

c and it is very important that suggestions are not put in an in-tray and forgotten

d and not just the quality control manager

e rather than a short period of big change or a yearly review of systems

Task tip

The text makes comparisons between companies which use *kaizen* and companies which don't. When filling the gaps, think about the comparison that particular sentence is making.

Kaizen

1 The word *kaizen* comes from the Japanese words for *school* and *wisdom*. It refers to a system for making improvements which aims to make sure that any business remains at the cutting edge in terms of quality, processes, technology and productivity.

2 Kaizen involves all employees, from top management to the cleaning and maintenance staff. Anyone can make a suggestion for improvement i __d__ . This is why implanting kaizen may involve a change in the corporate culture. It has to be something that employees do because they know it is good for them, not something which they do because management tell them they must.

3 One big difference between kaizen and other attempts to change a business is that kaizen is a continuous activity, ii _____ . Everyone is encouraged to think about the business and come up with suggestions for improvement all the time.

4 Kaizen generally focuses on solving a large number of small problems iii _____ . Usually the changes are to do with improving productivity or reducing waste. In addition, iv _____ kaizen does not involve just fixing problems. Even if something seems to be working well, staff should still think how they can make it even better.

5 In many companies which use kaizen, teams of employees can meet to put forward and discuss any possible suggestions for improvement in a forum known as a Quality Control circle. There are also other ways to collect employees' ideas, like putting suggestion boxes in the workplace.

6 Quite often about 90 per cent of employees' suggestions are implemented. The action should take place as soon as possible, sometimes that same day v _____ . Even if a particular suggestion is not implemented, it is important for the employees to know why.

7 The world has moved on since Japan's economic boom in the second half of the twentieth century but the principles of continuous improvement and reduction are still important for company managers. A number of Chinese companies are now interested in kaizen after seeing its effects in other companies. When the engineering company Huayu Cooper brought in the system, for example, output per workshift increased from 85 to 115 units.

5 Work in pairs and discuss the following questions.

- Is there a system in your company or place of study for employees or students to make suggestions?
- What do you think of the kaizen system for improving a company? Do you think there are any problems with it? If so, what?

Thinking globally

Getting started

1 Work in pairs. Read the following definitions and then discuss the question below.

Culture: *n.* the customs, institutions and achievements of a particular nation, people or group.

Cultural awareness: *n.* the ability to understand the culture of the people you are with and behave appropriately.

How important is it for business people to have good cultural awareness?

2 Read the following statements and decide which you agree with more. Discuss your ideas with your partner.

A
I don't think that studying different cultures is very important any more. The world is a much smaller place than it was fifty years ago. English has become an international language and many brands are known all over the world. Cultural differences have become smaller and people have become more similar to each other.

B
The fact that the world has become smaller means that it is more important to know about other cultures, not less. People still grow up within a particular culture and they are still influenced by it. That hasn't changed just because we now have international brands and an international language.

Global HR management

Reading

1 **You are going to read an article about the growing need for HR departments to think globally. Skim the article and answer the following questions.**

   1 Which paragraphs contain examples of Western HR managers who have worked in Eastern countries?
   2 Which paragraph contains an example of an Eastern HR manager who plans to move to the West?
   3 Which paragraph contains an example of why HR managers today have to think globally?

2 **Read the following statements (1–8) about the information in the text. If the text agrees, circle A. If it disagrees, circle B. If the information is not given in the text, circle C for doesn't say.**

   1 Human resources attracts people who are interested in travel opportunities.
      A right   (B) wrong   C doesn't say
   2 Fewer companies nowadays are moving their production offshore.
      A right   B wrong   C doesn't say

3 For many companies, there is greater growth potential at home than overseas.
   A right   B wrong   C doesn't say

4 Most HR managers believe that the best way to gain cultural awareness is to work in another country.
   A right   B wrong   C doesn't say

5 More people go to university in India than in most Western countries.
   A right   B wrong   C doesn't say

6 Western graduates are more likely to be unemployed after university than Indian graduates
   A right   B wrong   C doesn't say

7 Martin Poulsen was surprised to see how much time Chinese managers spent socialising with employees.
   A right   B wrong   C doesn't say

8 Jasmine Divedi's company is intending to move part of the HR department to the West.
   A right   B wrong   C doesn't say

The changing world of human resources

1 Human resources is not traditionally an area to work in if you want an international career. There are **not many** HR managers who have extensive experience of working overseas and only **a few** of them are truly globally mobile. But that could be changing.

2 This change is happening because in a great many companies, offshore operations are starting to play a different role to that of ten or twenty years ago. When they were first set up, they were usually just a low cost base for manufacturing. Now, however, **a large number** of them are involved in the innovation and creation of new products. For these companies, the biggest opportunities are in emerging markets abroad, not in their home country. This means HR managers have to know how to attract the best local talent for their overseas locations, and also how to develop their own staff for important posts there.

3 Of course members of an HR team can build up their cultural awareness without going to work long-term in another country. Even short visits abroad can help them gain **a little** more knowledge of overseas offices. But most companies do **not have much** money to spend on international travel for staff, and in any case, according to most international HR managers, it is not the same as gaining real experience of working there. For example, Tim Prendy, a HR manager who spent two years in India, came to realise that words like 'star performer' or 'high flyer' do not always mean the same thing in another culture. In the West, a high flyer usually means someone with special abilities and a **great deal** of determination; in India, it may

mean that the person attended one of the best universities. This often goes along with a different recruitment culture; in both China and India graduates rely more on university lecturers to place them in the right career than their CVs.

4 There can be other cultural differences too. For Martin Poulsen, a Danish HR manager who worked for a number of years in Shanghai, one of the biggest eye openers was to see **how much** of their personal time Chinese managers may spend with work colleagues. '**A lot of** time and effort in China goes into building up relationships with your team outside the workplace.' he reflects. 'The division between work and leisure time in Denmark is quite different.'

5 Of course, the movement is not just one way. Jasmine Diwedi, head of human resources of a software company in Jaipur, India, is planning to relocate to the US along with **several** members of her team. ' We have an international customer base so there are **lots of** advantages to having the HR department located outside India' she says. It seems that if they are working with a global pool of talent, then today's HR managers need to be globally mobile.

Grammar workshop

Quantity expressions

1   We use different quantity expressions for countable and uncountable nouns. Look at the expressions in bold in the reading text and write them in the correct place in the table.

For countable nouns	For uncountable nouns	For both
not many		

2   Underline the correct quantity expressions in the following sentences (1–7).

1   Only *a little/a few* customers have visited our website.
2   There aren't *much/many* opportunities for travel in my job.
3   Do you know *how much/how many* cash we'll need?
4   I don't have *much/many* information about Far Eastern markets.
5   I need *a little/a few* more time to complete the report.
6   I don't know *how much/how many* languages he can speak.
7   *A great deal of/several* people have applied to work in our US branch.

> *Much* and *many* are usually used in questions and negatives. In affirmative sentences, we usually use other expressions. In formal English we can use *a great deal of* + uncountable noun and *a great many / a large number of / several* + plural noun. In more informal English we use *a lot of / lots of*. (These expressions can also be used in questions and negatives.)

3 ⊙ Business English students sometimes find the use of *much* and *many* in sentences difficult. In the following sentences (1–8), decide if you need to replace *much* or *many* with one of the expressions from the box on page 77. THREE of the sentences are correct.

1 Our truck broke down and so we wasted ~~much~~ time. *a lot of / a great deal of*
2 We have invested much money in this market.
3 There hasn't been much interest in the new position.
4 He has much experience in this area.
5 Do you have many Chinese customers?
6 There isn't much space to store the new furniture.
7 There are many spare copies of the form in that cupboard.
8 Their employees need much training in health and safety procedures.

❯ page 81 Quantity expressions

International teams

Listening

1 **Discuss the following questions with a partner.**

1 What advantages do you think international teams have compared with teams in which all the members are from the same country?
2 What difficulties can international teams experience?

2 **Read the following statements and decide if they are true or false. Then compare your ideas with a partner.**

1 Teams where the members are from different cultures usually perform better than teams where people are from the same or similar cultures.
2 Employees are more likely to trust a manager who comes from the same country or culture as they do.
3 You can't build up a good relationship with members of a team just by communicating online.

3 ①30 **Listen to four people talking about international teams in their company. Listen and match each person (1–4) with the correct statement (a–f) at the top of the page. There are two statements you do not need.**

Person 1 .....e.....   Person 3 ....

Person 2 ....   Person 4 ....

Which person …

a works in a company which is planning to appoint a new HR director overseas?
b works in a company which categorises employees according to how globally mobile they are?
c works in a company which recently increased its number of vacant posts overseas?
d had a positive experience of working as part of a virtual team?
e successfully brought together an international team for a project?
f was a part of an online team who failed to work well together?

Global management

Vocabulary

Choose the word which best completes each sentence (1–8).

1 An international manager needs to be aware .... cultural and social differences.
   A on   B at   Ⓒ of   D about

2 Global managers have to deal with people who .... separated by time, distance and culture.
   A is   B are   C has   D have

3 It can be difficult to .... a balance between keeping a company's culture and responding to local conditions.
   A hit   B earn   C win   D strike

4 Effective global managers require .... skills, such as the ability to communicate and to understand different points of view.
   A soft   B light   C low   D smooth

5 Too many managers only start to think about cultural issues when things .... wrong.
   A come   B go   C run   D move

6 In some countries, people avoid open disagreement or saying no ....
   A direction   B directed
   C directing   D directly

7 Some countries favour .... timekeeping whereas others are much more flexible about this.
   A strict   B hard   C true   D severe

8 In some countries it's important to build .... a personal relationship before you do business with someone.
   A in   B out   C up   D off

Business tourism

Speaking

Read the following definition of business tourism.

> **Business tourism:** the activity of providing facilities and services for conferences, trade fairs and other business events in a town, city or region.

1 Choose either your own city or a city you have visited and liked. Imagine you are part of a project to promote this city as a centre for business tourism. You have to give a short speech about what the city can offer and why it is a good place for business events. Think about:

- good hotels and restaurants
- parks and large outdoor areas
- buildings where you can rent rooms
- transport links
- current small and large businesses in the city
- tourist attractions
- crime
- transport problems

2 Prepare your speech, saying how much/many there is/are of the above in the city you have chosen, and mentioning any other advantages.

Example: *There are several five-star hotels. There are not many large businesses at the moment, but there are lots of possibilities for companies to expand here.*

3 Work in groups of three and give your speeches to each other. Who gave the most convincing speech?

Requesting information

Writing

1 Read the advertisement below about a promotional organisation for a city.

Washington Partners

is the official promotional organisation for Washington DC. We aim to promote Washington DC as the city of choice for businesses, investors and business tourism.

So far, we have helped over 100 businesses who wanted to expand to Washington. Over 50 per cent of these came from overseas. We have a network of partners abroad who can be the point of contact for you if you are thinking of establishing your business in one of the top cities of the USA.

For information about our network, please contact Ronald Leman on info@washingtonpartners.com

2 You work for a company which is interested in making contacts and opening a branch in the USA. You decide to write an email to Ronald Leman. In your email you want to:

1 introduce your company
2 explain why you are thinking of expanding to the USA
3 ask what help Washington Partners can provide for your business
4 ask for contact details of a partner located in your country

3 Look at the beginnings of the sentences below and match each one (a–h) to one of the points (1–4) above. There are two for each point.

a We are interested in …
b Please could you also give me …
c We are a company …
d We hope to …
e Please could you tell me …
f I am writing to introduce …
g I would also be grateful if you could provide …
h I would also like to enquire …

4 Write your email, using some of the sentence beginnings above to help you. Write 60–80 words.

Grammar workshop 4

Units 13–16

Present perfect and past simple

1 Complete the following dialogue by writing the verbs in brackets in each gap (1–8) using either present perfect or past simple.

> **A:** Hi Nadia. I **1** _haven't seen_ (see) you for some time.
> **B:** No, well we **2** .... (just finish) moving to a new office. We're now based in Seamore Street.
> **A:** Oh really? How long **3** .... you .... (be) there?
> **B:** About three weeks. We **4** .... (move) on April 17. It was mad. We **5** .... (have to) pack everything into crates and we still **6** .... (not be) ready when the removal people **7** .... (arrive).
> **A:** But you're settled in now?
> **B:** No, that's the thing. We still **8** .... (not unpack) everything yet.

2 ☉ Business students at this level sometimes confuse the use of present perfect and past simple. Complete the following sentences (1–10) by putting the verb in brackets in the correct form, either present perfect or past simple.

1 As you _have_ already _heard_ , we have a new designer in the department. (hear)
2 Two months ago, our department successfully .... a new product. (launch)
3 As you .... just .... in the department, I think the seminar will be interesting for you. (start)
4 I .... this month's report yet. (not finish)
5 I .... already .... you an email regarding the subject of the meeting. (send)
6 The department .... very busy for the past few months as it is the end of the financial year. (be)
7 We .... some problems with our computers since yesterday morning. (have)
8 We .... your software during our visit to the computer show last month. (see)
9 Our current software has caused serious problems which .... us a lot of money. (cost)

10 I'd like to say something about what I .... before I .... to work for this company. (do, start)

a/an and some

☉ Business English students sometimes try to use a/an instead of some with uncountable nouns. Choose the correct word in the following sentences.

1 Please let me know if you need an /(some) overnight accommodation.
2 I would like a/some help from the sales manager.
3 I think you've done a/some very good job.
4 We have a/some very important work to do.
5 We would like to offer you a/some language training.
6 We run a/some course in basic Chinese for business people.
7 Our company has developed a/some new software.
8 This is a/some rather inconvenient moment to call.
9 I have a/some free time on Wednesday morning.
10 Please could you give me an/some information by the end of the week.

Articles

Read the following advertisement and put a/an, the or no article (-) in each gap.

> ## CULTURAL AWARENESS TRAINING
>
> Whether you are participating in **1** _a_ joint project or dealing with **2** .... overseas customer, it is very important to know something about your partner's culture. Our company delivers **3** .... training in **4** .... cultural awareness across **5** .... world. We guarantee that **6** .... knowledge you gain will help you do **7** .... business in today's global marketplace.
>
> **COMMENTS**
> 'It was **8** .... fantastic course and **9** .... tutor was really knowledgeable.'
>
> 'It was one of **10** .... best training days I've experienced. **11** .... content was excellent and I really enjoyed **12** .... activities.'

Quantity expressions

In the following sentences (1–6), one of the three alternatives is not possible. Circle the one which is NOT possible.

1 We have .... representatives based in the Far East.
   A a number of
   Ⓑ a great deal of
   C several

2 There aren't .... people who stock those products.
   A much
   B many
   C a lot of

3 Our Brazilian office has invested in .... state of the art equipment.
   A a great deal of
   B a lot of
   C a great many

4 Only .... our employees have expressed interest in moving to Tunis.
   A a little of
   B a few of
   C a small number of

5 There is .... money left in our travel budget.
   A not much
   B not many
   C only a little

6 I'm afraid I'm going to need .... help with this project.
   A a little
   B a few
   C some

Word types

1 ⊙ **Business English students sometimes make errors with word types (verbs, nouns and adjectives). In the following sentences one of the words is in the wrong form. Find the mistake and write the correct form at the end. TWO of the sentences are correct.**

   1 Thank you for your ~~inviting~~ to speak at the conference dinner. *invitation*
   2 The sales figures showed a small improving last month.
   3 We have made a few changes to the seminar programme.
   4 Ms Baker is a new member of our designing team.
   5 Please let me know if you have any questions or suggests.

6 I am pleased to announce the arrive of a new colleague.
7 He will be responsibility for all data systems.
8 You have made an excellent contribution to the department.
9 You can check the depart time of your flight on the website.
10 I would like to express my appreciate for your help last week.

2 ⊙ **Match each of the spelling rules (1–4) with the correct list of example words (a–d).**

   1 The *-ful* adjective suffix is always spelt with one *l*. _d_
   2 If you add a suffix beginning with a vowel, like *-ous*, to a word ending with silent *e*, you drop the *e* before it. ....
   3 If the suffix begins with a consonant like *-ment*, you keep silent *e* before it. ....
   4 If a word finishes with consonant + *y*, the *y* changes to *i* when you add a suffix. ....

   a improvement, management, hopeful
   b happiness, mysterious, various
   c famous, practical, storage
   d thoughtful, careful, wonderful

3 ⊙ **Business English students sometimes make spelling mistakes with words which contain suffixes. Find and correct the spelling mistakes in the following sentences. TWO of the sentences are correct.**

   1 She came up with some very ~~helpfull~~ ideas. *helpful*
   2 She felt very nerveous before the job interview.
   3 I would like to talk about our achievments over the past year.
   4 I would be gratefull if you could send me some information.
   5 Using the machines without protective clothing can be dangerous.
   6 We have a number of plans for staff developement.
   7 The report that you sent me was very useful.
   8 The product has been very succesful in our overseas markets.
   9 We would definitly like to see some samples of your products.
   10 It is not adviseable to buy the cheapest equipment you can find.

Describing statistics

Getting started

1 **Study the three diagrams (A–C) and answer the questions below.**

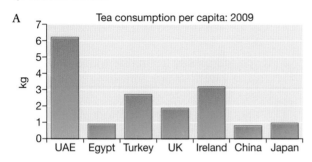

A Tea consumption per capita: 2009

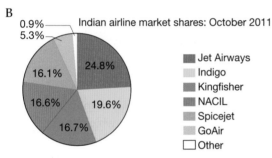

B Indian airline market shares: October 2011

- Jet Airways
- Indigo
- Kingfisher
- NACIL
- Spicejet
- GoAir
- Other

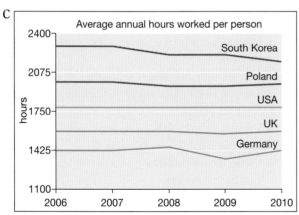

C Average annual hours worked per person

South Korea
Poland
USA
UK
Germany

1 Match each chart (A–C) with the following descriptions.
   1 pie chart ....
   2 line graph ....
   3 bar chart ....
2 Which chart(s) show trends (changes over a period of time)?
3 Which chart(s) show the situation at one point in time, like a photograph?

2 **Look at the charts and graphs again and decide if the following sentences are true (T) or false (F).**

1 People in Turkey drink more tea on average than people in Egypt. T ....
2 Between 2006 and 2010, the average Polish worker worked fewer hours a year than the average Korean. ....
3 From the seven countries shown, people in the UAE are by far the greatest consumers of tea. ....
4 The Indian air travel market is dominated by SpiceJet and Go Air. ....
5 In Germany, an employee's annual hours increased between 2006 and 2010. ....

3 **Did you find any of the information surprising?**

Describing trends

Vocabulary

1 **The graphs on the next page show the share prices of six different companies over the period of one week. Match the verbs and expressions in the box (1–6) with one of the graph movements (i–vi).**

> **1** rise/increase **2** fall/decrease **3** reach a peak
> **4** dip **5** fluctuate **6** level off

2 **Match each graph (a–f) to the correct description (1–6).**

1 There was a steady increase in the share price from Monday to Thursday but then it levelled off at the end of the week. c ....
2 Between Monday and Thursday, the share price showed only slight fluctuations but there was a sharp fall at the end of the week. ....
3 The share price reached a peak in the middle of the week. ....
4 The share price dipped slightly in the middle of the week but then showed signs of recovery after that. ....
5 The share price showed a downward trend throughout the week. ....
6 For the first four days the share price showed only slight changes, but at the end of the week it rose dramatically from around 200 to 500 pence. ....

a

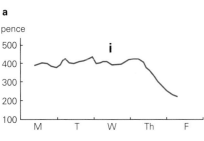

pence

b

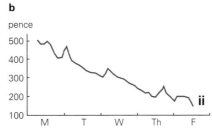

pence

c

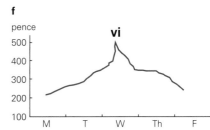

pence

d

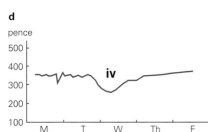

pence

e

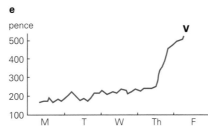

pence

f

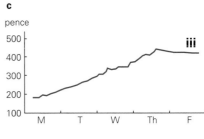

pence

3 Complete the following sentences about Graph f with the correct prepositions.

1 From Monday ___to___ Wednesday the share price rose.
2 On Wednesday it stood _____ 500 pence.
3 _____ Wednesday and Friday, it fell _____ 500 _____ around 200 pence.

4 What is the difference between *The share price fell to 200 pence* and *The share price fell by 200 pence*?

Grammar workshop

Adjectives and adverbs

- Trends can be described using a verb plus an adverb:
  *The share price **rose dramatically**.*

- You can express the same idea using an adjective and noun:
  *There was **a dramatic rise** in the share price.*

1 Complete the following table with the correct nouns. All except two are identical to the verb. Use the sentences in Vocabulary Exercise 2 to help you if necessary.

Verb	Noun
to rise	*a rise*
to fall	
to increase	
to decrease	
to dip	
to fluctuate	
to recover	

2 Study these spelling rules about turning adjectives into adverbs and then complete the table below.

- Most adjectives add *-ly* to form the adverb:
  e.g. sharp → sharply

- Adjectives ending in consonant + *y* change *y* to *i* before adding *-ly*:
  e.g. happy → happily

- Adjectives ending in *-ic* add *-ally*:
  e.g. automatic → automatically

- Adjectives ending in *l* also add *-ly*:
  e.g. beautiful → beautifully

- Adjectives ending in *-ble* make the adverb with *bly*:
  e.g. terrible → terribly

Adjective	Adverb
slight	*slightly*
sharp	
gradual	
steady	
dramatic	
noticeable	

3 Now change the following sentences (1–5) by completing them with either a verb–adverb or an adjective–noun phrase.

1 There was a steady increase in the share price for the first four days.
The share price *increased steadily* for the first four days.

2 The share price rose dramatically at the end of the week.
There was a .... in the share price at the end of the week.

3 There was a sharp fall in the share price on Friday.
The share price .... on Friday.

4 The share price showed only slight fluctuations.
The share price only ....

5 The share price dipped slightly on Wednesday.
There was a .... in the share price on Wednesday.

4 Think about the last thirty years in your country and write brief notes about changes during that time on one or more of the following topics.

- inflation
- the unemployment rate
- gross domestic product
- import and export figures

5 Work with a partner and take it in turns to tell each other about one or more of the above.

❯ page 98 Adjectives and adverbs

Speaking

1 Work in pairs.

Student A: look at the graph below.
Student B: look at the graph on page 119.

Take it in turns to describe your graph to your partner. Your partner draws the missing line on their blank graph.

Student A

Price of gold

Reporting figures

Writing

Look at the graph you drew when listening to your partner's information in the speaking task. Write a paragraph for a financial report describing how the price of gold or silver changed over the weeks. Begin with the following sentence:

In the first week, the price of gold/silver stood at …

Statistics

Listening

①31 You will hear some short recordings. Listen and choose the correct answer, A, B or C.

1 Which product has been the most successful?
A handbags
Ⓑ briefcases
C leather jackets

2 In which month were sales the highest?
A January
B February
C March

3 Which region has the greatest share of sales?
A Asia
B Europe
C America

4 Which line on the graph shows the pattern of sales in the supermarket on Saturdays?

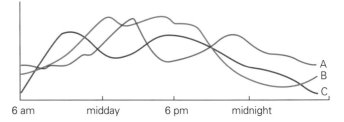

5 Which bar chart represents the sales figures for these three months?

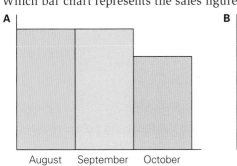
A

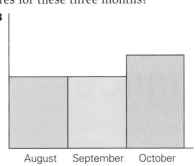
B

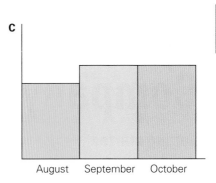
C

Reading

1 The bar charts below (a–f) show the revenue from sales of new technology and the revenue from after-sales service for six different software companies over a period of three years. Which company (a–f) does each of the sentences (1–5) describe? Write a–f next to the correct sentence. There is one chart that is not described.

1 Revenue from after-sales service rose steadily over the period while sales remained static. *a*

2 Revenue from after-sales service increased slightly in Year 2 and then levelled off whereas revenue from sales increased gradually throughout the period. ....

3 Although revenue from both sources declined over the period, the fall was more dramatic for sales. ....

4 Despite a slight dip in Year 2, revenue from after-sales service exceeded that for sales in all three years. ....

5 Revenue from sales fell sharply in Year 2 but then recovered to overtake revenue from after-sales service in the following year. ....

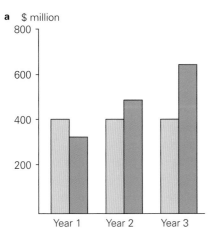
a $ million

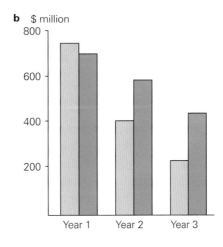
b $ million

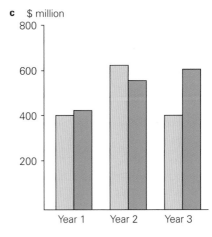
c $ million

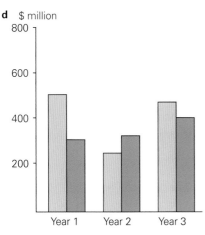
d $ million

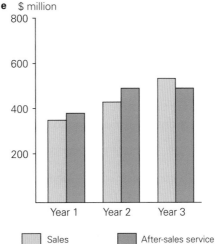
e $ million

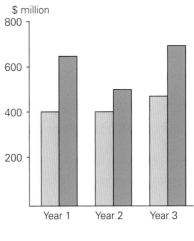
f $ million

Sales   After-sales service

2 Now write two sentences about the chart which is not described.

Company finances

Getting started

1 Work with a partner and discuss what qualities you think you need to be a successful accountant or financial officer. Choose the most important three qualities from the following:

- careful
- courageous
- creative
- enthusiastic
- good at communicating
- imaginative
- impatient with details
- focussed on details

2 Look at the qualities again. Which ones do you think are most important to be a successful company CEO?

3 How far do you agree with the following opinion? Discuss with your partner.

'When former financial officers or accountants become company CEOs, they don't usually do a very good job. This is because the personality and skills that you need for the two roles are completely different.'

Finance

Vocabulary

1 Match the financial terms (1–11) with the correct definition (a–k).

1	creditor	a	a person or organisation that owes money to the company
2	revenue	b	a person or organisation that the company owes money to
3	overheads	c	to legally stop doing business and close a company because of financial losses
4	to go bankrupt	d	the money that a company earns from its sales
5	to break even	e	to earn enough money to pay for the costs of running the company but no more (no profit is made)
6	debtor	f	how much a company earns before certain costs and taxes are deducted
7	net profit		
8	to overspend	g	the total amount of money that an organisation spends on something
9	gross profit	h	how much a company earns after all the costs and taxes are deducted
10	operating profit	i	to spend more than you originally planned in your budget
11	expenditure	j	the profit which comes from a company's usual activities of providing goods or services
		k	the costs of running the company, e.g. rent, electricity and water bills, etc.

2 The words in the box have similar meanings to three of the words from Exercise 1. Write the word with the similar meaning next to the one in the box.

to cover costs ....
to go into liquidation ....
turnover ....

3 Choose the correct expression from the box below to complete the definitions (1–3) You need to put the verbs in the correct form.

to chase payment   to pay off a debt   to write off a debt

1 If a company pays the money it owes to someone, then it ....
2 If a company tries to make a person or organisation pay the money that they owe (e.g. by sending out letters to remind them), then it ....
3 If a company decides to stop trying to get the money that a person or organisation owes it (because, for example, the company no longer exists), then it ....

4 Look at the following sentences (1–5) and choose the alternative, A, B or C, which is NOT possible.

1 I don't think we will make a profit next year but we hope to at least …
   A break even
   (B) go bankrupt
   C cover costs.

2 Operating profits fell last year but the company managed to save some money by reducing …
   A expenditure
   B overheads
   C revenue.

3 The company budgeted for $120,000 dollars, but the project cost them nearly $200,000. They … by nearly $80,000.
   A covered costs
   B overspent
   C exceeded their budget

4 The company was very successful last year, and increased their … from £290,000 to over £320,000.
   A debts
   B revenue
   C turnover

5 A great many people lost their jobs when the company …
   A went bankrupt
   B broke even
   C went into liquidation.

Working in finance

Listening

You will hear an interview with Steve Keley, who works for a company which provides auditing and financial advice for other businesses.

1 ①32 Listen to the introductory part of the interview and complete the following information:

Name: 1 *Steve Keley*

Name of company:
2 ....

Nature of work: working with failing businesses

Qualifications: trained as a/an 3 ....

2 ①33 Listen to the first part of the interview and decide if the following statements (1–5) are true or false. Write T for true or F for false.

1 Steve works with businesses that are experiencing financial difficulties. *T*
2 His department is expanding at the moment. ....
3 His company is a well-known accounting company. ....
4 You need to have a degree in accountancy to apply for work at his company. ....
5 Steve only works with retail businesses. ....

3 ①34 Listen to the second part of the interview and complete the following information. Write one or two words in each gap.

1 Steve has to follow guidelines about ___*ethics*___ and independence in his job.
2 Sometimes, Steve is shown information which is .... to the business he is working with.
3 There are times when the people in the companies he works with do not tell him ....
4 Sometimes he comes across businesses where .... has taken place.
5 Steve says it's amazing how people could .... if they want to.

4 ①35 Listen to the final part of the interview and write in the missing words (1–5). Write one word in each gap.

> **I:** What do you find most satisfying about your job?
> **S:** The most satisfying thing is probably when a job goes really well and a business that, when you first take it on, is in **1** ___*trouble*___, you work alongside the management and the lenders and come to a **2** .... outcome, and business is returned to a positive, **3** ...., cash-generative state and goes forward. Therefore no one loses any **4** ...., or the individuals involved don't lose their **5** .... and the owners don't lose their livelihoods, etc. Those kinds of positive stories are the most satisfying.

5 Look back at the adjectives in the *Getting started* section. Which of the qualities do you think are needed in Steve's job? Have you changed your mind about any of the qualities needed to be an accountant now you have heard the interview?

1 **Work in pairs and discuss the following questions.**

   1 In your country, where do people usually go to meet outside their home or place of work?
   2 Do older and younger people prefer to go to different places?

2 **You are going to read an article about an Indian chain of coffee shops called Café Coffee Day. Skim the article quickly to get an idea of the content. Which of the following does it NOT talk about?**

   1 how the company started up
   2 the effects of world coffee prices on the company
   3 the profile of the typical Café Coffee Day customer
   4 the future of the coffee market in India

THE GROWTH OF THE INDIAN COFFEE SHOP

The coffee shop as a place to meet goes back to the fifteenth century, and it is a familiar sight in most European cities. But over the past twenty years a coffee shop culture has started up in India as well. This is largely the result of one company, Café Coffee Day.

The company was founded by Mr V.G. Siddhartha in 1996. Mr Siddhartha began his career in financial services, but as he came from a family of coffee growers, he took out investments in coffee plantations. Then in 1993, he started the Amalgamated Bean Coffee Trading Company, or ABC. It started with an annual turnover of 60 million rupees but this has now grown to around 25 billion and it has become India's biggest coffee exporter.

But Mr Siddhartha also wanted to create his own chain of coffee shops. At that time, coffee drinking was not popular in India except among rich intellectuals and there was no coffee shop culture. When he opened his first coffee shop in Bangalore, it was marketed as an internet café. This was the bait, as few Indians had access to the Internet at that time and so many of them came to experience it. The coffee was a sideline.

The idea soon caught on and the coffee shop became a place for young people to meet. India has a young population with a median age of about 26. The typical Café Coffee Day customer is this age or younger, and normally comes with a group of friends in search of the same international coffee shop experience that they might find in other cities around the world. As the number of outlets has grown, so has the domestic consumption of coffee. According to India's Coffee Board, it stood at 5 thousand tonnes in 1990 but in 2009 it reached 120 thousand and is still rising.

This appeal to the young population is the main secret of the company's success but **(i) they** also enjoy a big financial advantage because they own their own plantations. This is not true of other chains. In addition, **(ii) they** make their own coffee machines and Mr Siddhartha has set up a college to train prospective employees. Café Coffee Day make about 10 to 12 per cent cash profit per annum, which Mr Siddhartha defines as net profit plus depreciation of assets. "If I am able to grow my business at 25 to 28 per cent and earn 10 per cent of **(iii) it** as cash profits, I am happy," he says.

However, there is a problem with this growth in the coffee shop culture. **(iv) It** has encouraged global brands to turn their attention to the Indian market. Some chains such as Britain's Costa Coffee have already started up in Indian cities and more big global players like Starbucks are predicted to arrive **(v) there** soon. Changes in the government's policy on foreign investment have probably encouraged **(vi) this**. But the team at Café Coffee Day are not especially worried. According to Mr Ramakrishnan, president of marketing, the coffee market in India is still growing and the arrival of a new brand may give **(vii) it** a further boost. What's more, these new brands may not know the Indian customer as well as Café Coffee Day. "In the US, 40 per cent of coffee sales occur before 11am," he says. "In India sales typically only happen after 11am. That's a huge shock for the Western brands." Indeed, with an annual revenue of 12 billion rupees and ambitious plans for expansion, Café Coffee Day may well become a serious global competitor to the big international coffee shop brands.

3 Now read the article more carefully and answer the questions. Circle A, B or C.

1 Annual turnover at ABC
   A has increased dramatically over the years. *(circled)*
   B is less than other coffee exporters in India.
   C is currently around 60 million rupees.
2 Mr Siddhartha's first cyber café was successful because
   A it sold coffee more cheaply than its competitors.
   B the Internet was not available to many Indians at that time.
   C there was a growing taste for coffee among the young.
3 The majority of Café Coffee Day's customers
   A come from the younger half of India's population.
   B come to the coffee shop on their own.
   C have visited other coffee shops around the world.
4 According to statistics from the Coffee Board, India's coffee consumption
   A has increased significantly since 1990.
   B peaked in 2009.
   C was static before 1990.
5 Café Coffee Day have a financial advantage over other coffee shops because
   A their machines are cheaper to maintain.
   B the government funds them to train staff.
   C they grow their own coffee.
6 According to Mr Ramakrishnan, international coffee chains may have difficulty in India because
   A the government may not allow them to set up there.
   B the market for coffee has already reached its peak.
   C they may not adapt to the habits of the Indian consumer.

4 Look at the pronouns (i–vii) in the text and decide what they refer to. Circle the correct answer, A or B for each pronoun.

> Task tip
>
> In order to follow the sense of a reading text, it is important to understand what the pronouns and reference words refer to. This can be confusing when the text is about a company because a company can sometimes be referred to in the singular (it) and sometimes in the plural (they) without much difference in meaning.
>
> Look back to the previous sentence and read it carefully. The pronoun doesn't always refer to the noun immediately before it.

(i)	they	A the young population
		B the company *(circled)*
(ii)	they	A other chains
		B Café Coffee Day
(iii)	it	A the business
		B 25 to 28 per cent
(iv)	It	A a problem
		B growth
(v)	there	A the Indian market
		B Britain
(vi)	this	A arrival of big global players
		B foreign investment
(vii)	it	A the coffee market in India
		B a new brand

5 Find words in the text with the following meanings.

1 areas of land where some types of crops are grown
   plantation
2 something attractive which is offered to persuade someone to do something ....
3 an activity which takes place in addition to the main business of a company ....
4 the average or middle number in a group

....
5 places where a particular product is sold

....
6 the gradual reduction in the value of something, such as a piece of equipment ....
7 something which helps something to expand or become more successful ....

❯ page 98 Reference words

Investments

Getting started

Work with a partner. Decide which of the following statements (1–6) are the three most important reasons for deciding to invest in a company.

1 The company has performed strongly in the past.
2 The company has set high profit targets for this year.
3 The company belongs to a growth sector.

4 The company does not have many competitors.
5 The company makes a diverse range of items.
6 You work for the company.

The stock exchange

Vocabulary

Imagine that you know nothing about shares or the stock exchange and have decided to look up information about both on the Internet. Read the following webpage and match the definitions (1–7) with the correct terms (a–g) on the next page.

HOW THINGS WORK

SHARES and the STOCK EXCHANGE

The stock market appears in the news every day. You hear about it all the time in statements like 'shares in this company rose' or 'shares in this group fell by 2%'. But what is a stock market? And what are people buying and selling?

If I own a business, then I will need money, especially if I want it to grow. I might have enough money to fund this

myself but it is more likely that I will need to get some from other people. This kind of money is called capital or financial capital.

If someone thinks that my business will grow and make money, then they may be willing to invest, that is, give me some money for a share in the profits that the business will make. For example, if I own a restaurant which I think is worth $1,000,000, I might divide it into ten and sell each piece for $100,000. Then each person who has bought a piece receives a tenth of the profits at the end of the year. Anyone who buys a piece of my restaurant has bought shares in it and is known as a shareholder. The restaurant will share out the profits among the shareholders at least once a year. This payment is called a dividend.

It really is that simple. The word stock is used to talk about a certain quantity of shares. When a company is large enough, it usually wants to sell stocks and shares to the public. This can be done through a stock exchange, which is like a big supermarket for stocks. However, you can't just walk into the stock exchange and buy shares. You have to do it through a broker who will buy and sell them for you and charge commission (a percentage of the price). There are famous stock exchanges in New York, London and Tokyo. Nowadays you can also buy and sell shares online by registering with special websites.

1. money which can be invested in a business to make profits   a   broker
2. the parts in which a company is divided so investors can buy them   b   shares
3. someone who owns part of a company   c   shareholder
4. part of a company's profits which is paid to the people who have bought shares in it   d   stock
5. a place where shares are bought and sold   e   capital
6. a person who can buy and sell shares for you   f   dividend
7. a certain number of shares   g   stock exchange

Financial news

Reading

1 **Read the following short articles (1–3) and choose the correct heading (a–h) for each. There are more headlines than you need.**

a   Commodity prices fall
b   High returns at Pine and Liddell
c   Japanese shares perform strongly
d   Commodity prices continue to climb
e   Disappointing results at Pine and Liddell
f   Commodity prices level off
g   Japanese buyers attracted to bonds
h   Japanese bond market crashes

Task tip

You have already practised skimming an article to decide if you want to read it in detail. When reading the newspaper, we often decide whether we want to read an article in detail by reading its headline (the title of an article) to see if it contains a company name we are interested in.

1

Pine and Liddell, the food company was *float*ed on the London stock exchange in May with a share price of 60p. The shares are attractive for their high *dividend yield* of 5.4 per cent. The company is chaired by Mahmoud Abbas, who has a personal 20 per cent *stake* in the company. Other shareholders to benefit include Spurdell Asset Management, the investment bank who handled the *flotation*.

2

Commodity prices have risen in recent years and, according to experts, this trend is likely to continue. Graham Mann at Harper's Gold General Fund says 'We are in a commodities *bull market*. This is because demand for many commodities is exceeding supply, especially in growing economies.'

3

The price of 10-year Japanese *bond*s rose yesterday after a fall in Tokyo shares. This preference for the government bond market instead of *equities* occurred as investors became less confident about the future of the Japanese economy, partly as a result of the yen's continued rise against the US dollar.

2 **Now match each of the words in italics from the newspaper articles above to the correct definition (1–8) below. Use the contexts in the articles to help you.**

1 A substance like gold or oil which can be bought and sold in large amounts.   *commodity*
2 A part of the total money invested in a company.
3 To start selling shares to the public for the first time.
4 The process of making shares available to the public to buy for the first time.
5 An amount of money borrowed by a government or organisation with a promise that it will pay the money back with interest at a fixed time.
6 A market in which the share prices are going up (the opposite of a *bear market*).
7 Another word for stocks.
8 The amount paid out on each share expressed as a percentage of the current share price.

Men and women's investments

Reading

1   Work in pairs and discuss the following questions.

- Do you think men and women have different approaches to investment?
- Do you think men and women prefer different types of investments?

2   Read the first two paragraphs of the article quickly and answer the following questions.

1   In general do men or women make better investors?
2   What differences have been found in the way that men and women handle investments?

MEN AND WOMEN'S INVESTMENTS

Have you ever heard that women are supposed to be better at managing money than men? Well, with regard to handling investments, there now seems to be some evidence to prove it.

In a well known piece of research, Brad Barber and Terence Odea from the University of California found that women's returns on their investments were higher than men's by an average of about 1 per cent each year. One reason for this seems to be that women trade their stocks less than men. The same study found that men sold their shares and bought different ones more often than women, which meant that their broker's fees were higher. They were also more likely to sell their shares in times of financial uncertainty, like the financial crisis of 2009. But of course, selling stocks when the market is low is not a good idea, as it means that the seller does not benefit from any *rally* in the market that may follow later. Men also do less research than women. Their investments are often based on *tips* they have received from friends but they fail to find out more about these tips before deciding to invest.

---

3   Now put the sentences below (a–f) in the correct order to make the final paragraph of the article by writing (1–6) in the boxes.

a   This means that they prefer safer investments and often go for investments which will give a fixed income, like bonds. ☐

b   and women sometimes lose out by avoiding risky funds. ☐

c   However, *with hindsight*, we can all see what too much risk taking can do to the global financial situation. A few more women working on Wall Street or in banking might help us to avoid such crises in future. ☐

d   Men, by contrast, tend to risk more and favour more *volatile* markets. ☐

e   Another general difference between men and women is that women are generally more *risk averse*. [1]

f   To some extent this is a good strategy because you need to take some risks with your investments if you want big returns ☐

---

4   Look at the words and expressions in italics in the paragraphs you have just read. You may not know the exact meanings of these words but you can use the context to guess. Choose the correct definition, A or B, for each word or phrase.

1   *rally*   (A) increase in value
                        B   decrease in value
2   *tips*   A   small pieces of advice
                        B   small sums of money
3   *with hindsight*   A   thinking about past events
                        B   thinking about future events
4   *volatile*   A   reliable
                        B   unreliable
5   *risk averse*   A   favouring risk
                        B   avoiding risk

5   Discuss the following questions in pairs.

1   Are there any other ways in which you think women do business differently from men?

2   Do you think companies should be required to have a minimum percentage of women (or men) on their board of directors? Why/Why not?

Working in investor relations

Vocabulary

Choose the word which best completes each sentence (1–5).

1 I introduce clients to people who are interested .... financing their operations.
  A to   B on   C (in)   D at

2 I try to get .... a positive message about the company through the media.
  A through   B across   C about   D along

3 Some of our clients are .... on the London Stock Exchange.
  A placed   B noted   C filed   D listed

4 Mining is generally considered to be a very capital .... industry.
  A heavy   B intensive   C serious   D dense

5 Analysts have to take an .... guess about what lies under the ground.
  A educated   B educator
  C education   D educational

Listening

1 **(1) 36 Listen to an interview with Matthew Beale, who works for an investor relations consultancy called Fortbridge. Number the following topics in the order that Matthew speaks about them.**

  a his interest in the mining industry ....
  b the public relations aspect of his job ....
  c running his own office ....
  d his global clients ....
  e the location of the company's offices ....
  f the investor relations aspect of his job ..1...

2 **(1) 36 Listen to the interview again and circle the correct answer, A, B or C, for questions (1–5).**

1 Matthew's work in investor relations involves
  (A) introducing clients to possible investors.
  B advising investors when to buy and sell shares.
  C calculating the cost of financing new operations.

2 According to Matthew, it is most important to communicate company news to
  A possible new investors.
  B current shareholders.
  C journalists.

3 Which of the following criteria does Matthew's company use to categorise clients?
  A where their head office is located
  B which stock exchange they are listed on
  C where most of their investors are based

4 What point does Matthew make about new mining ventures?
  A They require a high initial investment.
  B They need to be based on reliable research.
  C They are riskier now than in the past.

5 What does Matthew feel is the biggest advantage of working on his own?
  A He does not have to line manage others.
  B He is not distracted by colleagues.
  C He is able to work from home.

3 **(1) 36 Listen to the interview with Matthew again. Note down any other details you hear about the following areas of his job:**

1 investor relations and public relations
2 how clients are categorised
3 mining ventures
4 other people who work in the company

Compare your notes with a partner. Did you hear the same information?

Starting up

Getting started

Work with a partner. Look at the information and discuss the following questions.

Businesses always have a number of costs when they start up. Some of the most obvious include:

- premises costs
- legal costs (e.g. for a partnership agreement)
- utilities (e.g. electricity bills)
- insurance
- staff costs
- advertising and stock

1 How can you keep each of these initial expenses low?
2 What are some possible ways of getting the money to start up a new business?
3 Which do you think are the most common ways to fund a new business in your country?

Compare your answers with another pair.

Business support

Listening

1 **Complete the definitions (1–5) with the words and phrases from the box.**

1 If you obtain the money which you need to start your business, then you *raise capital* for it.
2 If someone gives you the money for your business, they _____ or _____ .
3 When someone lends you money, sometimes you have to promise to give them something, like your house, if you do not pay the money back. When you do this, you _____ .
4 Something of value that you or your business owns is a/an _____ .
5 The movement of money coming into and going out of a business is known as _____ .

> asset   cashflow   provide funding/capital
> ~~raise capital~~   secure a loan

2 (1)37 **Listen to an interview with Tara Ganesh, the marketing director of a business support service called *Entrepreneur*. How many ways to get money for a new business does she mention?**

3 (1)37 **Listen to the interview again and complete the notes.**

Which three kinds of advice can Entrepreneur give?
1 _legal_ 2 _____ 3 _____
Most common way to fund a new business:
4 _____
Bank managers want to see a 5 _____ .
The bank will look for realistic targets, steady growth and a strong 6 _____ .
Types of assets to guarantee bank loans:
7 _____ , 8 _____ .
A company which provides start-up money is a called a 9 _____ firm.
A business angel is a 10 _____ .
You can find business angels through
11 _____ .

Teenage entrepreneurs

Reading

1 Work in pairs. Each of you is going to read an article about a teenage entrepreneur who set up his own business. One student reads Text A, and the other Text B on page 120. First skim your text, and then look at questions (1–5) below and make notes on the answers.

1 What difficulties did the entrepreneur face when he was a child?
2 What projects or activities was he involved in before he set up the business?
3 When did he get the idea for the business?
4 How did he raise the money to start up?
5 How has the business grown?

TEXT A

Skydrop Enterprises

Joel Mwale was born in Kenya. His father died when he was seven and his family moved into a house with no electricity or running water. The water that people used in his village was often polluted and many people caught diseases from it. In 2007, Joel became ill from drinking polluted water and was taken to hospital. From his hospital bed, he decided to create a new borehole* which could provide the people in the village with clean water. He took the money that he was planning to use for his high school fees and set up the borehole on some nearby farmland. Over one hundred people came to collect water from it each day and the rates of infection from polluted water in the village dropped dramatically.

But now Joel had no money to pay his school fees. He needed to raise money, and so he started to think about using the rain as a source of drinking water he could sell. This was the beginning of Joel's business, Skydrop Enterprises. He borrowed $5,000 from a rich farmer who lived nearby and bought a water purifier which could be used for rainwater. The rainwater was then bottled and sold as drinking water. Joel admits he got the idea from other companies, like Coca-Cola, who have done something similar.

Skydrop Enterprises now sells thousands of bottles of water each month and the profits have allowed him to pay school fees for himself and for his brothers, as well as feed his family. He employs five full time workers at his production plant and the bottled water is sold as far away as Uganda.

*borehole: a deep hole made in order to get water out of the ground

---

2 Work in pairs. Take it in turns to tell each other in your own words about the entrepreneur you read about, using questions (1–5) to help you.

Grammar workshop

Which/who/that/where clauses

1 Study the information and answer the questions (1–5).

> **which/who/that/where clauses**
> The words in italics are relative pronouns. They are used in place of *he*, *she*, *it* or *they* to join two sentences together.
>
> **Subject relative clauses**
> *He was invited to attend the **Chocolate Experience show.***
> ***It** was held in Mexico.*
> *He was invited to attend the Chocolate Experience show **which/that** was held in Mexico.*
> *He borrowed $5,000 from **a rich farmer**. **He** lived nearby.*
> *He borrowed $5,000 from a rich farmer **who/that** lived nearby.*
>
> **Object relative clauses**
> ***The water** was often impure. People used **it** in his village.*
> *The water (**which/that**) people used in his village was often impure.*
> *He sent some samples to a **chocolate buyer**. He thought **he** would be interested.*
> *He sent some samples to a chocolate buyer (**who/that**) he thought might be interested.*
>
> **Relative clauses with *where***
> *He moved the chocolate-making operation into **his parents' garage**. There was more space **there**.*
> *He moved the chocolate-making operation into his parents' garage **where** there was more space.*

1 Which relative pronoun is used only for things?
   which
2 Which relative pronoun is used only for people?
   ....
3 Which relative pronoun is used only for places?
   ....
4 When is it possible to leave out the relative pronoun? ....
5 Find another example of subject and object relative clauses in the two texts.

2 The following letter was written to the owner of a cake shop which specialises in southern European products. Read the letter, and then rewrite the pairs of sentences in *italics* (1–5), joining them with a relative pronoun. Do not use *that*.

Dear Ms Tanzi,

1 *We are a new company. It specialises in the production of Greek pastries.* We are writing to ask if you would be interested in stocking our products. **2** *We were given your name by Ms Tina Furlan. We believe she is one of your regular customers.* She would be happy to recommend our products. **3** *We enclose a complete product list and three pastries. We hope you will enjoy them.*

Our products are all based on authentic Greek recipes. **4** *They are made from high quality ingredients. We import the ingredients from Greece.* **5** *We began selling our products six months ago at a local market. There, they proved to be very popular.*

We would very much like to meet you to discuss our proposal further. We can be contacted on the above number or by email.

We look forward to hearing from you.
Yours sincerely,

Kostas and Alex Niarchos

1   We are a new company which specialises in the production of Greek pastries.

2 ....

3 ....

4 ....

5 ....

3 🔘 Business English students sometimes forget to put relative pronouns in a sentence. In the following sentences, insert the missing relative pronoun in the correct place. TWO of the sentences are already correct *without* the addition of a relative pronoun.

which

1 We own a building to rent ^ is in a very convenient location.

2 This figure is a reduction in the amount was spent last year.

3 I would like to demonstrate a new product we have launched.

4 The training is for members of staff work in the customer services department.

5 I am writing to complain about the service I received.

6 There was a short delay occurred because of a computer failure.

▶ **page 98** *which*, *what* and *that*

Writing

Look back at the letter in Exercise 2. You are Ms Tanzi. Write a letter of reply to Kostas and Alex. In your letter:

- thank them for their letter
- say why you are interested
- suggest a time to meet
- enquire about discounts

Use the phrases in the box below to help you start your sentences. Write 60–80 words.

We would be very interested in …	We would be very happy to discuss …
Would you be free …	I would like to suggest …
I would also like to enquire …	I also wonder if you could offer …

Funding

Reading

Company background
Kalido is a company which provides software for data management. It has offices in the USA, the UK and India. Its clients include Shell and Unilever.

1 Work in pairs. Read the first paragraph of the text and discuss the question below.

KALIDO

1 Many entrepreneurs find unusual ways to finance their business if they cannot get help from traditional sources. However, the initial funding of the software company, Kalido, must definitely be one of the most unusual. Andy Hayler, the founder, got his employer to provide the capital for him.

Why do you think an employer might do this?

2 Skim the rest of the article to find the paragraph that gives the reason.

2 Kalido is the leading provider of data warehouse software that allows organisations to understand their business performance better. Unlike traditional software packages, Kalido systems are able to create reports on business information even if it comes in different formats. They also allow data analysis to continue during periods of organisational change such as relocation or mergers.

3 Andy Hayler worked for Shell, the petroleum giant, in the UK. While he was there, he spotted the need for a new data management package. Shell also realised that they needed a system that could monitor the vast amounts of data from their many different businesses, and so they agreed to act as venture capitalists and invest in his idea. For two years, they pumped money into Hayler's new software venture within Shell.

4 Hayler had to identify a market to tap into and produce a detailed business plan, just as if he was obtaining funding from anywhere else. The main difference was in the amount of funding that Shell provided. The first funding to launch the company was an astonishing $11 million.

5 As a result, Kalido expanded very quickly indeed compared with most new ventures. Just a year later, Kalido opened its first sales office in the USA. Then two years after starting up, it broke its ties with Shell. Kalido's software is now used by many large organisations including Unilever, Philips and Proctor and Gamble.

6 'Kalido was something of an unusual case in getting its initial funding from a large corporation,' Hayler admits. 'However, what we did was concentrate on a real customer problem and develop software directly to meet that need. Other companies starting up could do the same thing.'

3 Look at the article again and match the paragraphs (2–6) with the most suitable heading (a–f). There is one heading you do not need.

Paragraph 2   a   How the idea began
Paragraph 3   b   It could happen again
Paragraph 4   c   Who are Kalido?
Paragraph 5   d   The road to independence
Paragraph 6   e   New financial regulations
             f   Presenting the case for funding

4 Skim the article again to see if it contains any useful collocations and record them in your notebook.

Time and money

Vocabulary

1 Many of the words we use to talk about money are also used to talk about time. Complete the gaps (1–4) in the following text with a money word from the box.

> invest   save   ~~spend~~   waste

Having a great idea is not enough to start up a new business. You need to **1** ...*spend*... a great deal of time on market research and deciding who your customers will be. Doing this properly will **2** .... both time and money later. The most important thing is often belief. You need to believe in your product enough to be prepared to **3** .... time, effort and, yes, your own money in making it work.
And if the idea is not a success? Don't feel you have to **4** .... time and money on something of no benefit. You may be able to go back to your original idea later and change it or use parts of it for something else.

2 Look back at the text and underline the prepositions used after the following verbs.

1   spend   2   waste   3   invest

3 Verbs which usually describe water are also often used to talk about money or markets. *Cashflow* is an example of this. Look at paragraphs 3 and 4 of the text and <u>underline</u> two more water verbs.

4 Complete the following sentences (1–4) with a water verb from the box. Change the tense of the verb if necessary.

> dry up   flood   ~~pump/pour~~   tap into

1   The company has *poured/pumped* a lot of money into their South American venture.
2   The market has been .... with products imported from the USA.
3   The advertising campaign was designed to .... the new interest in healthy eating.
4   In the past there was government money available but this source of funding has .... now.

Grammar workshop 5

Units 17–20

Adjectives and adverbs

Rewrite the following sentences (1–7) by putting either a verb–adverb or an adjective–noun phrase in the gap.

1   There was a slight fall in house prices last year.
    House prices *fell slightly* last year.
2   Sales experienced a gradual decline in the second half of the year.
    Sales .... in the second half of the year.
3   Commodity prices have risen sharply since last year.
    There has been .... in commodity prices since last year.
4   There is often a sudden increase in demand just before the holiday period.
    Demand often .... just before the holiday period.
5   His presentation skills really improved after he did the training course.
    His presentation skills showed .... after he did the training course.
6   After a decline in the first quarter, the share price recovered dramatically in April.
    After a decline in the first quarter, there was .... in the share price in April.
7   There has been considerable fluctuation in the exchange rates this year.
    The exchange rates .... this year.

Reference words

Complete the following extracts (1–8) using a reference word from the box. You can use the same word more than once.

> it   one   them   these   they   this

1   I have had a look at the sales figures but I'm afraid *they* are not as good as we hoped.
2   Of course, you need a good idea to start a business but money is equally important. You can't start up without ....
3   Some entrepreneurs do not pass many exams at school. .... shows that you do not need a formal education to be successful.
4   Many of our smaller stores showed very weak sales last year. I am afraid some of .... outlets will have to close.
5   After you leave a post, previous colleagues can sometimes become your customers, so you should try to keep in contact with ....
6   Henshaw's attempt to merge with a Brazilian company failed. .... led to a sudden drop in the share price.
7   The business grew quickly from a small shop in the high street to .... with a number of stores across the country.
8   As an entrepreneur, you are certain to make some wrong decisions, but the important thing is to learn from .... mistakes.

Which, what and that

- **which** is a relative pronoun we use for things. It is also a question word. We use *which* instead of *what* when there is a limited number of choices.
  *This is the brochure **which** we give to all our customers.*
  *Could you tell me **which** model you ordered, regular or large?*
- **what** is a question word. It is not a relative pronoun.
  *I'd like to know **what** other services you offer.*
- **that** is a relative pronoun. We can use it instead of *which* or *who* in some clauses.
  *The company **which/that** he started went bankrupt after two years.*

1   ☉ Business English students sometimes confuse **which**, **what** and **that** at this level. Circle the correct alternative, **which** or **what**, in the following sentences (1–6).

1   Please let me know *which/(what)* time I should arrive.
2   You will find the office in West Street, *which/what* is in the fifth district.
3   *Which/What* of these two designs do you prefer?
4   I'm wondering *which/what* you hope to achieve in this meeting.

5 Do you know *which/what* of these two figures is correct?

6 The presentation will take place at the Hilton Hotel, *which/what* is a few minutes' walk from the station.

2 Circle the correct alternative, *what* or *that*, in the following sentences (1–6).

1 The information *what*/(*that*) you need is in my desk.

2 We are very unhappy with the software *what/that* we are using at the moment.

3 Please could you tell me *what/that* the subject of the talk will be.

4 They did not provide all the facilities *what/that* we expected.

5 I would like to know exactly *what/that* is included in this price.

6 I think a microphone is all *what/that* I will need for the talk.

Prepositions

Complete the following sentences (1–8) with either *in*, *on* or *with*.

1 We can't afford to spend a lot of money _on_ advertising.

2 We aim to supply our customers _____ top quality goods.

3 He invested a large sum of money _____ banking stocks.

4 Our success largely depends _____ reaching the right customers.

5 Our advertising campaign has certainly had an impact _____ sales.

6 The project was not successful and we wasted a lot of time _____ it.

7 Increasing the price now could result _____ a big drop in sales.

8 All shareholders are provided _____ a summary of the company's financial position.

Grammar and spelling revision

1 Read the following text and choose the correct word, A, B or C, to fill each gap (1–10).

ARTEMIS JEWELLERY

Artemis is a jewellery company which is based in Sweden. The company **1** __C__ set up in 1986 when Allan Nielsen opened a jewellery shop in Stockholm. Demand for the products increased, **2** _____ soon he opened a second shop in Copenhagen, Denmark. This was followed **3** _____ further locations in Switzerland, Germany and the UK. He also hired a new designer **4** _____ created the company's signature style. The company was floated **5** _____ the London Stock Exchange in 2005. Shortly after **6** _____ , the company brought out a line of Swiss-made watches, but they were **7** _____ less successful than their other products. An earnings report, published **8** _____ November last year, showed an unexpected drop in revenues at Artemis. **9** _____ then, the former CEO has left the company and Oscar Lindberg, a specialist in midmarket retailing, has taken over **10** _____ post.

1 A is	B has	C was
2 A and	B but	C also
3 A for	B at	C by
4 A who	B which	C what
5 A in	B on	C at
6 A it	B this	C these
7 A much	B very	C such
8 A in	B on	C at
9 A For	B By	C Since
10 A a	B the	C some

2 Find and correct the spelling mistake in each of the following sentences (1–8).

1 Demand for their products has increased ~~gradualy~~ over the year. *gradually*

2 Sales rose in the autumn and reached a pick in December.

3 The new data management system is a big improvment on the old one.

4 There are a number of diffrent software packages you can buy.

5 They have invested heavyly in their marketing campaign.

6 We have still not recieved payment for the last invoice.

7 Their raw materials can all be purchased localy.

8 When would be a convient time for the conference call?

Job applications

Getting started

1 Work in pairs. Make a list in your notebook of what you think a *curriculum vitae* (CV) or *résumé* should contain.

2 Look at the different sections (a–h) of a CV. Match each section with the correct title (1–8).

1 Referees
2 Achievements
3 Interests
4 Career history
5 Date of birth
6 Education and training
7 Skills
8 Contact details

a

David Haywood
P.O. Box 25127
Dubai
United Arab Emirates
Mobile: 09235 718221
Email: d_haywood11@gmail.com

b

- managed cost analyses for specific products and countries in relation to total consumption, market share and local production facilities.
- increased market share of an industrial paper product from 27% to 36% in a year.

c

2010–present:	Rahman Chemicals Dubai, sales product manager
2007–2010:	K–Chem Chemicals, Kuwait international sales representative
2006–2007:	hotel work and teaching English in Aswan, Egypt.

d

Excellent computer skills
Clean driving licence
Fluent German and conversational Arabic

e

Dr Kevin Smith Ph.D
Department of Business Studies
University of Southampton
kevinsmith@southampton.ac.uk

Mr Khaled Sayed
Managing Director
Rahman Chemicals
Dubai
UAE
K.sayed@rahman.ae

f

Basketball, fencing and photography

g

2006:	Degree BA (Hons) in Middle Eastern Studies, University of Leeds
2010:	MBA in International Business, University of Southampton
2010:	Training in advanced ExCel and database software

h

12 June 1984

3 Work with a partner and decide the best order for the sections (a–h) on a CV. Write numbers (1–8) in the boxes to show the order.

a ☐1 b ☐ c ☐ d ☐
e ☐ f ☐ g ☐ h ☐

Writing CVs

Reading

Look at this extract from a book which gives advice on how to write CVs. There is a list of headings in recommended order.

Writing your CV

A CV is an outline of a person's educational and professional background. In some countries, like the USA, it is known as a résumé. There is no one correct way to construct a CV, but remember the following two principles:

- Make it clear. Use direct, simple language, short headings and highlight the important things like the titles of previous jobs.

- Make it short, no more than two sides of paper. A busy personnel manager with 20 CVs to read in half an hour won't want to read anything longer.

Standard CVs are usually divided into a maximum of seven sections. One of the most common ways to order the sections is like this:

1 Personal details. These are facts about you and how to contact you. The section should include your name, address, and possibly date of birth and nationality. In the past people usually included their marital status (whether they were married or not) too, but this is not necessary nowadays.

2 Career profile. This is a short description of your skills and experience which is intended to get the employer's attention. It is usually written in complete sentences. It often includes phrases about what kind of person you are, like 'good team player'. You need to think carefully about what you write here. Try to make sure there is evidence for what you say from your achievements and work experience.

3 Education. This should outline your educational history and your qualifications. There is no need to give details about primary or elementary school! If you left school some years ago and have done company or professional training courses, it is more important to highlight this. In this case, you can call this section 'Education and training'.

4 Employment. This should include the different jobs you have done. Start with the most recent, as this is usually the one where you had the most responsibility. Give the main duties of each job, as it may not be clear from the job title. If you have only just left university and do not have much experience, think about any holiday jobs or voluntary work you have done. You have probably gained useful skills from these. For example, if you managed the money for a school society, this is good evidence of financial skills.

5 Skills. Here you should list any other skills that employers might be interested in, like computer skills or speaking another language.

6 Interests. This includes sporting and leisure interests. It is not strictly necessary to include these, but it can make the CV more interesting. Avoid obvious ones that most people share like reading and watching TV.

7 References. You should include two people who can provide you with a reference. One should be your last employer, if possible. Make sure you ask their permission first.

---

1. Skim the list to see if the writer agrees with the order you decided in the last exercise. Is there anything else that you think David Haywood should add to his CV?

2. Below are some short extracts from different CVs. Scan them quickly. Which follow the advice in the text above? Put a (✓) or (✗) in the box.

   1. I am a keen reader. ✗
   2. I speak fluent English, Spanish and some Arabic. ☐
   3. Marital status: single ☐
   4. EDUCATION: 1980–1985 Gutierrez elementary school. ☐
   5. Proven ability to build relationships with both corporate and individual clients. ☐
   6. A fantastic communicator and team player. ☐
   7. Clean driving licence. ☐

> **Task tip**
>
> Decide which heading you need to look under for each extract. Then read the advice under that heading, thinking about the extract.

Careers advice

Listening

1 **(2)01** You will hear an interview with Jacqui Miles, a careers adviser, about preparing CVs. Work in pairs and make a list of questions you would like to ask her. Then listen to the first part of the interview. Does she answer any of your questions?

2 **(2)01** Listen to the first part of the interview again and decide if the following pieces of advice are helpful in (A) the UK, (B) the USA or (C) Asian countries like India. Write A, B or C.

1 In the first few years after university, use a one-page CV. *B*
2 If you have only recently graduated, your CV should be two pages long. ....
3 If you don't have much work experience, emphasise research projects you have done. ....
4 If you don't have direct experience of the job, emphasise your transferable skills. ....
5 Be sure to include details of any academic prizes or scholarships. ....
6 Put details of your referees on a different sheet of paper from the CV. ....
7 You can send off letters of reference together with the CV. ....
8 Put details of two referees in the last section of the CV. ....
9 If you prefer, you can just write 'references available on request'. ....

3 **(2)02** Now listen to the second part of the interview and complete the notes. Write one or two words in each gap.

1 According to Jacqui, it is very important to treat your CV as a *marketing tool* .
2 The CV that you send should be a .... for the job description.
3 Jacqui's clients often do not put enough emphasis on their ....
4 Sometimes Jacqui's clients have used .... which is not suitable.
5 In the UK, a one-page CV is needed if you are applying for a job in ....
6 A CV can be longer than two pages if it is for a .... job.
7 CVs for academic jobs may contain a section on ....
8 CVs for jobs in IT need to list the .... that the applicant knows.

4 Discuss the following questions with a partner.

1 How do people usually write CVs in your country? Are they more similar to CVs in the USA or the UK?
2 Do you think the way in which people write CVs is changing in your country? How?
3 Jacqui says that your CV is a marketing tool. In what other ways can you market yourself for a job?

Corresponding with applicants

Writing

1 Work with a partner. What is the order that things happen when you apply for a job? Put the following actions (a–e) in the correct order by writing a number (1–5) in each box.

a You are shortlisted ☐
b You send in an application ☐ 1
c You are turned down/You are offered the job ☐
d You attend an interview ☐
e You are appointed/You apply for another job ☐

2 Read the following extract from an email of application:

I would like to apply for the post of marketing executive with WWT travel and tours, as advertised in the *Evening Post* of 12 November. I attach a copy of my résumé and the completed application form ...

3 Unscramble the phrases in the box and insert them in the letter below to create a reply.

> please us know let   meeting forward look we you to   that to am I pleased you inform
> to like would we you   ~~your thank interest in you for~~

Dear Mr Tang,

1 *Thank you for your interest in* the post of marketing executive.

2 .... you have been shortlisted for the post.

3 .... attend an interview at WWT at the above address on 28 November at 11.30 am. Please come to the reception desk in the main building.

4 .... as soon as possible if you are unable to attend at this time.

5 ....

Yours sincerely,

Tsui Ken Fung

Human Resources Manager

4 Study these phrases (1–3) used to introduce good and bad news.

> 1 I am **pleased** to inform you that …
> 2 I am **delighted** to inform you that …
> 3 **I am sorry / I regret** to inform you that …

5 Which of the phrases (1–3) above would you use if you wanted to do the following (a–c)? Write the phrase number in the correct box.

a let a customer know that he/she has won a prize? ☐

b tell a company that you have decided not to invest in their new project? ☐

c let a member of staff know that they have been accepted on a training course? ☐

6 Now read the following extract from a statement on an application form from Natasha Balabanovic, who is applying for a post with an IT company.

> I have worked for the last three years as an IT project manager for Cambers International Property Group. Although this has been an interesting and fulfilling job, I am now seeking to move into a more challenging role. I believe that a management post in the field of information technology would offer me this challenge …

Write a reply to Ms Balabanovic's application.
In your reply:

- thank her for the application
- give the news that she is not shortlisted for the post
- explain the main reason why
- express good wishes for the future.

Write 60–80 words.

Recruitment

Getting started

1 Complete the following definitions (1–4) with the correct verb from the box.

> dismiss ~~recruit~~ redundant resign

1 If you give someone a job, you __recruit__ them.
2 If you decide to leave your job, you ....
3 If staff need to leave because the company is reducing their workforce, they are made ....
4 If you tell someone they must leave because their work is unacceptable, you .... them.

2 What are the noun forms of the words in the box?

1 recruit __recruitment__ 3 redundant ....
2 dismiss .... 4 resign ....

3 Now match the words and expressions (1–7) below to the words (a–d) with approximately the same meaning. Some of the words on the right can be matched with more than one word on the left.

1 take on   a resign
2 quit   b make redundant
3 lay off   c dismiss
4 fire   d recruit
5 hand in your notice
6 hire
7 sack

Grammar workshop 1

First conditional

1 Read the extract from a book about interview techniques. What two things should a candidate read before attending an interview? Skim the text to find out, and write the answers below.

1 ....   2 ....

> The key to taking part in a successful interview is preparation. Before you attend the interview, be sure to find out the important facts about the company, its main activities, products and services. If you spend some time doing this homework, the interview is much more likely to be successful. Many candidates fail to do this thoroughly so if you are well-informed, you will look better than many other applicants. You can get most of the information from the company's website.
>
> Read over your own CV again before the interview, so that you are clear about which points you need to highlight. You should also refresh your memory about the basic facts of your current place of work. That way, if the interviewer asks about these, you'll be prepared.
>
> It goes without saying that you should arrive for the interview on time. That means knowing the exact location and how long it will take to get there. If you arrive late and out of breath, you will make a very poor impression.

2 Study the following sentence from the text and read the explanation below.

If you spend some time doing this homework, the interview is much more likely to be successful.

The second part (a successful interview) is the result or effect of the first part (doing the homework).

3 There are three more sentences like the example in the text. Look back at the text and complete the following table.

Cause	Effect
If you spend some time doing this homework	the interview is much more likely to be successful.
	you will look better than many other applicants.
	you'll be prepared.
If you arrive late and out of breath	

4 Use the completed table to answer the following questions.

1 What tense is used in the *if* or *cause* part of the sentence? ....

2 What tense is used in the *effect* part of the sentence? ....

> We use **first conditional** sentences to talk about possibilities in the future and their effects. Note that you do not use *will* in the first part of the sentence even though it is about a future possibility.

5 Complete the rest of the extract by putting the verbs in brackets (1–7) in either the present simple or the *will* future tense.

You also need to prepare questions to ask the interviewer. You should see the interview as a two-way process, partly for you to make sure that the job will give you the career development that you want. After all, if the company **1** doesn't suit (not suit) you, it is better to find this out at the interview, rather than after you have accepted the job. Besides, if you **2** .... (ask) intelligent questions, the interviewer **3** .... (be) impressed by your knowledge and interest in the company. Note down the questions that you want to ask beforehand; if you **4** .... (not write) them down, it is possible you **5** .... (forget) them during the interview.

Finally, remember that the interviewers may well ask other people for their opinions of you. This means you need to make a good impression on the employee who shows you around or on the receptionist as well. If they **6** .... (feel) that you are impolite or arrogant, probably the interviewers **7** .... (hear) about it.

Speaking

Work in pairs. You are going to interview some candidates for a vacancy in your department. If you do not work in the same department, or you haven't started work yet, invent a vacancy for a post in your company or college. Discuss the six qualities in a candidate below (a–f), and decide which are the most important for the role. Number them 1–6 (1 = most important; 6 = least important). Try to use some first conditionals in your discussion.

a good academic qualifications ☐
b relevant work experience ☐
c good communication skills ☐
d a smart appearance ☐
e a wide range of non-work interests ☐
f good computer skills ☐

> **Useful language**
> **Talking about candidates**
>
> If they have relevant experience, we know they can do the job.
> If he doesn't have the right computer skills, he'll have to be trained.
> She has to be able to …   They really need to …
> It's essential that they have …   If they don't have …

Interview questions

Reading

1 Read the article on page 106 quickly to get a general idea of the content. What is the main topic of the article, A, B or C?

A techniques to deal with difficult interview questions
B ways of assessing candidates before a job interview
C unusual questions that interviewers may ask

2 Look through the article again and match each of the paragraphs with the most suitable heading. There is one heading you do not need.

a Examples of strange interview questions. ...2...
b Essential skills for interview candidates. ....
c The biggest disadvantage of strange interview questions. ....
d The difficulty of finding the right person for a job. ....
e Do strange interview questions work? ....

PICKING THE RIGHT PERSON FOR THE JOB

1 When there are lots of good candidates for a post, it is not easy to choose between them. Faced with this problem, interviewers sometimes use strange methods in their attempt to pick out the right candidate for the job.

2 Sometimes this may take the form of a task, like finding the answer to a logical problem. More often it involves asking the candidates questions which are intended to give an idea of their skills or personality. 'How many houses do you think there are in your town?', for example, is intended to test the candidates ability to estimate numbers. Other questions require candidates to imagine themselves in a particular situation. 'If you had only six months to live, how would you spend them?' is a common one. This apparently shows whether candidates can set goals and prioritise. Perhaps the most difficult questions are those which are intended to show something about your personality, like 'If you were an animal, what animal would you be?' The answer, 'a horse', for example, might indicate that you are hard-working.

3 But do questions like these really help the interviewer to choose the best person? Surely you can find out more about a candidate by looking at their track record in previous jobs. In an interview, you want to find out if the candidate is a good communicator. You can only do this by having a normal conversation with them, not by asking questions like these.

4 Worst of all, odd questions like these may give the impression that the interviewer is not serious. I recently asked a friend, a successful business person who has often hired co-workers, if he ever used questions like these. Certainly not. Did he think they could be useful? No. In fact they were probably harmful because they could alienate good candidates. 'If someone asked me questions like that, I'd leave the interview' he said.

3 **Find words and phrases in the article with the following meanings.**

1 choose one person or object from a group
   pick out

2 make an approximate calculation of a number
   ....

3 to put things in order of importance so you do the most important first ....

4 a person's past achievements and failures
   ....

5 strange or unexpected ....

6 make someone feel or think something ....

7 make someone dislike you or feel they do not want to work with you ....

Grammar workshop 2

Second conditional

1 **Study this sentence from the text and answer questions (1–3).**

- *If someone asked me questions like that, I'd (I would) leave the interview.*

1 Is the speaker planning to attend an interview where someone will ask him these questions?
   ....

2 The tense in the *if* part of the sentence is in the past simple. Is it about the past? ....

3 In the result part of the sentence, what modal verb is used before the main verb? ....

> **Second conditional** sentences, unlike first conditional sentences, talk about an *imaginary situation* which cannot happen or which the speaker thinks will not happen.

2 **Two of the interview questions in paragraph 2 of the text are in the second conditional. Read the text again and <u>underline</u> the questions.**

Speaking

1 **Work in pairs.**

Student A: look at the question card below.
Student B: look at the question card on page 120.

Take it in turns to ask and answer the questions, writing down your partner's answers.

> **QUESTION CARD A**
> 1 If someone offered you a well-paid job in another city or country, would you take it?
> 2 If you could give one part of your job description/studies to another person, what would it be and why?
> 3 If someone gave you the money to set up a new business, what kind of business would it be?
> 4 If you were a man/woman, do you think your job would be easier or more difficult than it is now? Why?

2 **Write two more questions using the second conditional and ask and answer them with your partner. Choose your partner's two most interesting answers from both exercises and report them back to the class.**

> **❯** page 116 Conditionals

A recruitment agency

Listening

1 **(2)(03)** Listen to an interview with Simon Hale, who works for a recruitment agency, talking about his client base. In which order does he mention the following?

a age ☐ c nationality ☐
b gender [1] d qualifications ☐

2 **(2)(03)** Listen again and for questions (1–6), circle the correct answer, A, B or C.

1 Simon Hale's organisation places most people in
   Ⓐ large consultancies.
   B specialist jobs.
   C managerial posts.

2 According to Simon, attempts to attract more women into work
   A have not had much effect.
   B have brought benefits to companies.
   C have made recruitment more difficult.

3 What point does Simon make about the age of people he has placed?
   A The age range is wider than in some other agencies.
   B Most of the people he deals with are young.
   C He has never placed anyone over the age of sixty.

4 What does Simon say about the level of qualifications needed?
   A All his IT specialists need to have a degree.
   B A degree is preferred but not essential.
   C A vocational qualification is more important than a degree.

5 Why are a large number of the people from India?
   A There are cultural links between India and the UK.
   B There is high unemployment in India.
   C India has lots of IT specialists.

6 According to Simon, how has the recruitment industry changed?
   A It has higher standards than in the past.
   B It has become more competitive.
   C It has been affected by new legislation.

Writing

Read the advertisement below for another recruitment agency.

SANFORD RECRUITMENT

We are one of the leading recruitment agencies for IT professionals. Our consultants understand your IT needs and will find you the right person for the job.

If you are a company with a technical post you need to fill, or an IT professional looking for a job, fill in our online form or email us at info@sanford.com

You work for a company which needs to recruit an IT expert. Write an email to Sanford asking for their help. In your email:

* give details of the post you need to fill
* provide your contact details
* suggest times for Sanford to call and discuss your requirements
* enquire about their fees

Write 60–80 words.

Staff development

Getting started

Work in pairs. How can you let employees know if they are doing well at their jobs (give feedback on their work)? Try to think of at least three different ways. Then look at these suggestions (1–5) for giving feedback to employees and tick (✓) the ones which you think are a good idea. Try to agree on which method you think is the best.

1 The manager has a meeting with the employee in the office once a year to discuss their work. ☐

2 The manager has a meeting with the employee once a year as above, but outside the office (for example in a café). ☐

3 The manager only has a meeting with the employee if their work is not satisfactory. ☐

4 The manager gives the employee a grade at the end of the year (for example a number from 1 to 5, where 1 = very good and 5 = poor). ☐

5 The manager asks other members of staff to complete a questionnaire about the employee. ☐

Training

Reading 1

1 **Work with a partner and discuss the questions (1–4) which apply to you.**

   1 Have you ever attended any training courses with your company?

   2 If so, did you enjoy the course(s)?

   3 What kind of skills for your future job are you learning at the moment in your place of study?

   4 What kind of life/ professional skills do your present studies **not** provide you with?

2 **Opposite are four advertisements (a–d) for training courses. Read the titles and skim through the information in each to decide which would be most helpful for you in your work or study.**

a

DATA WAREHOUSE TRAINING

This course looks at the use of data warehousing and how to successfully design and manage a data warehouse. We will examine some of the practical experiences of real companies who have been involved in the implementation of data warehouse projects.

The course is presented in a non-technical way and no previous knowledge of data warehousing is needed. However, attendees are strongly advised to read our pre-course pack before beginning the training.

b

TIME-MANAGEMENT SKILLS

Kronos offers training in time-management skills and productivity. After completing the programme, trainees can take advantage of a refresher course in any of the countries where we operate at no extra cost.

Our programmes have proven effective for over 10,000 clients in the past 15 years. Independent surveys have shown that after the course, our clients achieve on average 70 minutes extra productivity each day. That's seven weeks each year!

c

UNDERSTANDING FINANCIAL STATEMENTS

This is a two-day workshop dealing with the basics of financial statement analysis for banks. The programme is designed for clients who have little or no experience of analysing financial statements for financial institutions. Trainees examine the components of a balance sheet and income statement and learn to identify the risks in the different business lines and products. The workshop leads into an intermediate level programme on Intensive Financial Analysis.

d

EMOTIONAL INTELLIGENCE

Emotional Intelligence (E.I.) is an essential quality for any successful leader. This course is for anyone in a management post who wishes to develop their self-knowledge and interpersonal skills. You will learn how to assess yourself accurately and how to use E.I. to influence and develop others. The impact can be dramatic on both your business and your personal life.

The course takes place at our New York or London training suites. We can also take group bookings and run the course in-company, or at a location of your convenience.

3 Look at the statements (1–7) below about the courses (a–d). Read the adverts again and decide which course each statement describes. Write the correct letter in each box.

1 After the course, trainees can do another follow-up course for free. `b`

2 The course changes more than the participants' working lives. ☐

3 After completing the programme, trainees can take a further course at a higher level. ☐

4 Research has been carried out into how the course has changed the clients' working practices. ☐

5 The course examines some case studies of actual companies. ☐

6 Trainees should do some pre-course study. ☐

7 The course can be held at your place of work. ☐

Reading 2

Read the following two texts and extract information from each to complete the form below them.

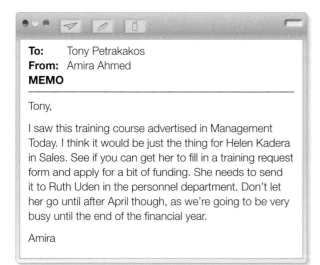

To: Tony Petrakakos
From: Amira Ahmed
MEMO

Tony,

I saw this training course advertised in Management Today. I think it would be just the thing for Helen Kadera in Sales. See if you can get her to fill in a training request form and apply for a bit of funding. She needs to send it to Ruth Uden in the personnel department. Don't let her go until after April though, as we're going to be very busy until the end of the financial year.

Amira

The Psychology of Selling

An exciting new course for anyone working in sales and marketing. You will learn how to:

- understand the factors which determine what customers buy and who from
- gain credibility with potential new buyers
- deal with buyers who hesitate

This could revolutionise your company's sales figures.

Course dates: 23–25 March
19–21 April
25–27 May
Price: Individual: £230
Corporate group rate: £190 per person

TRAINING REQUEST FORM

For the attention of:	1	Ruth Uden
Training requested for:	2	
Trainee's department	3	
Dates:	4	
Cost (excluding travel):	5	

Writing

Imagine you want to book places for some of the staff in your company on the 'Psychology of Selling' course. Write an email to the course organiser:

- saying how many members of staff you want to book for
- requesting a booking form
- telling him/her which dates you prefer
- asking if you can have the corporate rate

Write 60–80 words.

Sport and business

Reading

People often make comparisons between the world of business and the world of sport. For example, people who work well with their colleagues are often said to be good *team players*.

1 Work in pairs. You are going to read a text about football and business. Before you read, complete the following two sentences and then discuss your ideas with a partner.

Working in a company is like playing in a football team because ....
Managing a company is like managing a football team because ....

2 Skim the article to find out if it mentions your ideas.

THE WAY TO WIN

For a long time people have seen similarities between the world of sport and the world of business. In both cases, there is enormous pressure to win and, success depends on teamwork. Sports managers have often passed on ideas from the world of sport which help train business people. Will Carling, the former England rugby captain, set up a business consultancy and even co-wrote a book on the subject, called The Way to Win. International sports are always a good analogy to use in business training because people all over the world know their rules and their language.

Nowadays, the jobs of a football manager and a business manager are probably more similar than ever before. Chris Brady, an ex-footballer and football coach, is the author of The 90-Minute Manager, a book which shows how much business managers can learn by looking at what football managers do. For example, both have the job of keeping talented people with them when they could

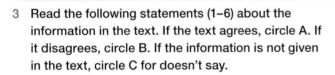

always leave and go somewhere else. The job of the manager in both cases is to make these talented people work for the good of the whole group. The results of a football team are transparent with the league tables showing the world how well they are performing. Again, big business is no different with share prices published in the media. As Chris Brady says, 'The role that modern business managers are increasingly being asked to play is the same one that football managers have always played.'

But perhaps one of the biggest lessons that football has for business is about the relationship between the manager and his team. A football manager does not sit in his office, separate from the players. When they have a football match, he is in the changing rooms beforehand talking to them and during the game he stands and watches everything. How different would companies be if CEOs had this close contact with their staff at work?

3 Read the following statements (1–6) about the information in the text. If the text agrees, circle A. If it disagrees, circle B. If the information is not given in the text, circle C for doesn't say.

1 Comparing sport and business is a new idea.
   A right   (B) wrong   C doesn't say
2 Will Carling is the only author of *A Way to Win*.
   A right   B wrong   C doesn't say
3 Football is a good example to use in business coaching because it is understood in many different cultures.
   A right   B wrong   C doesn't say
4 Company managers are better at keeping staff than football managers.
   A right   B wrong   C doesn't say
5 According to Chris Brady, the job of a business manager is becoming more similar to that of a football manager.
   A right   B wrong   C doesn't say
6 In the past, CEOs had more contact with their staff.
   A right   B wrong   C doesn't say

Vocabulary

1 Vocabulary from sports and games is often used in business situations. In each of the following examples (1–5), which sport or game does the expression in italics come from? Choose a sport from the box below. Sometimes more than one sport is possible and any sport can be used more than once.

> athletics   baseball   chess   football

1 Shall we *kick off* by looking at this month's sales figures? _football_
2 That new sales executive seems very good. He's really *on the ball*. _____
3 Neither side are willing to accept a compromise, so the negotiations have reached a *stalemate*.
   _____
4 I'm just writing to *touch base* with you. _____
5 A: All this paperwork has to be done by the end of the financial year.
   B: But that's only two weeks away.
   A: I know. It's a real *race against time*. _____

2 Now match the expressions (1–5) with their correct meanings (a–e).

1 kick off   a stay in contact
2 on the ball   b something that has to be done quickly to meet the deadline
3 stalemate   c a situation where no one can make any progress or gain anything
4 touch base   d efficient and aware of what is happening
5 race against time   e start (a meeting or a process)

Giving and receiving feedback

Vocabulary

In some companies, managers have a meeting with each member of staff once or twice a year when their achievements, strengths and weaknesses are discussed. This is sometimes called an *appraisal*.

> Many verbs add -*er* to make the name of the person who does the action. Some verbs can also add -*ee* to form the name of the person who is the object of the action. Two examples you know already are *employer* and *employee*.

What could you call the following people?

1 the manager who does the appraisal ....
2 the employee who receives the appraisal ....

Do you know any other business-related nouns which can finish in -*er* and -*ee*?

Listening

1 You are going to listen to an interview with Yvonne, who is talking about a system called *360 degree feedback*. Work with a partner and discuss what you think *360 degree feedback* means.

2 (2) 04 Listen to the interview and answer the following questions.

1 In the 360 degree system, who gives the feedback to an employee?
2 Who sees the feedback?

3 (2) 04 Listen again and complete the following sentences by choosing the correct ending. Circle A, B or C.

1 In 360 degree feedback, at least some of the appraisers must be chosen by …
   A the employee.
   (B) the employee's manager.
   C colleagues.
2 In the feedback, the employee is given …
   A a grade.
   B a written comment.
   C both a grade and a written comment.
3 The employee compares the feedback with …
   A his/her manager's appraisal.
   B his/her own self-assessment.
   C his/her development plan.

4 According to the speaker, linking the feedback to pay …
   A has never been tried.
   B is not recommended.
   C is usual.
5 The employee's manager must see …
   A the results of the feedback.
   B the employee's development plan.
   C the results of the feedback and the employee's development plan.
6 The speaker feels that feedback without the person's name on it …
   A is essential.
   B is more useful than named feedback.
   C is less useful than named feedback.
7 360 degree feedback is not recommended …
   A in times of major change.
   B in periods of growth.
   C in small companies.

4 Discuss the following questions with a partner.

1 How would you feel if someone asked you to receive 360 degree feedback? Do you think it is a good idea? Why/Why not?
2 Would you want to receive feedback with, or without, the person's name on it?

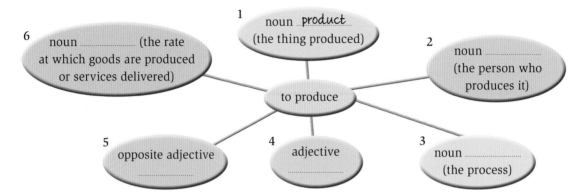

Employee productivity

Getting started

1 Complete the word diagram below with the correct forms of *produce*.

1 noun _product_ (the thing produced)

6 noun .... (the rate at which goods are produced or services delivered)

2 noun .... (the person who produces it)

to produce

5 opposite adjective ....

4 adjective ....

3 noun .... (the process)

2 You have asked your management team to suggest some ideas to improve employee productivity. Work in pairs and number the suggestions according to the effect you think they will have (1 = the best effect on productivity; 6 = the least, or perhaps a bad effect on productivity).

1 Stop paying employees by the hour and pay them according to how many goods they produce or how many sales they make.
2 Change employees' jobs around so that they do not get bored.
3 Offer a prize, like a free holiday, to the employee who is the most productive.
4 Introduce a scheme in which employees receive a fixed percentage of the company's profits.
5 Introduce flexible hours so employees can arrive at and leave the office when they want.
6 Share all the company's internal financial information with the employees so they know how the company is doing.

3 Compare your order with another pair and try to agree on the best order.

A meeting

Listening

1 ② 05 Listen to an extract from a meeting, where four managers are discussing possible ways of improving employee productivity. What action do they agree to take at the end of the conversation?

2 ② 05 Listen again and complete the following extracts (1–8) with one to three words.

1 We are planning _to upgrade_ the system next year.
2 How about .... the staff with smartphones?
3 .... people with a lot of gadgets isn't always a good idea.
4 We have to do something .... staff that we support them.
5 It's difficult .... people use smartphones properly.
6 How do you stop people .... games on them?
7 It might be possible .... the date of the system upgrade.
8 Before .... a lot of money on new equipment, we should find out how people really feel.

3 Discuss the following questions with a partner.

- Two people in the conversation disagree about the effect of giving company staff smartphones. One thinks it will help staff to do their job and make them more productive. The other thinks it will distract them and make them less productive. Who do you think is right? Why?
- Think of some new technology or software that has been introduced in your workplace or place of study. Does it just help people to work or study more efficiently or does it also have disadvantages?

Grammar workshop

Infinitives and -ing forms

1 Look again at the extracts from the Listening. Which gaps contain a verb in the infinitive form? Which gaps contain an -ing form?

2 <u>Underline</u> the correct alternatives in the following grammar rules. Use the examples from the Listening to help you.

1. We usually use <u>the infinitive</u>/the -ing form after adjectives (e.g. *difficult, possible, happy*).
2. We use the infinitive/-ing form after prepositions (e.g. *about, after, before*).
3. We use the infinitive/-ing form after some verbs, including most verbs about wishes or plans for the future (e.g. *plan, hope, want, would like, intend, expect*).
4. We use the infinitive/-ing form after some other verbs (e.g. *enjoy, finish, stop, mind, avoid, risk*).
5. We use the infinitive/-ing form when the verb is the subject of the sentence.
6. We use the infinitive/-ing form to talk about the purpose of an action.

3 Complete the following paragraph by putting the verbs in brackets in the infinitive or -ing form.

Some employers may think breaks are a waste of time but in fact **1** _providing_ (provide) staff with enough breaks is essential if you want them **2** .... (be) productive. Obviously, after **3** .... (concentrate) hard on something, everyone needs a few minutes away from their desk **4** .... (relax). But there is another good reason for **5** .... (give) employees enough breaks. The best ideas often come to people at these times. Sometimes it can be difficult **6** .... (see) a solution to a problem if you focus on it all the time. **7** .... (chat) to colleagues over coffee or even **8** .... (take) a walk in the park can free up your mind and allow you **9** .... (think) more creatively.

4 ⊙ Business English students sometimes confuse which verbs are followed by infinitives and which are followed by -ing forms. Circle the correct word to complete the following sentences.

1. We hope *to hear*/ *hearing* from you soon.
2. Do not hesitate *to call*/ *calling* me if you have any questions.
3. I would like *to suggest*/ *suggesting* a topic for the talk.
4. We really enjoyed *to meet*/ *meeting* your sales team.
5. The new equipment could help my company *to increase*/ *increasing* productivity.
6. They agreed *to accept*/ *accepting* a lower price.
7. I was preparing the report when suddenly my computer stopped *to work*/ *working*.
8. We look forward to *see*/ *seeing* you at the conference next week.

5 Look at the verbs before the words in *italics* in Exercise 4 and write each verb in the correct column below. Can you think of more examples for each column?

Verbs followed by infinitives	Verbs followed by -ing forms
hope	look forward to

6 **Work in pairs. Think of some reasons why you might do the following. Note down your ideas, using the purpose infinitive.**

1 go to work by bicycle instead of by car
   to save petrol, to avoid traffic jams, to keep fit

2 put plants around the office

3 keep a small knife in your office drawer

4 eat only an apple for lunch

5 switch off all the lights in the office

6 keep a rubber chicken in the office

7 **Compare your ideas with another pair. Who thought of the most unusual reasons?**

❯ **page 116** Infinitive and *-ing* forms

A report

Writing

1 **A week after the meeting about staff productivity, a report was written about the staff's opinions on technology. Look quickly through the report and answer the following questions.**

1 Where does the report say how the staff were contacted in order to get their opinions?

2 How are the staff's opinions organised?

3 What is the purpose of the final paragraph/conclusion?

> ### REPORT ON OFFICE TECHNOLOGY
>
> An all-staff email was sent out to ask staff their opinions about the office equipment. Staff were also invited to a meeting at Tuesday lunchtime to discuss possible improvements to the technology.
>
> **Current situation**
> There is a general feeling that the current computer system should be upgraded as soon as possible. The internet connection is often slow and unreliable. The IT support team are helpful, but cannot always respond to problems quickly enough.
>
> **Possible improvements**
> ....
> ....
>
> **Conclusion**
> I recommend that we research the cost of providing staff with smartphones and then make a decision on whether to purchase these and/or new presentation software. A further meeting with staff may be needed to discuss the company policy on how and when smartphones should be used.

2 **There are two paragraphs in the *possible improvements* section of the report. Write the phrases in the boxes below in the correct order to create the two paragraphs. The first and last phrases of each paragraph are marked. Then add the punctuation.**

1

which they felt would be very useful	however two members of staff were concerned
of having smartphones	for this reason, they wanted to agree on
1 in general staff liked the idea	that if they had smartphones
8 times when the phones could be switched off	the company would call them at weekends

2

for new presentation software which could be	James and Anisa agreed
to research the price of other software packages	**1** several requests were made
7 with some figures	and to get back to me after two weeks
an alternative to PowerPoint	

3 **Compare your two paragraphs with a partner. Do you have the same order and punctuation?**

Older employees

Reading

1 Use the adjectives in the box with *more, less* or other comparative forms, to complete the following sentence in three different ways. Then compare your ideas with a partner.

1 In general, I think older workers are more reliable than younger workers.

2 ....

3 ....

4 ....

> confident   enthusiastic   happy in their work   loyal   motivated   productive   ~~reliable~~   slow to learn

2 Read the following text to revise some grammar from earlier units by choosing the correct word, A, B or C to fill each gap (1–10).

1 A are	(B) have	C has
2 A in	B on	C by
3 A what	B that	C who
4 A Despite	B However	C Although
5 A which	B what	C where
6 A a	B the	C this
7 A too	B also	C ever
8 A than	B so	C as
9 A for	B of	C from
10 A because	B so	C therefore

The number of workers over the age of 50 or 60 is likely to increase in the future. We are all living longer and many businesses **1** __B__ decided to operate without a fixed retirement age **2** .... order to take advantage of the skills and experience **3** .... older workers can offer. **4** .... popular opinion, older workers are not less productive than younger ones. Indeed, in sectors **5** .... physical strength is not important, like **6** .... service sector, they may be more productive. They **7** .... tend to take less sick leave and do not have as many accidents **8** .... younger employees. Research also suggests that they do not suffer **9** .... stress so much. The reason for this may be that their children have left home, **10** .... it is easier for them to manage the work-life balance.

Listening

2 06 Listen to five older workers talking about their present employment situation. Match each person (1–5) with the correct statement (a–i) below. There are four statements that you don't need.

Person 1
Person 2
Person 3
Person 4
Person 5

a would like more job security
b feels that he/she is a victim of age discrimination
c works with people who are much younger than him/her
d did not spend a long time unemployed
e is planning to take early retirement
f works mainly with people of a similar age to him/her
g is short of money after being made redundant
h feels that his/her ability is not being exploited
i is waiting to hear the results of an interview

> **Task tip**
>
> Summarising the main point of what someone says is a useful skill in business. If you are writing notes on a candidate during an interview, it is better to summarise what they say in a few short sentences rather than write down every word. This exercise gives you practice in identifying suitable summarising sentences.

Grammar workshop 6

Units 21–24

Conditionals

1 ⊙ **Business English students sometimes make errors with the tenses in conditionals. Circle the correct alternative in the following conditional sentences (1–8).**

1 If you (require)/required further information, please feel free to contact us.

2 Please let me know if you *cannot / could not* attend the meeting.

3 It would be better if the sessions *are/were* held on our company premises.

4 If you *agree / will agree*, I will arrange your accommodation at the Hotel Flamenco.

5 We would be willing to increase our order if you *feel/felt* able to give a discount.

6 If you *have/will have* any questions, please log on to our website.

7 I hope that if we *order / will order* more than 100, we *receive / will receive* a discount.

8 If we *held / hold* the training session on company premises, it would be more convenient for everyone.

2 ⊙ **Business English students sometimes use the wrong tenses in second conditional sentences. Correct the tense mistakes in the following requests (1–8). TWO of the sentences are correct.**

1 I would be grateful if you ~~can~~ arrange a hotel room. *could*

2 I would appreciate it if all of you can attend a meeting at 3 pm.

3 I am very glad if you could change the date of the meeting.

4 I would be grateful if you could book me a standard room.

5 It will be helpful if you could contact the sales department about this matter.

6 I would be delighted if you are able to attend our meeting on 14 June.

7 I would appreciate it if you could send a company car to the airport.

8 I would be very much obliged if you can raise this issue in your meeting.

Infinitive and -ing forms

1 **Complete the following letter by putting one of the verbs from the box in each gap (1–8) in either the infinitive or the -ing form.**

> attend (x2)   come   complete   inform   see
> contact   invite

> Dear Mr Masters,
>
> Thank you for **1** _attending_ the interview on 28 June. We are writing **2** .... you that you have been shortlisted for the post. We would like **3** .... you **4** .... for a second interview on 12 July. We enclose a written task which you will need **5** .... before **6** ....
>
> If you have any queries, please do not hesitate **7** .... us. We look forward to **8** .... you again on 12 July.
>
> Yours sincerely,
> Pearl Makinson

2 ⊙ **Business English students sometimes wrongly use an infinitive instead of a preposition plus the -ing form of the verb. Correct the mistakes with infinitives in some of the following sentences by changing them to a preposition plus -ing. If the infinitive form is correct, write CORRECT at the end of the sentence.**

1 I apologise ~~to cancel~~ the meeting which was scheduled for today. *for cancelling*

2 We are interested to arrange a training course for our staff.

3 We are pleased to inform you that you have been selected for the post.

4 She will be responsible to create our new range of bracelets.

5 Many thanks to choose our company to give this talk.

6 My talk will be about the importance to prepare a development programme for staff.

7 Would it be convenient to hold the meeting at 12 o'clock?

8 Please accept my apologies for the delay to complete this project.

Grammar and spelling revision

1 Read the following text and revise some grammar by choosing the correct word, A, B or C, to fill each gap (1–12).

ONLINE RECRUITMENT

Most companies and organisations now recruit directly through the Internet. This is quicker and cheaper **1** __C__ paying a recruitment agency or placing an advertisement **2** _____ a newspaper. Often they recruit **3** _____ using the company website. They set up a page **4** _____ shows vacancies within the organisation and applicants can email the company directly with their CVs.

Some other websites just work **5** _____ databases for online CVs. These are used **6** _____ employers who are looking for candidates. Usually, you **7** _____ to put your CV on one of these sites but it can be an effective way **8** _____ finding out about new vacancies. **9** _____ employers access these sites, they search for keywords from your area of work so **10** _____ these on your CV is very important. If your CV does not contain the same words that the recruiter is using **11** _____ search the site, then you **12** _____ stand no chance.

	A	B	C
1	of	that	than
2	on	in	for
3	from	by	with
4	who	which	where
5	as	for	with
6	by	with	from
7	must	should	have
8	of	in	to
9	When	What	Which
10	include	included	including
11	for	to	in
12	will	would	should

2 Complete the following text by writing one suitable word in each gap.

According to many people, it's a good idea **1** __to__ have a section on your CV about your hobbies and interests because it can tell employers something **2** _____ the kinds of skills you have. For example, **3** _____ you like playing football, this shows you are a good team player.

Unfortunately, statements about unusual hobbies can often **4** _____ the wrong impression and even common hobbies can **5** _____ questions in employers' minds. A football player may have good team-building skills, **6** _____ what happens if you want him **7** _____ work late on an evening when there is an important match?

If you are applying **8** _____ your first job, you will have to list hobbies and interests on your CV **9** _____ of work experience. However, after you **10** _____ gained some relevant experience, you should think carefully about whether you **11** _____ to include them. After all, most people's hobbies **12** _____ not clearly related to the job they do, and listing too **13** _____ can suggest that you are not committed enough **14** _____ your work.

3 Complete the following sentences (1–6) with a noun formed from the word in brackets.

1 We need to find a way of improving staff __productivity__ . (produce)
2 The _____ did not put his contact number on the CV. (apply)
3 We are advertising for a new sales manager, following Ms Spencer's _____ last week. (resign)
4 He hopes to receive compensation for unfair _____ . (dismiss)
5 She made a very good _____ on the interview panel. (impress)
6 Unfortunately, a number of staff will face _____ if the merger goes ahead. (redundant)

4 ⊙ The following sentences contain spelling mistakes commonly made by candidates in Cambridge business exams. Find and correct the mistake in each one. One sentence has TWO mistakes.

1 The invoice was ~~payed~~ over a week ago. *paid*
2 One of your colleagues made a very usefull suggestion.
3 The price of the hole package is just under 100 dollars, wich is very reasonable.
4 We really need to find cheaper premises then these.
5 The new product is not very diffrent from the old one, despite the higher price.
6 A great many customers complaint about the poor service.
7 All applications need to be sent to the personal manager before the end of the month.
8 Please could you advice all your staff about the changes to the system.

Communication activities

UNIT 3

Growing pains

Speaking

Student B

Baja Fresh is a chain of restaurants which serves fresh food with a Mexican theme. The company began in 1990 when a husband and wife team opened the first restaurant in California. They paid for it by .... (how?).

Their selling point was the freshness of their ingredients and they refused to use .... (what?) in their kitchens. The restaurant was very successful and they gradually opened more. In 1997, they had 31 outlets.

Then in .... (when?), Wendy's, the international fast food restaurant, acquired Baja Fresh. They paid $275 million for it. They wanted to .... (what?) but unfortunately this didn't work out. They tried to expand every quickly but they didn't pay enough attention to the original business model. One year later sales began to decline and in 2004, they fell by .... (how much?). Faced with these figures, in 2006 Wendy's sold Baja Fresh for just $31 million to .... (who?).

After the sales, Baja Fresh closed a number of unprofitable restaurants and tried to .... (what?). Now the restaurant is doing well again. In 2010, they opened a new branch in Dubai and in 2011, David Kim, the Chief Executive, appeared on the TV programme .... (which?).

UNIT 6

Speaking

Student B

Ben and Jerry's ice cream:
It is manufactured in the USA.
It is sold on many Caribbean cruise ships.
The company is owned by Proctor and Gamble.
(**FALSE**: It is owned by Unilever.)

Puma sportswear:
The company is German but a lot of their sportswear is made in China.
They are best known for their baseball caps.
(**FALSE**: They are best known for running shoes and football boots.)
Their sportswear is distributed to over 100 countries.

UNIT 7

Telephoning

Role-play

Student B

You are the owner of Multipelli, a boutique specialising in leather goods. Three weeks ago you placed an order with Roco, one of your suppliers, for 120 leather jackets, 40 small, 40 medium and 40 large. You received the order today, but there are 40 small and 80 medium jackets!

Phone your suppliers to complain. Find out when they can deliver the large jackets and what they will do about the extra medium ones.

(The order number was 0043724).

UNIT 9

Making an appointment

Role-play

Student B

You are Carmen Vanegas, the sales representative from Medica from the Listening exercise on page 47. Your client, Stefano Cigada, phones to tell you that he cannot now make the meeting at 2 o'clock on Thursday as arranged. Here is an extract from your diary for the following week. Arrange a new time for the meeting that week when you are both free.

Monday	AM	*visiting new client*
	PM	
Tuesday	AM	
	PM	*out of area all day, return train 4.15*
Wednesday	AM	
	PM	*meeting with finance department*

UNIT 12

Booking a venue

Role-play

Student B

You work for Walfords Conference Centre, which has the following facilities:

- two lecture halls which can seat 120 people each
- five smaller seminar rooms which can each seat about 30 people
- an electronic whiteboard in each room
- car parking spaces for 150 cars

To book and pay, customers need to fill in the online booking form on the website. The first and third weeks in March are free, but you have bookings in weeks two and four.

A customer phones asking for information. Tell them about the facilities at the conference centre and advise them how they can book. Take their email address so you can follow up the enquiry.

UNIT 17

Describing trends

Speaking

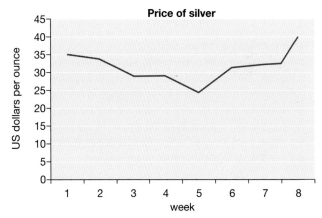

Teenage entrepreneurs

Reading

Text B

Chokolit

Louis Barnett left school at the age of 11 after he was diagnosed with dyslexia and a number of other disabilities, despite having a high IQ. His parents encouraged him to follow his own interests and one of these was baking. Louis started making chocolate cakes for family and friends and selling them to local shops and restaurants. After a while he moved on to making chocolates, which were so successful that he decided to start his own business. With the help of a small loan from his grandparents, he bought some new equipment and moved the chocolate-making operation into his parents' garage where there was more space. As demand grew, Louis then moved into a manufacturing site. He called the company 'Chokolit', because that was how he spelt 'chocolate' due to his dyslexia. Louis sent some samples of his products to a chocolate buyer for a local supermarket he thought might be interested. As a result, at the age of 14, he became the youngest ever supplier to Waitrose, a large UK retailer. He soon went on to supply other major retailers.

At the age of 17 Louis was invited, as a celebrity chocolate maker, to attend the Chocolate Experience show which was held in Mexico. He has been back many times since on business and is planning to open a restaurant and retail outlet there. On his return from Mexico, he decided to write his first book, as he felt he needed to show others that with determination and hard work anything is possible. Now at the age of 20 Louis is a well-known entrepreneur, a published author and motivational speaker. On his speaking tours, he informs young people that 'you don't make mistakes, you only learn lessons'.

UNIT 22

Grammar workshop 2

Speaking

QUESTION CARD B

1 If your best friend wanted you to set up a new business with them, would you accept? Why?/Why not?
2 If you could create a new post in your department, what would it be and why? / If you could add a new subject to the one your place of study offers, what would it be and why?
3 If you could go on any training course you wanted, what course would you choose and why?
4 If you were much older or younger than you are now, do you think your job would be easier or more difficult? Why?

Writing reference

Levels of formality

1 It is important to write an email or a letter in a style suitable for the person who will read it. What style should you use if you are writing to the following people? Write F (formal) or I (informal).

1 a friend or colleague you know well ....

2 someone outside your company you have not met ....

3 someone senior to you in your company ....

4 someone junior to you in your company ....

2 The table shows some of the differences between formal and informal English. Put each of the examples (a–j) opposite in the correct place in the table.

More formal	Less formal
No contractions 1	Contractions 2 ....
Complete sentences, with no missing words 3	Sometimes sentences with small grammar words, such as *the*, *is* and *are* missing (especially in notes) 4 ....
Full stops and commas 5	Sometimes dashes instead of full stops (especially in notes) 6 ....
No abbreviations 7	Some abbreviations may be used 8 ....
Longer ways of making requests and enquiries 9	Shorter ways of making requests and enquiries 10 ....
Begin: *Dear Sir/ Madam/ Dear Mr/Mrs/ Ms* +surname, *Dear Sirs* (for a company)	Begin: *Dear* + first name / *Hi/Hello* +first name (emails)/ first name only (notes and some emails)
End: *Yours faithfully / Yours sincerely / Kind regards* (emails) *Many thanks*	End: *Best wishes / All the best / Thanks* (emails)/ just with your name (notes and some emails).

a Goods ready for collection.

b Please find the agenda for the staff meeting this afternoon attached. If you would like to add anything, let me know.

c Pls cd you phone back asap?

d I'm, we've got, it's

e The goods are ready for collection.

f Staff meeting this afternoon – agenda attached. Let me know if anything to be added.

g I would be grateful if you could ...

h Please could you phone back as soon as possible?

i I am, we have, it is

j Please could you ...

3 Read the two emails below without paying attention to the gaps. Which is more formal? Which is more informal?

A
....
I'm going to be at our Heliopolis office on Monday morning. Please can you type up the sales report while I'm away and send it to Duncan in the marketing department?

Andrew

B
....
Thank you for the information on your conference facilities. I would like to book 120 rooms for the night of March 15 including breakfast. I would be grateful if you could give me a quotation for this.

....
Denise Wilson

4 Which of the beginnings and endings in the box would be suitable for each email?

A: Beginnings: Hi Louise, Dear Louise, Dear Miss Louise, Louise,
   Endings: Thanks, Cheers, Yours sincerely, Kind regards
B: Beginnings: Dear Mr Ford, Hi Mr Ford, Mr Ford,
   Endings: Yours sincerely, Kind regards, Thanks, Many thanks

5 The phrases in the box make two emails asking for a project update. Separate the phrases and then write them in your notebook in the correct order to create two emails, one formal and one informal.

> drop me a line and let me know
> Do you think you'll finish on time
> ~~Hi Sam,~~   ~~Please could you~~
> on the data management project.
> you are likely to finish on time
> or do we need to look at the deadline again?
> ~~I would be grateful if you could~~
> how things are going
> ~~Dear Sam,~~   or if the deadline needs to be revised.
> send me a short progress report
> with the data management project?
> Please could you let me know whether

More formal	More informal
Dear Sam, I would be grateful if you could …	Hi Sam, Please could you …

6 Choose a suitable sign-off for each email.

Emails

The most common kind of communication for business people is an email. Read the following statements (1–6) about emails and decide if they are true or false. Write T or F.

1 Emails are usually not very long. ....
2 Emails are usually more informal than letters. ....
3 Emails can contain very informal grammar like *gonna* for *going to*. ....
4 Emails should start with a greeting like 'Hi John'. ....
5 It is acceptable to write an email completely in capital letters. ....
6 Emails usually use the same abbreviations that you find in text messages like *b4* for *before*. ....

Emails: Requests

1 Look at the three emails (1–3) and match each one with these subject headings (A–C).

A Subject: Help request
B Subject: Premises enquiry
C Subject: Hotel booking

1 ....

Hi Selva
Mr Chen is arriving from Beijing on Monday 13 January. Could you book three nights at the Hilton for him please, and make sure we get the discounted rate? Let me know if there are any problems.
Cheers
Kingsley

2 ....

Dear Joel
I wonder if you could find half an hour this week to give me a hand with the quarterly reports? I'm afraid I'm having a lot of problems with the spreadsheets.
Yours
Chris

3 ....

Dear Mr White,
I am writing with regard to your office space to rent in Seamore Street.
I am the owner of a small cleaning agency and I am currently looking for an office in this area. I would be grateful if you could arrange an appointment for me to view this space. Please could you also tell me if it includes private bathroom facilities?
Yours sincerely
Jane Rowe

2 All three emails ask the reader to do something. Find and underline the language used to make the requests. (There are two in Email 3.)

3 Which requests are more formal? Which are more informal? Why?

4 Complete the following reply to Email 3 using the phrases in the box.

> I also attach   I can confirm   Please call our office
> Thank you for your enquiry
> We would be grateful if you could
> We would be happy

Dear Ms Rowe,
1 .... about the office space in Seamore Street. 2 .... to arrange a viewing of the premises. 3 .... on 01343 758495 to fix a suitable time. 4 .... that the office space includes private bathroom facilities.

5 .... a copy of our request form.
6 .... complete this and return it to us so that we can inform you of any other suitable office space which may be available.

Yours sincerely,

Patrick White

Emails: Invitations

1 **Read the following email invitation. In which order does the writer:**

a make the invitation ☐

b refer to his company by name ☐

c express hope for a positive reply ☐

d say why they have chosen to invite this person ☐

e give details about the event ☐

Dear Mr Langridge,

We at Hawthorn Publications are writing to inform you about our new health and fitness magazine, *Wellbeing*. This is an exciting new venture and will be launched in October of this year.

We are planning an event on 5 October at the Madison Hotel to celebrate the launch and we would like to invite you to give a short talk. We feel that your status as a local sports personality and your work on promoting sporting activities to young people make you an ideal choice as keynote speaker.

We hope you can accept our invitation and look forward to hearing from you.

Yours sincerely,

Robert Moreno

2 **Order the sentences below to create an acceptance email for the above invitation.**

Dear Mr Moreno

a Please could you let us know how long the talk should be. ....

b Thank you for your invitation to the launch of *Wellbeing*. ....

c We would also like to see an advance copy of the first issue of the magazine. ....

d Mr Langridge will be very happy to accept the invitation and give a talk. ....

Yours sincerely

Ulrike Bauer

(PA to John Langridge)

Emails: Enquiries

1 **Read the following email enquiry about training courses, and put the words in phrases (1–5) in the correct order.**

Dear Sirs,

1 *reference am to I writing with* your advertisement in *Business World* for corporate and business training courses.

2 *am I in interested especially* your customer service and customer management courses. **3** *also notice that I However* you offer a free consultation service to discuss training needs. **4** *like I definitely would to* make use of this service.

5 *me Please send you could* some further information about dates and prices? **6** *like enquire I would to also* if you can run the courses on our company premises.

Yours faithfully,

Carol Thompson
Training Manager

2 **Match the two halves of each sentence and complete the reply from the training company.**

Dear Ms Thompson,

1 Many thanks for your enquiry …

2 I attach our brochure …

3 If you would like to arrange a consultation …

4 All of our courses can be delivered …

5 We look forward …

 a … please call us on the above number to fix a date and time.

 b … about our training courses.

 c … either at our offices or at your premises.

 d … to hearing from you.

 e … which gives full details including dates and prices.

Yours sincerely,

Simon Bennett

Emails: Other functions

Sometimes we write emails for other reasons. Usually the writer gives the reason in the first sentence.

1 **Complete emails (1–3) on the next page with the phrase which gives the reason for writing.**

A thank you for

B congratulations on

C I'm sorry about

1

> Hi Lee
>
> .... your promotion! I was delighted to hear the news. Very much deserved!
>
> Steve

2

> Hi Bruce
>
> Just a quick message to say .... all your hard work on the website. Everyone agrees it looks excellent and is definitely much more user friendly than before.
>
> Lotte

3

> Dear Nihat
>
> .... my late arrival this morning. Unfortunately my childminder was sick and I couldn't leave on time. I hope giving the presentation on your own wasn't too difficult.
>
> Valerie

2 In emails like these we may also give the reason again before we sign off. Match each ending to the correct email.

A Good luck with the new post!
B Apologies again,
C You're a star!

Memos

Memos are messages giving information or instructions to one person or a group of people in the same organisation. They are often sent by email.

1 Read the following memos without paying attention to the gaps. Match each one with its main purpose below.

a giving an instruction ....
b making a request ....
c giving good news ....
d giving bad news ....
e giving information about working conditions ....

1

> **Subject:** IT system
> **To:** all staff
>
> Please note that the internal email system will be unavailable on Tuesday from 9 am **1** .... we are upgrading the software. Hopefully we will complete this by 3 o' clock.
>
> The IT department

2

> **Subject:** Meeting on 16 May
> **To:** staff
>
> There will be a meeting on 16 May at 9.00 am **2** .... discuss the rebranding project. All department managers are required to attend.
>
> Gabrielle

3

> To: Tracy Best
>
> Dave Collins, our new systems administrator will be here at 9 o'clock on Monday **3** .... I've just realised I'll be with the accountant at that time. Please could you give him a tour of the office when he arrives? With luck, I'll be free by about 9.30.
>
> Thanks
> Matt

4

> Dear all
>
> Re: our new training programme: I am sorry to say that we have had a number of complaints. Please see the attached feedback from participants. There will be a meeting next week **4** .... we can discuss this together and decide what changes we need to make.
>
> Abi

5

> To all staff:
>
> I am happy to tell you that James Winter has now accepted the post of Human Resources Manager **5** .... will take over from Marcus Doel next month.
>
> Wendy

2 Complete each memo with the correct link word or phrase from the box. There is one you do not need.

> and   because   but   despite   in order to   so that

3 Find the following in the memos.

1 A phrase to tell the reader that s/he needs to know and remember this information.
2 Two words or phrases meaning that this is what the writer hopes will happen.
3 A two-letter word which is used to announce the subject of a memo.
4 A phrase used to introduce bad news.
5 A phrase used to introduce good news.

Notes

Notes are brief informal messages, usually written to people in the same organisation.

1 Look quickly at the notes near the top of page 125 and decide if statements (1–4) are true or false. Write T or F.

1 Notes sometimes miss out small grammar words like pronouns and articles. ....

2 Notes are always written in full sentences. ....

3 Notes often use dashes instead of full stops. ....

4 Notes sometimes use abbreviations. ....

> Tim Wallace 1 *telephoned/ phoned* in sick this morning – injured his leg in a bike accident last night. Pls could you 2 *let his line manager know/ inform his line manager?*

> Jacqui,
> Have borrowed your copy of the database instructions. Hope you don't 3 *mind/object* – will put it back as soon as I've finished.
> 4 *Thank you / Cheers*
> Vince

> Roda,
> Mr Nkumba emailed me – says the order still hasn't arrived. Could you 5 *get in contact with / call* the warehouse and find out what's 6 *happening / going on?*
> Thanx.
> Luse

2 Notes are usually written in an informal style. In the above examples, circle the best alternatives (1–6).

3 Read the following extracts from a telephone conversation.

> Hello Rina, it's Paul. Can I speak to Koji please?

> ... well, when he gets back, can you ask him to call me straight away? It's quite urgent ...

> ... I need to check some of the figures on this spreadsheet he's sent me.

4 Write a note for Koji from Rina about Paul's telephone call. Use a maximum of 15 words.

Letters and more formal emails

Emails have replaced letters in many business situations today. However, letters are still sometimes used for promotional purposes, and often accompany legal documents like contracts.

There are some rules you need to follow when writing a formal letter. Many of these are also true for more formal emails, such as those that accompany job applications.

1 Match the sentence halves to create rules for letter/ formal email writing.

1 Start your letter *Dear Sir/Madam* ....

2 Start your letter *Dear Mr/Mrs/Ms/Dr* + surname ....

3 Start your letter *Dear* + the person's first name ....

4 If you start your letter *Dear Sir/Madam,* ....

5 If you start your letter *Dear Mr/Mrs/Ms/Dr* + surname, ...

6 If you start your letter *Dear* + the person's first name, ...

7 If you are writing for your company, ...

a put your name and job title under your signature.

b you should finish *Yours sincerely*.

c when you do not know the person's name.

d you can finish *Kind regards* or *Best wishes*.

e you should finish *Yours faithfully*.

f if the person is a friend or colleague.

g if you know the person's name but have not met them, or want to keep the letter formal.

2 Read the email below without paying attention to the gaps. What is its main purpose?

a to promote a product

b to make a request

c to apply for a job

> Dear Ms Munro,
>
> I am writing 1 .... the Guilden Business College. We are a well-established provider of business courses and we hope to organise a programme of visits for our students next term. I wonder if it would be possible to arrange for a small group of students to visit your company, preferably during the month of May?
> 2 .... and 3 ....
> 4 ....
> 5 ....
> 6 ....

3 Complete the email by putting the words and phrases in the box in the correct place. There are two you will not need.

> Anna Furlan   Course Director   on behalf of
> thank you in advance
> We look forward to hearing from you   with regard to
> Yours faithfully   Yours sincerely

4 Read the following letter of application. In which order does the writer give the following information?

a details of her qualifications ☐

b the reason for writing ☐

c a phrase showing that she expects a reply ☐

d details of other documents that she is sending ☐

e details of her relevant skills ☐

f times when she will be available for interview ☐

---

34 North Street
South Penrith
Sydney NSW 2750
d.lundy@yahoo.com
12.3.13

Personnel Department
Milton Event Management
Glenmore Park
Sydney NSW 2745

Dear Mr Spearing,

I am writing to apply for the post of Personnel Manager's Assistant as advertised in the Sydney Guardian. I enclose a completed application form.

I graduated in June 2011 with a Bachelor's degree in business administration and since then I have worked as an executive assistant with Ringfields. I believe my experience of office administration and my strong written and spoken communication skills make me an excellent candidate for the post you are advertising.

I am available for interview at any time and look forward to hearing from you.

Yours sincerely,

Deborah Lundy
Deborah Lundy

---

5 Normally business letters are written on headed paper so the company's address and contact details are already there. However, if you are writing a letter of application or enquiry for yourself, you will need to put the information in the correct position. Circle the correct rules for laying out formal letters. Use the above letter to help you.

1 You write your address in the *top left hand / top right hand* corner of the letter.

2 You write the address of the company you are writing to *on the left / on the right* above the start of the letter.

3 You write your email address *above / below* your home address.

4 You write the date *above / below* your address.

5 You write your name *above / below* your signature.

6 Write out the following letter of application with the correct layout, punctuation, capital letters and paragraphing. Use the letter in Exercise 4 to help you.

59 cranmore street manchester m39 8gw 12.2.13 personnel department boltons electronics new road salford m47 2eb dear mr campbell i would like to apply for the post of customer service officer which you are advertising on jobsearch.com you will see from my cv that i have a degree in english and economics i have also completed a course in it applications including spreadsheets i have good communication skills and a wide knowledge of electronic goods as i previously worked at weekends in an electronics store i am available for interview at any time and look forward to hearing from you yours sincerely martin hope

Statistics and reports

The following tables give some information about the profits and numbers of guests at a hotel.

Eastern Ranger Hotel, Leigh-on-Sea: Annual profits

Year one	Year two	Year three
£32,924	£33,143	£35,096

Average monthly room occupancy rate in Year three

Jan	Feb	March	April	May	June
56%	63%	69%	79%	77%	94%
July	*Aug*	*Sept*	*Oct*	*Nov*	*Dec*
98%	100%	82%	66%	54%	58%

Restaurant: average percentage of restaurant diners not staying in hotel in Year three

Jan–Mar	April–June	July–Sept	Oct–Dec
67%	51%	47%	52%

1 Complete the following description of the statistics in the tables using the words and phrases in the box.

> decline   decreased   high   however   increased
> lower   lowest   reach   slight   slightly   stood at

In Year one, profits **1** .... £32,924. This figure rose in Year two and again in Year three to **2** .... just over £35,000.

Room occupancy rates were generally **3** .... in June, July and August, but much **4** .... during the winter months. The rate for January was just 56%. This percentage **5** .... steadily throughout the first part of the year despite a **6** .... dip in the month of May. In August it hit 100% but after that it experienced a rapid **7** .... The **8** .... rate was recorded in November at 54%.

With regard to the restaurant, in the first quarter of the year, on average 67% of diners were from outside. This percentage **9** .... in the second quarter and again to just 47% in the third quarter. **10** .... , the percentage in the final quarter was **11** .... higher, at 52%.

Reports often summarise the performance of a company over a period of time. They can also be the results of market research and may make recommendations for the company's future.

2 Read the following statements about reports and decide if they are true or false. Write T or F.

1 Reports are usually written in a formal style. ....
2 You finish a report by writing *Yours sincerely* and signing your name. ....
3 Reports are divided into sections with subheadings. ....
4 The first section of a report usually states its aim or purpose. ....
5 Reports often contain direct requests. ....
6 The ideas in a report should be supported by facts and figures. ....

Read the following report on the hotel without paying attention to the gaps and check your answers to Exercise 2.

> **The aim of this report is to summarise the annual performance of our Eastern Ranger hotel in Leigh-on-Sea.**
>
> **Profits and occupancy**
> In Year three, the hotel made a profit of just over £35,000, which was slightly under target. Room occupancy rates fell considerably after the summer season. **1** .... Room occupancy in November, however, dropped to an average of 54%. **2** ....
>
> **Specific facilities**
> Facilities such as the restaurant, bar and health club are popular with guests but a large part of the clientele is from the local population, especially for the restaurant. **3** .... The bar is also a popular venue for local office workers on weekdays in the evenings. **4** .... The hotel has a well-equipped conference room but this is seriously underused.
>
> **Recommendations**
> We recommend that the hotel should target the events market by developing the conference facilities page of the website more, and possibly rebranding as a centre for training events. **5** ....

3 Place each of the following sentences (a–e) in the correct gap in the report.

a In the first three months of the year, on average 67% of restaurant diners were not staying in the hotel.
b These two facilities help to increase profits during the low season.
c We should continue to build on the success of the restaurant by advertising it locally as a separate venue.
d The most successful month was August when the hotel was running at full capacity.
e Seasonal bookings resulted in only a slight improvement for December.

Functions bank

Starting a note/ informal email
Just a note/ quick message to say …
Just thought I'd let you know that …

Starting a letter/ formal email
I am writing to enquire about / apply for / inform you of / about …
I am writing with regard to / with reference to … (subject / a previous letter)
I am writing on behalf of … (person/institution)

Referring to a previous communication/ previous information
Re: With reference to / Further to … (your enquiry, telephone call etc.) (formal)
Thank you for your email/ letter/ enquiry …
I see/ notice that …

Referring to previous information
I see/notice that …
In your email/letter you refer to …

Referring to additional documents
I attach …/ Please find attached (email)
I enclose …/ Please find enclosed (letter)
Please refer to …

Referring to future communications
We will contact you again …
We will be in touch within … (5 working days)

Asking for a reply
I am looking forward to hearing from you.
I look forward to hearing from you. (more formal)
Please get back to me. (informal)
Please let me know … (informal)

Inviting future communications
Please feel free to contact me if …
Please do not hesitate to contact me if … (more formal)

Making a request
Please can/could you … (informal)
I wonder if you could … (formal/for a more difficult request)
I would be grateful if you could … (formal)
I would appreciate it if you could … (formal)

Making a suggestion
Perhaps we/you could …
How about …
I suggest/recommend …

Requesting information
Please could you tell me / let me know …
I would like to enquire … (more formal)
Please confirm. / I would be grateful if you could confirm … (formal)

Giving information
Please note/ be aware that …
I would like to inform you that … (formal)

Giving good news
I am happy / pleased to tell you …
I am pleased / delighted to inform you … (formal)

Giving bad news
I'm afraid … (informal)
I am sorry to tell you that …
I am sorry to inform you that … (formal)
I am very sorry to have to inform you that … (formal, for serious bad news)

Inviting
We would like to invite you to …
We would be delighted if you could attend … (more formal)

Accepting an invitation
I'd love to come … (informal)
I am/ would be (very) happy to accept …
I would be delighted to attend … (more formal)

Thanking
Thank you/ Many thanks for …
Cheers (informal)
Thank you in advance for … (when making a request)

Congratulating
Congratulations on …
I would like to congratulate you on … (formal)

Apologising
Sorry about … (informal)
Please accept my/our apologies for … (formal)

Word lists

The numbers in brackets indicate the page on which the word first occurs. Some of these words appear in the transcripts at the back of the book. CD1 T1 means that the word appears in Track 1 on CD1.
n = noun, *n phr* = noun phrase, *pl n* = plural noun, *v* = verb, *v phr* = verb phrase, *phr v* = phrasal verb, *adj* = adjective, *adj phr* = adjectival phrase, *adv* = adverb, *adv phr* = adverbial phrase, *prov* = proverb

UNIT 1

accountant *n* (10) someone whose job is to keep or examine the financial records of a company or organisation

area of responsibility *n phr* (10) a part of your job that is your particular duty to deal with

be left in charge *v phr* (CD1 T2) to be the person who is responsible for someone or something

bookkeeping *n* (10) recording the money that an organisation or business spends and receives

Chief Executive Officer (CEO) *n phr* (12) the main person respnsible for managing a company or organisation, who is also sometimes the company's president or chairman of the board

co-ordinate *v* (11) to make different people or things work together effectively, or to organise all the different parts of an activity

correspondence *n* (CD1 T2) letters or emails from one person to another, or the activity of writing and receiving letters or emails

deal with *phr v* (10) to do business with a person or organisation

flipchart *n* (13) large pieces of paper attached to a board on legs, which you write or draw on when you are talking to a group of people

human resources *n phr* (10) the department of an organisation that deals with finding people to work there, keeping records about all the organisation's employees, and helping them with any problems

in charge of *adj phr* (12) responsible for something or someone

invoice *n* (11) a list that shows you how much money you owe someone for work they have done or for goods they have supplied

keep track of *v phr* (CD1 T2) to continue to know what is happening to someone or something

lead the team *v phr* (10) to be in control of a group of people who work together to do something

look up information *v phr* (11) to look at a book or computer in order to find facts about a situation, person, event, etc.

low-end worker *n phr* (12) a person whose job is not well paid

machinist *n* (10) someone whose job is operating a machine in a factory

monitor *v* (12) to watch something carefully and record your results

organogram *n* (10) a diagram that shows the structure of an organisation and the relationships between the different people, departments, and jobs at different levels within that organisation

payroll *n* (10) the activity of managing the money that is paid to employees

personal assistant (PA) *n phr* (11) a person who organises letters, meetings and telephone calls for someone with an important job

personnel *n* (11) the department of an organisation that deals with finding people to work there, keeping records about them, etc.

prioritise *v* (11) to decide which of a group of things are the most important, so that you can deal with them first

promote a product *v phr* (10) to advertise something that is made or grown to be sold

purchase *v* (10) to buy something

quality control *n phr* (11) the process of looking at goods when they are being produced to make certain that they are of the intended standard

recruitment *n* (10) when you try to persuade someone to work for a company or to join an organisation

reference *n* (13) a letter that is written by someone who knows you, to say if you are suitable for a job or course

reputation *n* (12) the opinion that people have about someone or something based on their behaviour or character in the past

research and development (R&D) *n phr* (10) the part of an organisation that works to improve its existing products and develop new ones

responsible for *adj phr* (10) having a duty to deal with or manage someone or something

retailer *n* (11) someone who sells products to the public

staff welfare *n phr* (10) the health and happiness of the people who work for an organisation

stock *n* (10) all the goods that are available in a shop

stock *v* (11) to have something available for people to buy

supervisor *n* (10) someone who watches a person or activity and makes certain that everything is done correctly, safely, etc.

supplier *n* (10) someone who provides things that people want or need, often over a long period of time

to the required standards *adv phr* (13) to the level of quality that is officially demanded of something

working relationship *n phr* (CD1 T2) the way two people or groups who work together feel and behave towards each other

UNIT 2

accept an apology *v phr* (17) to allow someone to say sorry

assist *v* (17) to help

attach *v* (14) to add a computer file to an email message

be a hit *v phr* (15) to be a very popular person or thing

booked up *adj phr* (17) someone who has arranged a lot of things to do and is very busy

brand *n* (16) a product that is made by a particular company

enclose *v* (16) to send something in the same envelope or parcel as something else

forward *v* (16) to send a letter, email, etc. that you have received to someone else

get in touch *v phr* (17) to communicate with someone by telephone, or by writing to them

get together *v phr* (17) to meet in order to do something or spend time together

grievance *n* (15) a complaint, especially about unfair behaviour

hard copy *n phr* (16) information from a computer that has been printed on paper

highlight *v* (14) to make something a different colour so that it is more noticable, especially written words

inclusive *adj* (16) including the first and last date or number stated

look forward to *phr v* (16) to feel happy and excited about something that is going to happen

offer an apology *v phr* (17) to say or write something to say that you are sorry about something you have done

pie chart *n phr* (14) a circle divided into several parts to represent how the total amount of something is divided up

public relations (PR) *n phr* (15) writing and activities that are intended to make a person, company, or product more popular

relevant *adj* (16) related or useful to what is happening or being talked about

schedule *n* (17) a plan of events or activities and the times that they will happen or be done

set up *phr v* (15) to start a company, system, way of working, etc.

share price *n phr* (15) the price of one of the equal parts that the value of a particular company is divided into when it is owned by a group of people

social networking site *n* (14) a website for communicating with friends and for meeting other people

spread information *v phr* (16) If information spreads or if someone spreads it, it is communicated from one person to another.

threat *n* (15) someone or something that is likely to cause harm or damage

unload *v* (10) to remove things from a vehicle

warehouse *n* (10) a large building for storing goods that are going to be sold

word of mouth *n phr* (15) the process of telling people you know about a particular product or service, usually because you think it is good and want to encourage them to try it

UNIT 3

acquire *v* (18) to buy or take control of a company or part of a company

branch *n* (20) one of several shops, offices, etc. that are part of a company or organisation

break into an area *v phr* (CD1 T7) to suddenly start an activity

broaden your product range *v phr* (18) to increase the number of different things made by your business

chain *n* (20) a number of similar shops, restaurants, etc. owned by the same company

classic example *n phr* (CD1 T6) something that is very typical of a group of things that you are talking about

come up with an idea *v phr* (21) to think of a suggestion or plan

competitive market *n phr* (20) the buying and selling of something when other businesses are trying to be more successful than yours

consultant *n* (CD1 T5) someone who advises people about a particular subject

corporation *n* (20) a large company or group of companies

deadline *n* (CD1 T6) a time by which something must be done

decline *v* (20) to become less in amount, importance, quality, or strength

discounted *adj* (18) cheaper than usual

electrical appliance *n phr* (18) a piece of electrical equipment with a particular purpose in the home or office

empire *n* (21) a large group of businesses that is controlled by one person or company

entrepreneur *n* (18) someone who starts their own business, especially when this involves risks

expand *v* (20) to increase in size or amount, or to make something increase

face collapse *v phr* (20) to have to deal with the sudden failure of a system, organisation or business

founder *n* (19) someone who establishes an organisation

insight *n* (21) the ability to understand what something is really like, or an example of this

launch a product *v phr* (22) If a company launches a product or service, it makes it available for the first time

leadership *n* (18) the job of being in control of a group, country, or situation

lose custom *v phr* (CD1 T6) when people stop buying things from shops or businesses

maintain quality *v phr* (18) to make something that is good or well-made continue in the same way

merger *n* (19) when two or more companies or organisations join together

mortgage *n* (20) money that you borrow to buy a home

novelty *n* (CD1 T6) the quality of being new or unusual

on the back of a previous success *adv phr* (CD1 T6) soon after an earlier success, and as a result of it

outlet *n* (20) a shop that sells one type of product or the products of one company

overtake *v* (18) to become more successful than someone or something else

private investor *n phr* (20) a person who invests money, rather than a company or financial organisation that does this for a client

profitable *adj* (CD1 T7) making or likely to make money from selling goods or services for more than they cost to produce or provide

recall *v* (CD1 T6) to order the return of someone or something

record profits *n phr* (20) more money made from selling goods or services than ever before

selling point *n phr* (20) a characteristic of a product or service that will persuade people to buy it

spectacular growth *n phr* (CD1 T5) when something grows, increases or develops in an extremely good or surprising way

start up *phr v* (19) to create and start a new business or organisation

state owned enterprise *n phr* (18) a business that is owned and controlled by a country's government

stuck on a problem *adj phr* (21) not able to solve a difficult situation

substandard *adj* (18) something that is not as good as it should be

trading company *n phr* (18) a business that buys and sells goods

turn a company around *v phr* (18) to change an unsuccessful business so that it becomes successful

UNIT 4

apply for a job *v phr* (CD1 T8) to ask officially for regular work

better safe than sorry *prov* (23) said when you think it is best not to take risks even when it seems boring or difficult to be careful

bonus *n* (CD1 T8) an extra amount of money that you are given, especially because you have worked hard

build up a good relationship *v phr* (24) to develop successfully the way in which two or more companies, countries, or people behave towards each other

clearly defined role *n phr* (23) the exact job that someone is expected to do in a particular situation

cut costs *v phr* (23) to reduce the amount of money that you need to buy or do something

cutting edge technology *n phr* (24) the use of all the best developments in scientific discoveries

demonstration *n* (24) showing how to do something, or how something works

family commitments *n phr* (25) things that you must do with the people who are related to you that take up your time

fix a time *v phr* (22) to decide a certain and particular point in the day or night to do something

health and safety *n phr* (24) making sure that people are safe and healthy at work or in public places

invest heavily *v phr* (23) to give a lot of money to a business, or buy something which costs a lot, because you hope to get a profit

jobseeker *n* (22) someone who is trying to find a job

keep up with the times *v phr* (22) to change your ideas, opinions or way of living or working to make them modern

meet a deadline *v phr* (23) to finish work at the time or by a date that has been previously agreed

meet your needs *v phr* (23) to be a big enough amount or of a good enough quality for someone

nothing ventured nothing gained *prov* (22) You have to take a risk in order to get something good.

opportunities for promotion *n phr* (22) the chance to get a more important job

package *n* (CD1 T8) the pay and other advantages that a worker receives

promote growth *v phr* (24) to encourage business activities to develop

set up *phr v* (23) to arrange for something to happen

set up a meeting *v phr* (25) to arrange for an event to happen where people come together to discuss something

staff representative *n* (24) someone who speaks or does something officially for the people who work for an organisation

standard procedure *n phr* (22) the official or usual way of doing something

strategy *n* (22) a plan that you use to achieve something

supportive *adj* (CD1 T8) giving help or encouragement

take a serious risk *v phr* (23) to do something although something very bad might happen because of it

take on a challenge *v phr* (22) to accept a difficult job or responsibility

target driven *adj phr* (CD1 T8) wanting very much to achieve a particular thing

tough *adj* (CD1 T8) difficult

wide range *n phr* (23) a lot of different types of thing

work closely *v phr* (23) If you work closely with someone, you work together a lot.

workforce *n* (25) all the people who work for a company or organisation

UNIT 5

adjust *v* (31) to change something slightly so that it works better, fits better or is more suitable

assemble *v* (31) to build something by joining different parts together

be made up of *v phr* (29) to be arranged by putting different things together

blade *n* (28) the flat, sharp, metal part of a knife, tool or weapon

boardroom *n* (31) a room where the people who control a company or organisation have meetings

bulb *n* (28) a glass object containing a wire which produces light from electricity

cable *n* (CD1 T9) a wire covered by plastic that carries electricity, telephone signals, etc.

charge *v* (30) to put electricity into something

craftsman *n* (CD1 T11) someone who uses special skill to make things, especially with their hands

dismantle *v* (31) to take something apart so that it is in several pieces

drop down menu *n* (CD1 T10) a pop-up menu: a list of choices on a computer screen which is hidden until you choose to look at it

fasten *v* (31) to close or fix something together, or to become closed or fixed together

filing cabinet *n* (29) a piece of office furniture with deep drawers for storing documents

fit *v* (31) to put or fix something in a particular place

gadget *n* (31) a small piece of equipment that does a particular job, especially a new type

goods *n* (CD1 T10) items which are made to be sold

handle *n* (31) the part of something that you use to hold it or open it

hanger *n* (CD1 T9) a wire, wooden or plastic object for hanging clothes on

headphones *pl n* (28) a piece of equipment that you wear over your ears so that you can listen to music without anyone else hearing it

in stock *adj phr* (CD1 T10) to be available in a shop

jam *v* (30) to get stuck, or to make something get stuck

lens *n* (28) a curved piece of glass in cameras, glasses and scientific equipment used for looking at things

mouse mat *n* (29) a flat piece of material on which you move the mouse of your computer

pliers *pl n* (31) a tool for holding or pulling small things like nails, or for cutting wire

plug *n* (28) a plastic or rubber object with metal pins, used to connect electrical equipment to an electricity supply

process an order *v phr* (CD1 T10) to deal with a request for goods in an official way

remove *v* (31) to take something away

rivet *n* (31) a metal pin used to fasten pieces of metal together

run out *phr v* (30) to use all of something so that there is none left

screen *n* (28) the part of a television or computer which shows images or writing

seminar *n* (31) a meeting of a group of people with a teacher or expert for training, discussion or study of a subject

stand *n* (28) a piece of furniture for holding things

steel *n* (29) a very strong metal made from iron, used for making knives, machines, etc.

stick out *v* (CD1 T9) If part of something sticks out, it comes out further than the edge or surface it is on.

switch *n* (28) a small object that you push up or down with your finger to turn something electrical on or off

tool *n* (30) a piece of equipment that you use with your hands in order to help you do something

UNIT 6

aim at *v phr* (33) to produce something for a particular purpose, or a particular group of people

audit *n* (35) when an independent person examines all the financial records of a company to produce an official report

average *adj* (32) usual and like the most common type of something

blend *v* (CD1 T12) to mix two or more things together completely

component *n* (32) a part of something, especially a machine

corruption *n* (35) dishonest or immoral behaviour, usually by people in positions of power

counterfeit *adj* (35) made to look like the real thing, in order to trick people

distribute *v* (32) to give something out to people or places

hold up *phr v* (35) to make something or someone slow or late

in-house production *n phr* (35) done in the offices of a company or organisation by employees of that company

industrial action *n phr* (35) when workers stop working or do less work because they want better pay or conditions

insurance *n* (35) an agreement in which you pay a company money and they pay your costs if you have an accident, injury, etc.

labour costs *n phr* (34) the money needed to pay workers in a company or a country

license *v* (32) to give someone official permission to do or have something

life cycle *n* (32) the changes that happen in the life of an animal, plant or product

lifespan *n* (32) the amount of time that a person lives or a thing exists

logo *n* (32) a design or symbol used by a company to advertise its products

loss *n* (35) when you do not have someone or something that you had before, or when you have less of something than before

outsource *v* (34) If a company outsources work, it employs another organisation to do it rather than using its own employees.

production plant *n phr* (34) a large factory where an industrial process happens

put off *phr v* (35) to decide or arrange to do something at a later time

raise productivity *v phr* (34) to increase the rate at which goods are produced

shred *v* (32) to tear or cut something into small, thin pieces

strike *n* (35) a period of time when people are not working because they want more money, etc.

vat *n* (34) a large container used for mixing or storing liquid substances, especially in a factory

wall planner *n* (29) a large piece of paper showing the days, weeks and months of the year, in which you can put the dates of events, meetings, etc.

withdraw *v* (32) to remove something, especially because of an official decision

UNIT 7

banker's card *n phr* (37) a small plastic card from your bank which you show when you write a cheque

courier *n* (36) someone whose job is to take and deliver documents and parcels

cover your expenses *v phr* (36) to have enough money to pay for the things you need

customer base *n phr* (36) the group of people who usually buy or use a company's products or services

customs *n* (38) the place where your bags are examined when you are coming into a country, to make sure you are not carrying anything illegal

delivery charges *n phr* (37) the amount of money that you have to pay for taking things such as letters, parcels or goods to a person or place

depot *n* (CD1 T13) (US) a small bus or train station

distributor *n* (38) a person or organisation that supplies goods to shops and companies

domestic market *n phr* (38) the number of customers who buy or may buy products and services offered by companies within their own country

freight *n* (38) goods that are carried by trains, trucks, ships or aircraft

helmet *n* (37) a hard hat that protects your head

Incoterms *n* (38) International Commercial Terms: a set of rules used in the trade of goods from one country to another

intellectual property (IP) *n phr* (38) someone's idea, invention, etc. that is protected by law from being copied by someone else

lease *v* (36) to make an agreement by which someone pays you money in order to use something for a particular period of time

legal requirements *n phr* (36) official rules about something that it is necessary to have or to do

packaging *n* (38) the paper, box, etc. that something is inside so it can be sold or sent somewhere

paperwork *n* (38) the part of a job that involves writing letters and emails, organising information, etc.

patent *n* (38) a legal right that a person or company receives to make or sell a particular product so that others cannot copy it

receipt *n* (36) a piece of paper that proves that you have received goods or money

stationery *n* (CD1 T13) things that you use for writing, such as pens and paper

trade fair *n phr* (38) a large event at which companies show their products to people who might buy them

trademark *n* (38) the name of a particular company or product which cannot be used by anyone else

UNIT 8

ad *n* (40) an advertisement: a picture, short film, song, etc. which tries to persuade people to buy a product or service

advertising agency *n phr* (40) a company that produces advertisements

brand identity *n phr* (42) a set of ideas and features that a company wants people to connect in their minds with its products or brand

brand management *n phr* (41) the process of controlling the way in which a company markets a product or brand so that people continue to buy it or buy more of it

brand new *adj phr* (43) completely new

brand values *n phr* (42) good qualities that a company wants consumers to connect with its brand

campaign *n* (41) a series of organised activities or events intended to achieve a result

channel of distribution *n phr* (41) one of the methods that are used for selling a company's products or services

core brand *n phr* (43) the most important name of a product produced or sold by a particular company

demand *n* (41) a need for something to be sold or supplied

forecast *v* (41) to say what you expect to happen in the future

market leader *n phr* (41) the company that sells most of a product or service in a particular market

market research *n phr* (41) the activity of finding out what people like about products and what things they want to buy

market share *n phr* (41) the number of things that a company sells compared with the number of things of the same type that other companies sell

sample *n* (43) a small amount of something that shows you what it is like

slogan *n* (42) a short phrase that is easy to remember and is used to make people notice something

sponsor *n* (41) a person or organisation that gives money to support an activity, event, etc.

stand out *phr v* (42) to be very easy to see or notice

target *v* (41) to aim advertising, criticism or a product at someone

UNIT 9

agenda *n* (49) a list of subjects that people will discuss at a meeting

catering *n* (47) providing food and drinks for people at social events

compact *adj* (46) small and including many things in a small space

connecting flight *n phr* (CD1 T16) a journey by aircraft that arrives at a particular time so that passengers can get onto another aircraft

go smoothly *v phr* (CD1 T16) to happen without any problems or difficulties

gross domestic product (GDP) *n phr* (49) the total value of goods and services produced in a country in a year

meet and greet *n phr* (CD1 T18) an arrangement for one person to formally meet and talk to another person

rep *n* (47) someone whose job is to sell things for a company

retirement *n* (CD1 T18) when you leave your job and stop working, usually because you are old

review *n* (48) the process of considering something again in order to make changes to it

roadshow *n* (49) a radio or television programme broadcast from a public place

stylish *adj* (46) fashionable and attractive

type up *phr v* (CD1 T19) to make a typed copy of a piece of text that is written by hand

user-friendly *adj* (46) a machine or system that is easy to use or understand

UNIT 10

aisle seat *n phr* (50) a seat beside the passage between the lines of seats in a plane

check in *phr v* (50) to go to the desk at an airport in order to say that you have arrived and to get the number of your seat

departure lounge *n phr* (50) a large room in an airport where passengers wait to take their flight

fall short of *v phr* (52) to not reach a particular level, but only by a small amount

fee *n* (53) an amount of money that you pay to do something, to use something, or to get a service

flight attendant *n phr* (50) someone whose job is to look after passengers on an aircraft

go ahead *v phr* (52) to start to do something

hold *n* (50) an area on a ship or aircraft for storing things

locker *n* (50) a small cupboard in a public area where your personal possessions can be kept

luggage *n* (50) bags and cases that you carry with you when you are travelling

reschedule *v* (50) to agree on a later date for something to happen

setback *n* (52) a problem that makes something happen later or more slowly than it should

swap *v* (50) to give something to someone and get something from them in return

time management *n phr* (53) the practice of using your time effectively, and the study of this

upbeat *adj* (52) positive and expecting a situation to be good or successful

venue *n* (52) a place where a sports game, musical performance or special event happens

UNIT 11

24/7 *adv phr* (CD1 T22) done, lasting, etc. for twenty-four hours a day, seven days a week

annual leave *n phr* (55) a paid number of days each year that an employee is allowed to be away from work

assembly line *n phr* (55) a line of machines and workers in a factory which a product moves along while it is being built or produced

autonomy *n* (57) the right of a country or group of people to govern itself

backlog *n* (CD1 T22) uncompleted work that should have been done earlier

diverse *adj* (57) including many different types

entitled to *adj phr* (55) If you are entitled to something, you have the right to do or have it.

flexible *adj* (55) able to change or be changed easily according to the situation

full capacity *adv phr* (CD1 T22) the greatest amount possible of something

headquarters *n* (57) the place from where an organisation is controlled

innovation *n* (55) a new idea or method that is being tried for the first time, or the use of such ideas or methods

office politics *n phr* (57) the relationships in a group of people who work together which allow particular people to have power over others

set aside *v phr* (CD1 T22) to save something, usually time or money, for a special purpose

spread rumours *v phr* (57) to cause information which may not be true to

be communicated from one person to another

subscriber *n* (55) someone who pays to receive a newspaper or magazine regularly or to use a phone line or internet service

switch off *v* (CD1 T22) to stop giving your attention to someone or something

team building activities *n phr* (57) organised events that help a group work together more effectively as a team

think outside the box *v phr* (57) to use new ideas instead of traditional ideas when you think about something

under pressure *adv phr* (CD1 T22) required to do something in a limited amount of time

UNIT 12

capacity *n* (58) the largest amount or number that a container, building, etc. can hold

case study *n* (58) a report about a particular person or thing, to show an example of a general principle

corporate event *n phr* (61) an activity that is planned for a special purpose involving people from a large company or group

delegate *n* (58) someone who is sent somewhere to represent a group of people, especially at a meeting

fill in a form *v phr* (61) to write the necessary information on an official document

floor *n* (60) an area where a particular activity happens

format *n* (60) the way something is designed, arranged or produced

lecture *n* (58) a formal talk given to a group of people in order to teach them about a subject

panel *n* (60) a group of people who are chosen to discuss something or make a decision about something

participant *n* (59) someone who is involved in an activity

plenary *adj* (58) relating to a meeting at which all the members of a group or an organisation are present, especially at a conference

promote growth *v phr* (58) to cause an increase in the ability of an economy or business to produce goods and services

social media *n phr* (CD1 T24) forms of media that allow people to communicate and share information using the Internet or mobile phones

staff retention *n phr* (58) the ability of a company to keep its employees and stop them from going to work somewhere else

web conferencing *n phr* (59) a system by which many computer users can communicate with each other at the

same time on the Internet, using webcams

webinar *n* (58) an occasion when a group of people go online at the same time to study or discuss something

work-life balance *n phr* (58) the amount of time you spend doing your job compared with the amount of time you spend with your family and doing things you enjoy

UNIT 13

apply *v* (64) to ask officially for something, often in writing

be thrown in at the deep end *v phr* (64) to start a new and difficult job or activity without having help or preparation

concerned *adj* (65) worried

CV *n* (64) a document which describes your qualifications and the jobs you have done, which you send to an employer that you want to work for

degree *n* (CD1 T25) a qualification given for completing a university course

demanding *adj* (CD1 T25) needing a lot of your time, attention or effort

field *n* (64) an area of study or activity

interpersonal skills *n phr* (64) particular abilities connected with relationships between people

jump in at the deep end *v phr* (CD1 T26) to do something without thinking or preparation

learning curve *n phr* (66) how quickly or slowly someone learns a new skill

manual *n* (64) a book that tells you how to use something or do something

mining company *n phr* (66) an organisation involved in the industrial process of digging coal or other minerals out of the ground

overlap *n* (CD1 T25) the amount by which two things or activities cover the same area

personable *adj* (CD1 T25) having a pleasant appearance and character

postgraduate *n* (CD1 T25) a student who has one degree and now studies at a university for a more advanced degree

promotion *n* (66) when someone is given a more important job in the same organisation

put your foot down *v phr* (66) to tell someone in a strong way that they must do something or must stop doing something

reverse side of the coin *n phr* (66) a different way of considering a situation, making it seem either better or worse than it did originally

settle in *phr v* (65) to begin to feel relaxed and happy in a new home or job

transition *n* (CD1 T25) when something changes from one system or method to another, often gradually

turn out *phr v* (65) to happen in a particular way, or to have a particular result

UNIT 14

back-up copy *n phr* (69) a computer file, document, etc. that is created to be exactly the same as another one

consumables *pl n* (69) goods that are quickly used and need to be replaced often

cultural awareness *n phr* (CD1 T27) knowledge and understanding of the habits, traditions and beliefs of a country, society or group of people

customise *v* (69) to change something to make it suitable for a particular person or purpose

department store *n* (CD1 T28) a large shop divided into several different parts which sell different types of things

desalination plant *n* (71) a factory or other place where salt and other minerals are removed from water

device *n* (70) a piece of equipment that is used for a particular purpose

glassware *n* (69) drinking glasses or other objects made of glass

in due course *adv phr* (71) at a suitable time in the future

irrigation *n* (71) when water is provided for an area of land so that crops can be grown

modestly priced *adj phr* (71) not expensive

promotional item *n phr* (69) an object that is made for the purpose of advertising something

rank *n* (CD1 T27) a position in society or in an organisation, for example the army

survey *n* (69) an examination of people's opinions or behaviour made by asking people questions

tight budget *n phr* (CD1 T27) when you have only just enough money to buy or do something

token *n* (71) something that you give to someone in order to show them love, to thank them, etc.

wrap *v* (68) to cover something or someone with paper, cloth, etc.

UNIT 15

block booking *n phr* (73) a large number of tickets for a particular event, hotel, flight, etc. that are sold to one person or organisation

break down barriers *v phr* (72) to improve understanding and communication between people who have different opinions

break the ice *v phr* (73) to make people who have not met before feel relaxed with each other, often by starting a conversation

dominate *v* (CD1 T29) to control or have power over someone or something

economic boom *n phr* (75) a period when there is a big increase in sales or profits

forum *n* (75) a situation or meeting in which people can exchange ideas and discuss things

handout *n* (CD1 T29) a copy of a document that is given to all the people in a class or meeting

implement a suggestion *v phr* (75) to put a plan or idea into action

in-tray *n* (75) a container where you keep letters and documents that need to be dealt with

maintenance staff *n* (75) the people whose job is to keep a building, vehicle, road etc. in good condition by checking it regularly and repairing it when necessary

management consultancy *n phr* (74) a company that offers other companies advice about the best ways of managing and improving their businesses

outcome *n* (74) the final result of an activity or process

put forward a suggestion *v phr* (75) to suggest a plan or idea so that it can be considered or discussed

reach full potential *v phr* (73) to develop, achieve or succeed in the most complete way

UNIT 16

conference call *n phr* (CD1 T30) a telephone call between three or more people in different places

emerging market *n phr* (77) a part of the world where a product or service is starting to be sold

evaluate *v* (CD1 T30) to consider or study something carefully and decide how good or bad it is

eye opener *n phr* (77) something that surprises you and teaches you facts about life, people, etc.

globally mobile *adj phr* (77) able to change your way of working to suit many different countries

graduate *n* (76) someone who has studied for and received a degree qualification from a university

growth potential *n* (76) the ability of an economy or business to produce a greater number of goods and services

high flyer *n phr* (77) someone who is very successful or who is likely to be very successful, especially in business

long-term *adj phr* (77) continuing a long time into the future

offshore operation *n phr* (76) a company that is based in a different country to the one in which it does most of its business, often for tax reasons

pool of talent *n phr* (77) the suitable, skilled people who are available to be chosen to do a particular type of job

soft skills *n phr* (78) people's abilities to communicate with and work well with other people

star performer *n phr* (77) the person judged to be the best worker in a company or organisation

strike a balance *v phr* (78) to give two things the same amount of attention, or find a compromise between two things

UNIT 17

bar chart *n phr* (82) a drawing that uses thick lines of different heights or lengths to show how different pieces of information are related to each other

briefcase *n* (CD1 T31) a flat, rectangular case with a handle for carrying documents, books, etc.

Christmas rush *n phr* (CD1 T31) when a lot of things are happening and a lot of people are trying to do something at the time of the Christian period of celebration around 25 December

dip *v* (82) to become lower in level or amount

exceed *v* (85) to be more than a particular number or amount

fluctuate *v* (82) to keep changing, especially in level or amount

inflation *n* (84) the rate at which prices increase, or a continuing increase in prices

level off *phr v* (82) If a rate or amount levels off, it stops rising or falling and stays at the same level.

line graph *n phr* (82) a drawing that uses lines to show how different pieces of information are related to each other

make inroads *v phr* (CD1 T31) to start to become successful by getting sales, power, votes, etc. that someone else had before

peak *n* (82) the highest level or value of something

per capita *adj phr* (82) for each person

pick up *phr v* (CD1 T31) If a business or social situation picks up, it improves.

stand at *phr v* (83) to be at a particular level, amount, height, etc.

static *adj* (85) not moving or changing

trend *n* (82) a general development or change in a situation

unemployment rate *n phr* (84) the number or percentage of people in a country or area who do not have jobs

UNIT 18

bait *n* (88) something that you use to persuade someone to do something

boost *n* (88) an act or event that increases or improves something

break even *v phr* (86) to not make money but also not lose money

broad spectrum *n phr* (CD1 T33) the many different ideas, opinions, possibilities, etc. that exist

cash-generative *adj* (CD1 T35) producing a profit for a business

chartered accountant *n* (CD1 T32) in the UK, a person who has finished three years of work and training and passed an examination to become a member of the Institute of Chartered Accountants

chase payment *v phr* (86) to try to get an amount of money owed that has not been paid back by the expected time

confidentiality *n* (CD1 T34) the fact of private information being kept secret

cover costs *v phr* (86) to be enough money to pay for something

creditor *n* (86) a person or organisation that someone owes money to

debtor *n* (86) someone who owes money

depreciation *n* (88) a loss of value, especially over time

distressed *adj* (CD1 T32) foreclosed and offered for sale, usually at a price below market value

expenditure *n* (86) the total amount of money that a government or person spends on something

fraud *n* (CD1 T34) when someone does something illegal in order to get money

go bankrupt *v phr* (86) to be unable to continue in business because you cannot pay your debts

go into liquidation *v phr* (86) to close a business because it has no money left

gross *adj* (86) money that has not had taxes or other costs taken from it

livelihood *n* (CD1 T35) the way that you earn the money you need for living

median *adj* (88) relating to the middle number or amount in a series

net *adj* (86) money that has had costs such as tax taken away from it

operating profit *n phr* (86) the money that a company makes from its normal business activities

overheads *pl n* (86) money that a company spends on its regular and necessary costs, for example rent and heating

overspend *v* (86) to spend more money than you have, or more than was planned or agreed

owe *v* (86) to have to pay money back to someone

pay off a debt *v phr* (86) to finish paying back money that you owe for something

plantation *n* (88) an area of land in a hot country where a crop is grown

prestigious *adj* (CD1 T33) respected and admired, usually because of being important

prospective *adj* (88) Prospective buyers, employers, parents, etc. are not yet buyers, employers, parents, etc. but are expected to be in the future.

recession *n* (CD1 T33) a time when the economy of a country is not successful

restructuring *n* (CD1 T32) the act of organising a company, business or system in a way to make it operate more effectively

revenue *n* (86) large amounts of money received by a government as tax, or by a company

sideline *n* (88) a job or business in addition to your main job or business

turnover *n* (86) how much money a business earns in a period of time

write off a debt *v phr* (86) to accept that an amount of money has been lost or will never be paid to you

UNIT 19

assets *pl n* (CD1 T36) things such as money, property or land owned by a person, company or organisation

bear market *n phr* (91) a time when the share prices of a company are falling as a lot of people are selling them

bond *n* (91) an official document from a government or company to show that you have given them money that they will pay back with a certain amount of extra money

broker *n* (90) someone whose job is to buy and sell shares equal parts of a company's total value

bull market *n phr* (91) a time when the share prices of a company are rising as a lot of people are buying them

capital *n* (90) an amount of money that you can use to start a business or to make more money

capital intensive *adj phr* (93) A capital intensive business needs to spend a lot of money on buildings, equipment, etc. before it can start.

co-worker *n* (CD1 T36) someone that you work with

commodity *n* (91) a product that you can buy or sell

dividend *n* (90) an amount of money paid regularly to someone who owns shares in a company from the company's profits

educated guess *n phr* (93) a guess which is made using judgement and a particular level of knowledge and is therefore more likely to be correct

equities *pl n* (91) shares in companies, especially ordinary shares, or the activity of trading these shares

float *v* (91) to start selling a company's shares to the public

get the message across *v phr* (93) to tell other people what you think about something

rally *v* (92) to improve after a period of falling share prices or of low activity

returns *pl n* (91) the profits that you get from an investment

risk averse *adj phr* (92) not wanting to take risks

shareholder *n* (90) someone who owns shares in a company

stake *n* (91) a part of a business that you own, or an amount of money that you have invested in a business

stock *n* (90) the value of a company, or a share in its value

stock exchange *n* (90) the place where stocks and shares in companies are bought and sold

UNIT 20

business angel *n phr* (94) a person who invests money in a new business to help it get started

cashflow *n* (94) the movement of money in and out of a business or bank account

corporation *n* (97) a large company or group of companies

data warehouse *n phr* (97) a large amount of information stored on one computer, or on a number of computers in the same place

flood the market *v phr* (97) to provide too much of a product so that there is more of this product available than there are people who want to buy it

giant *n* (97) a very large and important company or organisation

partnership *n* (94) a company which is owned by two or more people

pump money into *v phr* (97) to spend a lot of money trying to make something operate successfully

raise capital *v phr* (94) to manage to get money to invest in a business, project, property, etc.

savings *pl n* (CD1 T37) money that you have saved, usually in a bank

secure a loan *v phr* (94) to manage to borrow money, usually from a bank

tap into a market *v phr* (97) to find a particular group of people who might buy something and use this to your advantage

utilities *pl n* (94) organisations that supply the public with water, gas or electricity

venture capital *n phr* (CD1 T37) money that is spent on a new activity or company, especially when there is a chance that the activity or company will not be successful

UNIT 21

appoint *v* (102) to officially choose someone for a job

fulfilling *adj* (103) something that satisfies you and makes you happy

qualifications *pl n* (101) the skills, qualities or experience that you need in order to do something

referee *n* (100) a person who knows you and who is willing to describe your character and abilities in order to support you when you are trying to get a job, etc.

research project *n phr* (102) a detailed study of a subject, especially in order to discover information or understand the subject better

résumé *n* (100) a document which describes your qualifications and the jobs that you have done, which you send to an employer that you want to work for

scholarship *n* (102) an amount of money given to a person by an organisation to pay for their education, usually at a college or university

shortlist *v* (102) to put someone on a list of people who are competing for a prize, job, etc., who have already been chosen from a larger list

specifications *pl n* (CD2 T2) a description of the exact tasks involved in a particular job, and of the skills, experience and personality a person needs in order to do the job

transferable skills *n* (102) particular abilities used in one job or career that can also be used in another

turn down *phr v* (102) to refuse an offer, a job or a request

voluntary work *n phr* (101) work that is done without being paid and usually involves helping people

UNIT 22

alienate *v* (106) to cause someone or a group of people to stop supporting and agreeing with you

dismiss *v* (104) to officially make someone leave their job

fire *v* (104) to tell someone they must leave their job

give something a bad name *v phr* (CD2 T3) If something is given a bad name, people have a bad opinion of it based on what has happened in the past.

hand in your notice *v phr* (104) to tell your employer that you intend to leave your job after a particular period of time

hire *v* (104) to begin to employ someone

lay off *phr v* (104) to stop employing someone, usually because there is no more work for them

make redundant *v phr* (104) If you are made redundant, you lose your job because your employer no longer needs you.

resign *v* (104) to officially tell your employer that you are leaving your job

sack *v* (104) When someone gets the sack or is given the sack, they are told to leave their job.

take on *phr v* (104) to begin to employ someone

track record *n phr* (106) how well or badly you have done in the past

two-way process *n phr* (105) a situation in which two people or groups both work towards something, where both expect rewards from the efforts they make

vocational qualification *n phr* (107) an official record showing that you have skills and education that prepare you for a job

UNIT 23

anonymous *n* (CD2 T4) not giving a name

appraisal *n* (111) when you examine someone or something and judge how good or successful they are

balance sheet *n phr* (108) a document that shows what a company has earned and what it has spent

coach *v* (110) to teach someone so they improve at a sport, skill or in a school subject

corporate rate *n phr* (109) an amount of money that is charged to or paid by a business

credibility *n* (109) when someone can be believed and trusted

kick off *v phr* (111) starting a discussion or activity

mistrust *n* (CD2 T4) when you do not believe or have confidence in someone or something

on the ball *adj phr* (111) quick to understand and react to things

refresher course *n phr* (108) a course to practise and improve skills, usually

because you have not used them for a long time

revolutionise *v* (109) to change something in every way so that it is much better

stalemate *n* (111) a situation in which neither side in an argument can win

touch base *v phr* (111) to talk with someone for a short time

UNIT 24

age discrimination *n phr* (115) unfair treatment of a person because of their age

confident *adj* (115) certain about your ability to do things well

exploit *v* (115) to use or develop something for profit or progress in business

fixed retirement age *n phr* (115) the arranged or decided age when you have to leave your job and stop working

free up *phr v* (113) to make something available to be used

go down *phr v* (CD2 T5) If a computer goes down, it stops working.

loyal *adj* (115) always liking and supporting someone or something, sometimes when other people do not

service sector *n phr* (115) the part of a country's economy that is made up of businesses that provide services

sick leave *n phr* (115) when you are away from your work because you are ill

state-of-the-art *adj phr* (CD2 T5) using the newest ideas, designs and materials

stereotype *n* (CD2 T6) a fixed idea that people have about what a particular type of person is like, especially an idea that is wrong

surveyor *n* (CD2 T6) someone whose job is to examine the structure of buildings or measure and record the details of an area of land

take advantage of *v phr* (115) to use the good things in a situation

upgrade *v* (112) to improve something so that it is of a higher quality or a newer model

Exam skills and Exam practice

Contents

About Cambridge English: Business Certificates

Recognition of *Cambridge English: Business Certificates*, also known as *Business English Certificates* (*BEC*), is rapidly growing, as a number of companies are using the examinations as a focus for in-company training courses. A list of companies that use *Cambridge English: Business Certificates* for a variety of purposes including recruitment can be found at www.cambridgeesol.org.

The *Cambridge English: Business Certificates* suite is linked to the five ALTE/Cambridge levels for language assessment, and the Council of Europe's Common European Framework of Reference for Languages (CEFR).

Cambridge English: Business Certificates	Equivalent Main Suite Exam	ALTE Level	Common European Framework of Reference for Languages (CEFR) Level
	Cambridge English: Proficiency (CPE)	Level 5	C2
Business Higher	Cambridge English: Advanced (CAE)	Level 4	C1
Business Vantage	Cambridge English: First (FCE)	Level 3	B2
Business Preliminary	Cambridge English: Preliminary (PET)	Level 2	B1
	Cambridge English: Key (KET)	Level 1	A2

At all three levels, the 'business' aspect of this examination affects the vocabulary, the types of texts selected and the situations presented in the tasks. In addition, as in the Cambridge ESOL Main Suite exams, other skills, such as understanding the gist of text and guessing unfamiliar words in a listening situation are tested.

The table below shows the common characteristics at the different levels of *Cambridge English: Business Certificates*.

	Business Preliminary	Business Vantage	Business Higher
Reading	• 7 parts/45 items • 1 hour 30 minutes for reading *and* writing	• 5 parts/45 items • 1 hour	• 6 parts/52 items • 1 hour
Writing	• 2 parts • 1 hour 30 minutes for reading *and* writing	• 2 parts • 45 minutes	• 2 parts • 1 hour 10 minutes
Listening	• 4 parts/30 items • about 40 minutes, including transfer time	• 3 parts/30 items • about 40 minutes, including transfer time	• 3 parts/30 items • about 40 minutes, including transfer time
Speaking	• 3 parts • 12 minutes • 2:2 format*	• 3 parts • 14 minutes • 2:2 format*	• 3 parts • 16 minutes • 2:2 format*

* two examiners, two candidates (2:3 format used for the last group in a session where necessary)

Reading Paper Part 1: Exam skills

Part 1 consists of:

- five short texts such as notices, advertisements, memos, emails, etc.
- five multiple choice questions, one for each text. You must choose the correct answer, **A**, **B** or **C**.

You practised similar skills in Unit 6 (page 35), Unit 7 (page 37), Unit 10 (page 51) and Unit 12 (page 60). This type of question tests your ability to understand the meaning and purpose of short texts.

> **Short texts**
> Short texts give the information in very few words and some, such as notices and phone messages, often leave out the non-essential words like *the*. This means that you need to read the words that are there very carefully and think about the exact meaning.

Suggested exam technique

1 The texts are very short, so you need to read each one slowly and carefully.
2 Before you look at the three alternatives, think for a moment. What is the main information that the text gives? Or what does the text ask the reader to do?
3 Read all three alternatives carefully before you finally decide (even if you immediately think that A is correct).
4 Be careful! The three alternatives will not usually use the same language as in the text. You must look for one which expresses the same idea as in the text using different words.

Exercises

1 **The following two notices give three alternative sentences to choose from. The correct answers are already given to you. Write why the other two are incorrect.**

1
> **Sales representative required**
> Closing date for applications: 24 April.
> Previous experience of working in sales essential. Own car an advantage.

   A Applicants must have experience of this type of work.
   B Applicants need to own their own car.
   C Applicants have to be free to start work on 24 April.
   A is correct.
   B is not correct because ....
   C is not correct because ....

2
> Subscribe to *Business Today* for twelve months and save 50 % off the normal price! Offer ends March 1. Valid for new subscriptions only.

   A You can renew your subscription to *Business Today* for half the normal price.
   B *Business Today* will be cheaper after March 1.
   C If you start subscribing to *Business Today* before March, you will save money.
   C is correct.
   A is not correct because ....
   B is not correct because ....

Sometimes the three alternatives are answers to a question or endings to a sentence. In this case, read the question or the first part of the sentence carefully as well, as in this example.

3
> Julia Ryan, the current marketing assistant, is replacing Claire Anderson in accounts while she goes on maternity leave.

   What is Julia Ryan going to do?
   A She is going to work in marketing
   B She is going to work in accounts.
   C She is going on leave.
   B is correct.
   A is not correct because ....
   C is not correct because ....

2 **In the following two examples, identifying the correct answer depends on understanding an idea which is expressed in the question, using different words.**

1
> Tim – order 1241 held up in customs. Please phone agent ASAP (before they collect the next batch)

   What is the problem with the order?
   A It is damaged
   B It is delayed.
   C It has not been collected.

2
> Tony – couldn't get hold of Mario. His office number was engaged. Could you try?
> Elaine

   Why couldn't Elaine speak to Mario?
   A The phone line was in use.
   B He was out of the office.
   C The number was wrong.

In these two questions, which words in the texts are expressed differently in the correct alternatives?

To try a real exam task, go to page 140.

Reading Paper Part 1: Exam practice

Questions 1–5

- Look at questions **1–5**.
- In each question, which sentence is correct?
- For each question, mark one letter (**A**, **B** or **C**) on your Answer Sheet.

EXAMPLE

> ### Telephone message
>
> Bill Ryan caught 9.30 flight – due here 11.30 now, not 12.30

When does Bill Ryan expect to arrive?

A 9.30
B 11.30
C 12.30

The correct answer is **B**, so mark your Answer Sheet like this:

0	A	B	C
	▭	▬	▭

1

> ### MEMO
>
> **TO:** Chris
> **FROM:** Sandy
> **SUBJECT:** Order
> The new consignment of parts hasn't arrived yet. Please contact the suppliers and ask them why.

Sandy is asking Chris to contact the suppliers and

A find out if some parts are in stock.
B report a mistake in a recent order.
C enquire about the delay of a delivery.

2

> ### NETWORK DIRECT
>
> Fastest-growing online business directory
>
> **ADD YOUR COMPANY NOW**
>
> Click, fill in the form, our staff will do the rest
>
>

Network Direct will help companies to

A promote their business.
B improve their administration.
C expand their workforce.

3

> ### NOTICE
>
> To all staff:
>
> Please stay out of this area unless invited to the Health and Safety enquiry

A This area is only open to the enquiry organisers.
B It is not safe for anyone to enter this area.
C Only certain people are admitted into the area.

4

> ### NEWS
>
> Eurest wins big contract worth £6 million with expanding insurance provider.
>
> Tillman to provide maintenance service at Tillman's 55 office locations
>
> **CLICK HERE FOR FULL STORY**

A Eurest's insurance bill is expected to rise by a large amount.
B Eurest has announced plans to expand its office locations.
C Eurest has signed an important deal with a new client.

5

> **To:** All staff
> **From:** HR Manager
> **Subject:** Training courses
> _____
> Please inform your line manager this week of any new training needs for the next quarter.

Staff must tell management

A what courses they are currently taking.
B what professional development they require.
C how they could help train new employees.

Reading Paper Part 2: Exam skills

Part 2 consists of:

- one list of eight items that form part of a set, such as book titles or job titles
- five sentences, which may describe, for example, people in five different situations.

You must match each one to one of the items on the list.

You practised similar skills in Unit 1 (page 11) and in Unit 8 (page 41). This part of the exam tests:

- your knowledge of vocabulary
- your scanning skills.

Paraphrases

In many parts of the reading paper, the reading text will not use the same language as in the questions. When you read the questions, try to think of what different words might be used to express the ideas. For example:

- the text might use a synonym (e.g. *take on* instead of *recruit*)
- the text might express the same idea in a negative way (e.g. *it was unsuccessful* instead of *it failed*.)
- the text might say something more precise than the question (e.g. if the question says *most* or *a majority*, the text might give an exact percentage).

Suggested exam technique

1 Read the list of eight items quickly.
2 Read the first of the five sentences carefully. It can be useful to underline the most important words.
3 Scan the list again to find an item which matches.
4 Again, the items in the list will not use the same words as the sentence. Look for words which express a similar idea in a different way.
5 Follow the same procedure for the other four sentences. Be prepared to go back and change your mind if necessary.

Exercises

1 a **Read the following three sentences. The most important words are underlined.**

1 Mr Rodriguez runs a <u>factory</u> and wants to find out how he could make the business more <u>environmentally friendly</u>.
2 Ms Shirzad is <u>buying a house</u> and wants to know what kind of <u>mortgage</u> she should get.
3 Mr Cairns wants to find a company who can <u>provide the food</u> at a <u>corporate event</u>.

b **It can be useful in this exercise to think of associated words and ideas when you read each sentence. Match the words and phrases in the box with one of the sentences in Exercise 1a.**

buffet   green products   interest rate   loan
property   reduce pollution   set menu

The following list shows the titles of five magazines (A–E). Decide which one would be most useful for each of the three people in Exercise 1a.

A *Computing Advisor*   D *Ecology Today*
B *Personal Finance*   E *Catering Monthly*
C *Personnel Management*

2 a **Read the following three sentences and underline the most important words.**

1 Mauricio has the job of managing the advertising budget for the next year.
2 Ruth is giving a talk at a conference and would like some advice on how to make it memorable.
3 Luana is a human resources manager who wants the staff to work together and share ideas more.

b **Write down any other words you know associated with the words and phrases that you underlined. (Take no more than a minute over this.)**

c **The following list shows the titles of six business books (A–F). Which one should each of the people in Exercise 2a read?**

A *Successful Negotiations*
B *Financial Planning and Monitoring*
C *Building a Winning Team*
D *The Art of Manager-Employee Relations*
E *Effective Presentations*
F *Analyzing Market Research Data*

3 **Look at the list below. It shows a number of forms used within a company. For sentences 1–4 decide which of the forms each person needs.**

A incident report form   D expenses claim form
B order form   E customer feedback form
C disciplinary form   F training request form

1 Naoko went to a meeting in another city and wants to get her train fare back. ....
2 Debra wants to know what opinions clients have about the company service. ....
3 Daniel wants to buy some new office equipment. ....
4 Faisal wants to go on an IT course. ....

To try a real exam task, go to page 142.

Reading Paper Part 2: Exam practice

Questions 6–10

- Look at the list below. It shows study programmes available online.
- For questions **6–10**, decide which study programme (**A–H**) is most suitable for each person.
- For each question, mark one letter (**A–H**) on your Answer Sheet.
- Do not use any letter more than once.

Online study programmes

A Small Business Accounting – New tax laws

B Doing Business in the USA – Strategies for small businesses

C Marketing – Key legal issues

D Sales Management Training – Customer care

E Information Management – Getting started

F Human Resources Management – Employment law

G Workplace Skills – Working together

H Finance – International corporate issues

---

6 The head of a small law firm wants one of his employees to do a course on teambuilding.

7 A human resources director is looking for a course which will help her to set up a computer database.

8 The director of an American firm wants to learn how the law affects the way its products are promoted.

9 An accounting software company executive is keen to improve the way his company handles clients buying its products.

10 A US finance company director needs someone from her organisation to go on a course about workers' rights.

Reading Paper Part 3: Exam skills

Part 3 consists of:

- eight graphs or charts, or a graph dealing with eight areas of information, for example eight months or eight years.
- five sentences describing the information.

You must match each sentence with the correct graph or part of the graph.

You practised similar skills in Unit 17 (page 85). This part of the exam tests your ability to understand descriptions of graphs and statistics.

> **Link words**
>
> Link words allow you to follow the argument of a text and can also help you to check your understanding of words and phrases. For example, if you see *but, although* or *despite* in the middle of a sentence, you know that the idea after it will **contrast** with the idea in the first part.

Suggested exam technique

1   Study the graphs carefully. Read the introduction, the keys and the figures on them so you are sure that you understand the information that they give.
2   You may find it useful to make some quick sentences in your head describing the graphs so you are quite clear about what they describe.
3   Read the first sentence and then look back at the graphs and match.
4   The sentences often have two parts which are linked with a word like *while* or *although*. They may refer to two, or even three different figures on the graph. Make sure that **all** parts of the sentence are true for the graph that you choose. It can be useful to underline the most important words.
5   You may find it useful to identify possible graphs for the first part of the sentence and then see which one of these matches the second half.

Exercises

1   **For the following graphs and charts, choose the sentence which is completely correct, A, B or C. Be careful because many of the sentences are partly correct.**

1   The following graph shows the price of gold and platinum over a period of six months.

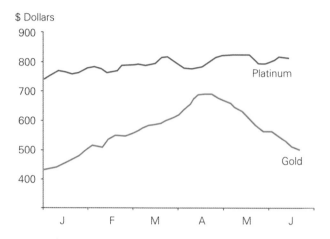

A   The price of gold climbed steadily from January to April but the price of platinum saw a dramatic fall at the beginning of the year.

B   The price of gold reached a peak in April whereas the price of platinum fluctuated only slightly throughout the period.

C   The price of gold rose during the first four months and the price of platinum followed a similar trend.

2   The following table shows passenger numbers on two different airlines over a period of three years.

	Year 1	Year 2	Year 3
Airline A	1,759,652	1,941,849	2,116,708
Airline B	2,461,580	2,231,092	2,254,661

A   Passenger numbers on airline A rose throughout the period and overtook numbers for airline B in year 3.

B   Both airlines experienced a drop in passenger numbers in year 2, but airline B showed signs of recovery the following year.

C   Although passenger numbers on airline B fell in year 2, they remained higher than airline A throughout the period.

3   The following pie charts show distribution outlets for a brand of sun cream in two different years.

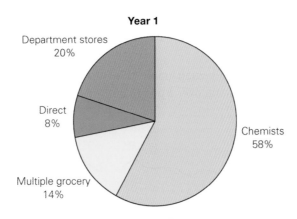

Year 1

Department stores
20%

Direct
8%

Multiple grocery
14%

Chemists
58%

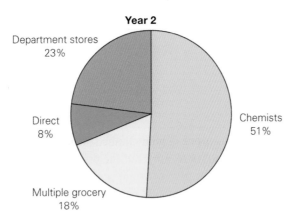

Year 2

Department stores
23%

Direct
8%

Multiple grocery
18%

Chemists
51%

A   The percentage sold through department stores increased slightly although chemists remained the main retail outlet.

B   The proportion which was sold direct remained negligible despite a slight increase in Year 2.

C   The percentage sold through chemists showed a slight decrease, unlike the percentage sold through multiple groceries, which experienced a significant rise.

2   **Study the graph and match each of the three sentences to the correct month.**

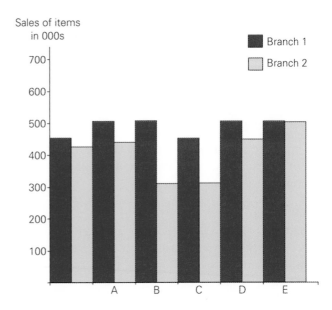

Sales of items in 000s

■ Branch 1
▫ Branch 2

1   Even though sales at Branch 2 increased considerably, the figure still remained below that for Branch 1.

2   Sales at Branch 1 of the store showed no significant change from the previous month, in contrast to sales at Branch 2, which experienced a sharp fall.

3   Sales at Branch 1 levelled off in this month, whereas sales at Branch 2 continued their strong performance.

To try a real exam task, go to page 145.

Reading Paper Part 3: Exam practice

Questions 11–15

- Look at the graph. It shows the percentage change in the values of three different types of investment over a nine-year period.
- Which year does each sentence (**11–15**) describe?
- For each sentence, mark one letter (**A–H**) on your Answer Sheet.
- Do not use any letter more than once.

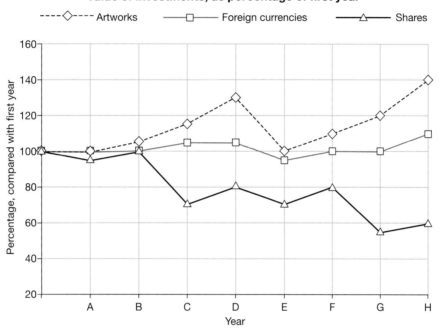

11 In this year, despite a continuing upward trend in artworks, the investment in foreign currencies was unchanged and share values dropped sharply.

12 Shares declined in value in this year, while there was a slight rise in the value of currencies and a large one in artworks.

13 This was a good year for investors in general, with all three indexes rising, artworks showing the most impressive growth.

14 Shares and artworks both showed an increase in value, unlike currencies, which remained steady after rising in the previous two years.

15 Although both artworks and shares enjoyed small gains in this year, these were not matched by the value of currencies, whose level did not change.

Reading Paper Part 4: Exam skills

Part 4 consists of:

- one text of about 150-200 words.
- seven questions where you have to decide if the statement is *right, wrong* or if the text *doesn't say* (i.e. the text does not give us enough information to make a decision).

You practised similar skills in Unit 11 (page 57), Unit 13 (page 65), Unit 16 (page 76) and Unit 23 (page 110). This question tests your ability to read and pick out specific information in a text.

Doesn't say

Be careful of the difference between ***wrong*** and ***doesn't say***. **Wrong** means that the sentence **cannot** be true according to the text. ***Doesn't say*** means that we **cannot know** from the text if it is true or not.

Reference words

In order to follow the argument of a text, you will need to understand the reference words. These are the words and phrases which refer back, or sometimes forwards, to another part of the text.

- often they are pronouns such as *he, this, the one* (e.g. *The new storeroom has a much bigger capacity than **the** old **one**).
- sometimes they are nouns with a similar or a more general meaning. In this case, they are often preceded by *this* (e.g. *Nestlé took over Perrier, the French producer of mineral water. **This acquisition** caused problems with the trade unions*).

Suggested exam technique

1 Read the text through once without worrying about unknown words.
2 Read the first statement carefully and then go back to the text and look for the information there. The answers to the question usually come in the same order in the text, so when you have found the answer to one, move on to the next part of the text.
3 If the information in the text has the same meaning as the statement, then the answer is *right*.
4 If the information is different, think carefully. Do we know that the statement is untrue (*wrong*), or is it still a possibility (*doesn't say*)?
5 If you find nothing similar in the text, then the answer is *doesn't say*.

Exercises

1 **In the following exercise, one of the statements is right, one is wrong and for one, the text does not say. Mark each statement *R, W* or *DS*.**

Example: Sales of the product rose.
A *Sales of the product increased.* This is *R*, because *rose* and *increased* have the same meaning.
B *Sales of the product decreased.* This is *W*, because *rose* and *decreased* have opposite meanings.
C *Sales of the product doubled.* This is *DS* because all we know is that sales rose. It is possible that they doubled but we cannot know this.

1 Richard is disappointed at the sales figures for the new product.
  A Richard thought that more customers would buy the product.
  B There has been disappointingly little interest in the product from retailers.
  C Richard is pleased at how well the product is selling.
2 He approached the bank for a loan.
  A The bank lent him money.
  B He asked the bank if he could borrow money.
  C He decided not to request a loan from the bank.
3 You can contact our 24-hour information service.
  A The information service is not available after 12p.m.
  B The information service is free of charge.
  C The information service is available at any time.
4 Judith no longer works for MTV.
  A Judith was dismissed from her job at MTV.
  B Judith used to work at MTV.
  C Judith is currently employed by MTV.
5 Michael has only worked in our marketing department for three weeks.
  A Michael only joined our marketing department three weeks ago.
  B Michael has only three weeks' experience of marketing.
  C Michael starts work in our marketing department in three weeks' time.

6 I intend to start a diploma in international business in September.
   A I obtained a diploma in international business in September.
   B My plan is to begin a course in international business in September.
   C I will start studying full time in September.

7 Sales have been lower than usual for December.
   A December sales have shown an increase on previous years.
   B The sales figures are the lowest ever recorded for December.
   C Sales are down compared with previous December figures.

8 The team consists of staff from the production, sales and marketing departments.
   A The team includes employees who work in marketing.
   B The team is made up entirely of staff from the sales department.
   C The majority of the team members are from the production department.

2 **Sometimes answering this type of question means you must put together the information in the passage to follow the sense of the text. This means that you must understand the pronouns and reference words. You practised this in Unit 18 on page 89.**

Example:

> The engineering company Orwells have reported a decrease in profits of 8 per cent. However the CEO is optimistic about the future. The main reason for the fall was the rising cost of steel, but improving sales in the automobile industry are expected to compensate for this.

Higher steel prices have caused a decrease in profits at Orwells.

This is *R*, because *the fall* in the third sentence is the same as *a decrease* in the first sentence.

Now decide if the statements below are *R*, *W* or *DS* for the following passages.

1
> Fun Drinks are to launch a new soft drink, *Energise*, in the autumn. Unlike most of its drinks which target 11–16 year olds, this product will be aimed at the adult consumer, especially sportspeople. It will compete directly with the highly successful sports drink, *Sportsade*.

R, W or *DS*?: *Energise will target the 11–16 age range.*

2
> There were a number of applicants for the post of accounts clerk but only three were chosen for interview. Mr Wright, who did the interviews, felt that all three candidates were suitably experienced but the post was offered to the one with a diploma in bookkeeping.

R, W or *DS*?: *Mr Wright has a diploma in bookkeeping.*

3
> Under the new leadership, Ancots Telecom is planning to raise its capital expenditure to $2.5m this year. This strategy goes against what is happening in the telecommunications field as a whole, with most other carriers preparing for an overall decrease in spending.

R, W or *DS*?: *Ancots Telecom is managing its finances differently from most other telecommunication companies.*

To try a real exam task, go to page 148.

Reading Paper Part 4: Exam practice

Questions 16–22

- Read the article below in which investors are given advice on buying shares in a market research company.
- Are sentences **16–22** on the opposite page 'Right' or 'Wrong'? If there is not enough information to answer 'Right' or 'Wrong', choose 'Doesn't Say'.
- For each sentence **16–22**, mark one letter (**A**, **B** or **C**) on your Answer Sheet.

SHARES IN SHARP INFO

Companies need to find out how their products are performing compared with those of their competitors. Sharp Info carries out such research for businesses in a wide range of industries, including healthcare, telecommunications and sporting events, and has built up a strong position in the field of market research.

Fund manager Brian Hawkes recommends shares in Sharp for two reasons. Firstly, he points out that Sharp has an international customer base, protecting it from local economic conditions. He also refers to Sharp's recent acquisition of MEM, a competitor specialising in obtaining market information from the internet. This was part of

Sharp's strategy to move further into online market research. Hawkes notes that management expects to make annual savings of £15m as a result of the takeover, adding significantly to the £25m that Sharp is already likely to make in profits.

Another fund manager, Debra Hansen, takes a different view. 'Sharp shares look attractive because they are currently trading below those of their competitors. However, the long-term potential of the market research industry is unclear. Analysts predicting minimum growth of 4% in this field next year could well be disappointed. You should avoid putting money into this sector for the moment.'

---

16 Sharp Info carries out research for businesses that want to know about sales in their sector.

  A Right   **B** Wrong   **C** Doesn't say

17 Sharp carries out more market research for healthcare companies than for any other industry.

  A Right   **B** Wrong   **C** Doesn't say

18 Hawkes believes one of Sharp's strengths is that it has clients in several countries.

  A Right   **B** Wrong   **C** Doesn't say

19 Hawkes claims that Sharp acquired MEM in order to make annual profits of £15m.

  A Right   **B** Wrong   **C** Doesn't say

20 Online market research is now Sharp's main activity.

  A Right   **B** Wrong   **C** Doesn't say

21 According to Debra Hansen, Sharp shares are cheaper than others in the same sector.

  A Right   **B** Wrong   **C** Doesn't say

22 Hansen believes that the market research sector will grow by at least 4% next year.

  A Right   **B** Wrong   **C** Doesn't say

Reading Paper Part 5: Exam skills

Part 5 consists of:

- one text of about 300 to 400 words.
- six multiple-choice questions where you must choose A, B or C.

You practised questions like this in Unit 2 (page 16) and Unit 18 (page 89).

This section tests your ability to:

- skim
- scan
- read for gist, especially opinions
- read for specific information.

> **Unknown vocabulary**
> The text may contain words you don't know. Do not spend too much time trying to understand their exact meanings. You may well find you can answer the questions without knowing them. If there is a question which uses this new vocabulary, use the context in the passage to try to guess the meaning. An approximate meaning is often all that is needed to get the right answer to a question.

Suggested exam technique

1. Skim the text first to get a good general idea of what it says and the topic of each paragraph.
2. Read the beginning of the first question and underline the most important words.
3. Find where the question is answered in the text. Then read the three alternatives and decide which is correct. Sometimes you may find it easier to decide which ones are not correct.
4. The answers to the question usually come in the same order in the text so when you have found the answer to one question, move on to the next part of the text.
5. Think about the link between the first part of each question and the three alternative answers. For example, if the question asks about the reasons for something, the alternatives may be three possible causes. In this case, make sure that the answer you choose is definitely given as a cause in the text.
6. The text will usually not use the same language as in the question. You need to look for the same idea expressed in a different way.

Exercises

1. a **Skim the text about Anwar's restaurant and decide which of the following it talks about.**

   a The original idea
   b Raising the money to start up
   c Taking on employees
   d Advertising the restaurant
   e Buying the equipment
   f Expanding the business

ANWAR'S RESTAURANT

Anwar Salama worked for a number of years in the restaurant trade. During this time, he learnt about health and safety, dealing with suppliers and all the issues that come up in the day-to-day management of a restaurant. After five years, he felt sure that he could successfully run a restaurant of his own, specialising in Middle Eastern food. However, as it turned out, he underestimated how difficult it would be to obtain the initial funding.

Anwar found a small café that he could take over and approached his bank for a loan. However, they were less helpful than he had hoped. They were reluctant to offer him a loan because he had no property or equipment which he could use to secure it. Eventually, he put together a detailed business plan with the help of a friend and persuaded the bank to lend him £5,000.

Purchasing the equipment to set up was a further difficulty. He had originally intended to buy second-hand equipment but he had difficulties finding anything suitable. It was also more expensive than he had thought. The bank refused him a further loan so in the end he found a local firm who were willing to let him buy equipment on hire purchase. Looking back, he feels that this was a better solution as the equipment was new and was less likely to break down.

Despite the initial problems, Anwar's restaurant was a success and three years later it had a turnover that was almost double the original estimate. Anwar wanted to expand. Most of his customers were shoppers who wanted a lunchtime snack but he had seen a property that was ideally situated to capture the trade of workers leaving the office in the evening. The bank was much more willing to listen to Anwar's proposal now that he could show the impressive figures from his first venture and he was able to use the lease on his current restaurant as security. The new restaurant opened last year and is already doing well.

---

b **Now choose the correct answer, A, B or C. Use the questions and instructions in italics to help you.**

1. Why did Anwar feel confident about running his own restaurant? (paragraph 1)
   (i Find a phrase in the paragraph which means 'he felt confident about ...'
   ii Does the answer to the question come before or after this phrase?)
   A He had training in restaurant management.
   B He had built up a lot of experience in the trade.
   C He had a number of contacts who were willing to invest.

2 Why did Anwar's bank not want to give him a loan? (paragraph 2)

(i Find an adjective meaning they did not want to.
ii What link word is used to introduce the reason why the bank did not want to?)

A He had never run a restaurant before.

B His business plan was badly written.

C He had no assets which he could offer as security.

3 According to Anwar, buying the equipment on hire purchase (paragraph 3)

(i Scan the paragraph for the phrase 'hire purchase'.
ii Are A, B and C reasons why he bought equipment on hire purchase, or results of buying it this way?)

A caused him to overspend on his budget.

B meant that the equipment was less suitable.

C saved him money on repair bills.

4 Anwar was keen to move into the new premises because (paragraph 4)

(i Find a noun in the paragraph which refers to the new premises.
ii Does the reason why he wanted to move come before or after this noun?)

A it would expand his customer base.

B his first property was too small.

C the lease on the first property was coming to an end.

2 a **Skim the text opposite and then read questions (1–4). Do not answer the questions yet.**

1 Invesco reduced its absenteeism rates by

A offering a company health provision.

B taking advice from psychologists.

C making staff more motivated.

2 Restricting sick pay is likely to be less effective than some other measures because

A it encourages employees to be absent for longer periods.

B it is not supported by research.

C it ignores the reasons why staff go off sick.

3 The Royal Mail workers' union felt that their company's attempts to reduce absenteeism

A had no effect on the absenteeism rate.

B did not solve the real problem.

C increased job satisfaction.

4 According to Anne Rogers, problems with absenteeism

A only affect a minority of companies.

B are ignored by too many companies.

C are difficult to solve.

The right treatment for absentees

Taking a day off sick may seem a small thing but days absent from work are a huge financial problem for businesses. Although many absentees are genuinely ill, there can be other reasons why people decide to stay away from the office, such as stress. In these cases, absenteeism rates can often be improved by better management and company policies which promote respect.

Some institutions have taken further steps to deal with the problem of workplace absence. After investigating how much was being paid in wages for sick employees, the investment company, Invesco, decided to invest in a private doctor for its staff. They also offered free medical tests and counselling. Research carried out a year later found that one-day sickness absences were down by 6 % as a result. Other companies have used more aggressive policies, such as not paying employees for the first two or three days that they take off sick. However, if one reason for absenteeism is stress, then policies like these are not likely to solve the problem as they make no attempt to understand why employees take days off sick.

Other approaches to the problem involve rewarding the employees who have good attendance records. For example, you might offer an extra day's leave to an employee who has taken no time off sick during the year. Royal Mail, the UK post office, has gone further by offering the prize of a new car to employees with 100% attendance. However, the Royal Mail workers' union have argued that the company should focus on improving job satisfaction, rather than gimmicks like these, even if they reduce the absenteeism rate in the short term.

Anne Rogers, executive director of an agency which provides personnel support, is convinced that the problem affects a large number of businesses. Although many companies report that they have no significant problems with absenteeism, according to her, they have quite often simply failed to look at the figures. Indeed, many companies do not know precisely what they are. Meanwhile, one-day absences continue to cost businesses vast amounts of money each year.

---

b **Which question is about:**

i how something was done?

ii the results of something?

iii the reasons why something may not work.

c **Now read the text again and choose the correct answers, A, B or C.**

To try a real exam task, go to page 151.

Reading Paper Part 5: Exam practice

Questions 23–28

- Read the report below about the performance of an Irish manufacturer of paper goods.
- For each question **23–28** on the opposite page, choose the correct answer.
- Mark one letter (**A**, **B** or **C**) on your Answer Sheet.

Company Performance

The first half of this financial year seemed promising for the company after several difficult years. The results for our Dublin and Cork branches have greatly improved, but this is mainly due to the restructuring that took place at the end of last year in Dublin. Despite improved sales for the second quarter, the retail business ended the half-year slightly behind plan. However, branded sales were in line with targets for both large and small notebooks, with the majority of sales losses due to own-label products. Selling prices met planned targets.

The consolidation of other notebook manufacturers across Europe continues. The recent purchase of Wells Stationery by German group Schröder is an example. Schröder is currently restructuring its business in Germany, transferring equipment and reducing staff levels with the expectation that it will target high street retailers in the UK and Ireland.

On a positive note, sales of our *University* notebook brand increased by 11 per cent compared to this time last year. Our Brand Marketing Programme continues to increase the notebook's profile among our target dealers and we have also won orders from leading retailer Smiths. However,

the increase in sales was mainly due to the notebook's introduction in the USA, together with the new *Calculator* notebooks.

Over-production of envelopes across Europe resulted in a price war over the first half of the year. This has resulted in a loss of some £2m worth of our envelope business from UK retailers Paper Express and TSD.

However, the first half of the financial year at our site at Hampton was reasonably promising, despite the loss of a number of 'special envelope' contracts. In an effort to increase the level of business in the 'specials' sector, we have restructured our team and created a new customer service department.

There have been a number of changes to our senior management team. Our Financial Director, Mark Shaw, left the company in October to become a director of BVN, and Tony Tripp, previously Operations Director, was appointed in his place. As to the next six months, the market will be tough in all sectors in which we operate. But by keeping control of costs and focusing on important purchasers, we should be able to maximise our return on sales of our products.

---

23 What do we find out about the company's performance in the first paragraph?

   A Not all targets were met.

   B Its results were unexpected.

   C The recent restructuring had a negative effect.

24 What has Schröder decided to do?

   A sell its German operation

   B look at markets outside Germany

   C transfer some of its staff from Germany

25 The most important factor in the success of the University notebooks was

   A the Brand Marketing Programme.

   B a large order from a leading retailer.

   C their launch in a new market.

26 Why did the company lose money on its sales of envelopes?

   A It had to lower its prices.

   B It wasn't able to meet demand.

   C It lost contracts in several European countries.

27 What caused the changes in the senior management team?

   A Someone new was taken on.

   B Someone was promoted.

   C Someone resigned.

28 What does the company have to do in the next six months?

   A expand marketing

   B launch new products

   C target key customers

Reading Paper Part 6: Exam skills

Part 6 consists of:

- one text of about 150 words
- twelve multiple-choice gaps where you must choose the correct word, **A**, **B** or **C**.

You practised similar skills in Grammar Workshop 5 (page 99), Unit 24 (page 115) and Grammar Workshop 6 (page 117).

This part of the exam tests your knowledge of

- vocabulary (especially collocations)
- prepositions
- grammar (tenses, comparatives, modal verbs, etc.)
- pronouns and reference words
- link words (*and, although, despite,* etc.)

Suggested exam technique

1 Before you look at the alternatives, read the text through and try to think which word will go in the gap. You may find that you think of one of the alternatives.
2 The three alternatives may have similar meanings, but look at the words either side of the gap. The right answer will often depend on these.
3 If you are not sure of the answer, try to eliminate a wrong alternative.
4 When you have finished, read the text through again with your answers to check.

Exercises

1 **The gaps in this exercise test your knowledge of verb forms. Put the correct letter in each gap.**

> The shoe company Gean **1** .... founded in 2006 by Mr Daniele Bani. Since then, it **2** .... expanded rapidly and now it has 15 per cent of the Italian market share. In order to expand further, Mr Bani **3** .... to target markets outside Europe where there **4** .... expected to be a growing demand for luxury footwear.

1	A has	B is	C was
2	A has	B is	C was
3	A must	B needs	C should
4	A is	B will	C has

2 **The gaps in this exercise test your knowledge of pronouns and reference words. Put the correct letter in each gap.**

> A recent UK study has revealed that 65 per cent of CVs **1** .... are submitted to employers contain inaccuracies. Although some of **2** .... are simple mistakes, many of **3** .... are deliberate lies. Employers are responding to **4** .... situation by carrying out more detailed checks on **5** .... job candidates.

1	A who	B which	C what
2	A this	B these	C them
3	A this	B it	C them
4	A this	B these	C those
5	A his	B they	C their

3 **In this text, choose the correct prepositions to fill the gaps. Look especially at the verbs and adjectives before each one.**

> **THE *GREEN* OFFICE**
>
> There are a number of simple steps you can take to make your office more environmentally friendly. Most of them are not just about looking **1** .... the environment. They are useful for anyone who is interested **2** .... running their office more efficiently. For example, has anyone in your workplace ever left their computer switched **3** .... all night? Making sure that everyone shuts **4** .... the computer **5** .... the end of the day will save energy and reduce your electricity bills too. Many office workers also depend too much **6** .... hard copies of documents, which means that the office spends far more than it should **7** .... paper. Encourage staff to create files and store emails on the computer so that they do not have to print everything **8** ....
>
> A truly green office will have a system for recycling different materials. Try to persuade your boss to set **9** .... a system with different bins for paper, cardboard and plastic and make sure everyone is aware **10** .... it . If colleagues complain **11** .... the extra time and trouble, you may be able to invest **12** .... individual recycling containers which can be placed next to everyone's desk. These are available from many recycling companies.

1	A for	B after	C up
2	A at	B about	C in
3	A on	B off	C down
4	A on	B off	C down
5	A in	B on	C at
6	A on	B of	C from
7	A on	B for	C from
8	A up	B on	C out
9	A up	B on	C out
10	A at	B of	C in
11	A of	B from	C about
12	A on	B at	C in

To try a real exam task, go to page 153.

Reading Paper Part 6: Exam practice

Questions 29–40

- Read the article below about cash flow management.
- Choose the correct word to fill each gap, from **A**, **B** or **C** on the opposite page.
- For each question **29–40**, mark one letter (**A**, **B** or **C**) on your Answer Sheet.

Managing your Cash Flow

Managing cash flow is probably the least exciting aspect of running a business. It is, however, a key area, and one (**29**) .... can make the difference between the success and failure (**30**) .... your business.

As part of good cash flow management, John Reid of JRA Finance advises start-up businesses to avoid investing (**31**) .... too much equipment, and to hold money back for unexpected events. He (**32**) .... recommends establishing a good relationship with your bank, (**33**) .... payment terms clear to clients, and following up efficiently on (**34**) .... who do not pay on time.

Periods of high growth will (**35**) .... cash flow management difficulties for small- or medium-sized enterprises, as this phase typically involves high expenditure (**36**) .... raw materials and labour costs. Business consultants (**37**) .... that steady growth ought to be the (**38**) .... goal of any company. (**39**) .... borrowing is often essential to fund business growth, very high borrowing (**40**) .... lead to higher interest rates and tighter repayment schedules.

29	**A** that	**B** what	**C** where
30	**A** by	**B** of	**C** from
31	**A** in	**B** with	**C** by
32	**A** even	**B** also	**C** still
33	**A** putting	**B** making	**C** doing
34	**A** they	**B** these	**C** those
35	**A** rise	**B** increase	**C** grow
36	**A** at	**B** on	**C** for
37	**A** analyse	**B** allow	**C** agree
38	**A** complete	**B** total	**C** overall
39	**A** Whether	**B** Because	**C** Although
40	**A** may	**B** would	**C** should

Reading Paper Part 7: Exam skills

Part 7 consists of:

- two short texts such as memos, emails or advertisements.
- one form which you must fill in with information taken from the texts.

You practised similar skills in Unit 5 (page 31) and Unit 23 (page 109).

This part of the exam tests your ability to identify relevant information in a short text.

Suggested exam technique

1. Look at the form and read the headings carefully.
2. Look at the texts and think who would complete the form. For example, an order form would obviously be completed by the company who needs the goods, not by the company who supplies them.
3. Scan the two texts to find the relevant information.
4. If the information you need is a name, for example, then the texts are likely to contain two or three names. In this situation, it is a good idea to underline all the names you can find and then decide which is the correct one.

Exercises

1. The travel claim form at the top of the page asks for the names of three different people. Scan the two emails and underline all the names. Then decide which name corresponds to which heading to complete the form.

To: Maureen Kirk
From: Mahbub Dharmen
Re: travel expenses

Dear Maureen,

I'm meeting Erica Ray at our new office on Tuesday 16 March to check everything is ready for the opening. How do I claim travel expenses?

Mahbub

To: Mahbub Dharmen
From: Maureen Kirk
Re: travel expenses

I'm attaching a travel claim form. If you complete it and send it to Daniel Musser in finance, he'll prepare you a travel warrant. It's just like a cheque that you can take to the railway station. Please send the form today if you can as I'll need to approve it before you go.

Maureen

TRAVEL CLAIM FORM

For the attention of:	**1** ....
Ticket required for:	**2** ....
Authorised by:	**3** ....
Date of travel:	Tuesday 16 March

2. Sometimes you will need to take information from one of the texts to work out which is the correct information in the other. In the following exercise, complete the conference booking form with the missing information. To do this, you need to look both at the list of conference fees and the email to Simon Roberts.

To: Simon Roberts
From: Carmel Volponi
Re: conference booking

Dear Simon

Please fill in the conference booking form below for me and book me a night in the hotel. I'm only going for one day so I'll only need to stay Friday night. If you send it in this week, we can still get the early booking rate. Don't forget to tell them I need a vegetarian lunch.

Thanks,

Carmel

Conference fees:

	early booking	standard
Full conference delegate:	£280	£310
Day delegate:	£150	£185
Block booking rate per delegate:	£240	£290

Fees include registration, conference materials, lunch and tea and coffee.
Block bookings can only be made for groups of six or more and are only available for the full three days.

CONFERENCE BOOKING FORM

Name:	Carmel Volponi
Company:	Tele 43
Job title:	marketing manager
Delegate type	**1** ....
Special requirements (e.g. dietary)	**2** ....
Payment:	I authorise you to charge my credit/debit card
	£ **3** ....

To try a real exam task, go to page 155.

Reading Paper Part 7: Exam practice

Questions 41–45

- Read the memo and the advertisement below.
- Complete the form.
- Write a word or phrase (in CAPITAL LETTERS) or a number on lines **41–45** on your Answer Sheet.

PHILLIPS
MANUFACTURERS OF FINE FURNITURE SINCE 1830

MEMO

To: Kevin Carlton
From: Jane Wright
Subject: Recruitment Fair

I think we should book a stand at one of these recruitment fairs. We need to take on more store assistants for the busy season – management's set a very high sales target in our retail stores this year. Book a stand in my name, and try to get the biggest one they can provide, while keeping the expense to a minimum.

SAVILLES RECRUITMENT FAIRS

IN YOUR AREA SOON
LET US PUT YOU IN TOUCH WITH THE STAFF YOU NEED!

For:
Manufacturing Staff: October 15
Retail Staff: November 1
Management: December 2

BOOK NOW!
Small, Medium, or Large stand included in admission fee.
Super Large available at extra cost.

COMPANY STAND BOOKING FORM

Complete the form below to book a stand at one of our recruitment fairs.

Date required:	(41)	
Size of stand required:	(42)	
Name of company:	(43)	
Type of product:	(44)	
Full contact name:	(45)	

Listening Paper Part 1: Exam skills

Part 1 consists of:

- eight short conversations or monologues.
- eight multiple-choice questions. These may be texts, pictures, graphs or diagrams. You must choose **A**, **B** or **C**.

You practised similar skills in Unit 7 (page 39), Unit 9 (page 47 and 48) and with statistics in Unit 17 (page 84).

This part of the exam tests your ability to listen for specific information in a short extract.

> **Multiple-choice questions in the Listening paper.**
> Each question has three alternatives. One is the correct answer, the other are 'distractors'. You have to distinguish the relevant information from the distractors. Be careful when you listen because the speakers will usually mention something connected with the distractors. You must be alert in order to decide that they are the wrong answers.

Suggested exam technique

1 **Use the pause** before each recording to read the beginning of the question and the three alternatives carefully. You may find it useful to underline the important words.
2 The speakers will probably say something about all three alternatives or something similar to them. Listen carefully to decide which is correct.
3 The speakers will not use exactly the same words as in the questions. Listen for the same idea expressed with a different word or phrase.
4 If the alternatives are words and phrases, not numbers, try to think of alternative words for these ideas before you hear the recording.
5 If you find a question difficult, use the pause between listening the first time and listening the second time to read it again and think about what you have heard.

Exercises

1 **②07** Listen to the following two short extracts and fill in the gaps. Then answer the multiple-choice question at the end.

   1 **Man** Do you want to meet sometime to discuss the market research survey? I could do next **1** .... morning.

      Woman Yes, I could as well, but I was hoping we could meet earlier than that. How about **2** .... this week or **3** .... morning?

   Man Sorry, I can't make either of those. I'm in meetings both days.

   Woman OK, then, next week it is.

   What day are the speakers going to meet?

   A Monday

   B Thursday

   C Friday

  2 **Man** Has there been much interest in the new post?

      Woman Yes, we've had about **1** .... applicants, some very good ones too. I'm choosing them for interview at the moment and it looks like I'll be seeing about **2** .... of them.

      Man So we should probably always advertise in that paper from now on. When we put the advert online, only about **3** .... people contacted us.

   How many candidates is the woman going to interview?

   A 60

   B 30

   C 10

2 **②08** Listen to the next two extracts and answer the following two questions.

  1 How much will the woman pay for the hotel room?

   A £140

   B £175

   C £125

  2 Where is Mr Sullivan going to have lunch?

   A Greek restaurant

   B steak bar

   C staff canteen

3 **②09** Listen to two more extracts and answer the questions below. For these two questions you need to think about other words you might use to talk about the three alternatives.

  1 What has been changed about the packaging for the sweets?

   A the shape

   B the material

   C the colour

  2 What did the man think about the presentation?

   A The content was boring.

   B The presenter spoke clearly.

   C The ideas were original.

To try a real exam task, go to page 157.

Listening Paper Part 1: Exam practice

(2) 10 Questions 1–8

- For questions **1–8** you will hear eight short recordings.
- For each question, mark one letter (**A**, **B** or **C**) for the correct answer.

> **Example:**
> Who is Emily going to write to?
> **A** the staff   **B** the supplier   **C** the clients
> The answer is **A**.

- You will hear the eight recordings twice.

1 What time will Jim's flight be?

A

B

C

2 When will the sales conference take place?
- **A** September
- **B** October
- **C** November

3 Which graph is correct?

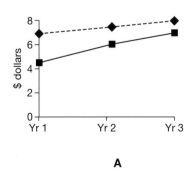

A

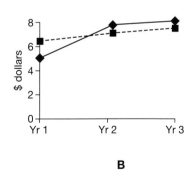

B

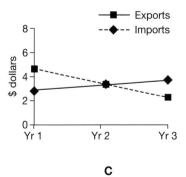

C

4 What does the woman say about the staff's telephone skills?

   A They are slow answering the phone.

   B They are very impolite.

   C They give incorrect information.

5 Where should the presenter go first tomorrow?

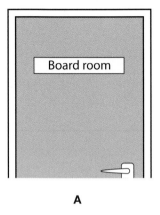

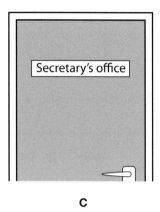

       A   **B**   **C**

6 What is the main problem with the new product components?

   A They are the wrong colour.

   B They are the wrong size.

   C They are the wrong material.

7 Which chart shows the company's expected sales figures?

Quarterly Sales Figures

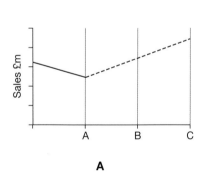
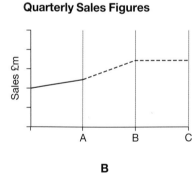
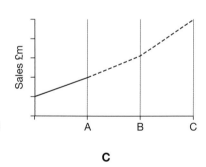

       A   **B**   **C**

8 Which job will the man apply for?

   A area manager

   B branch manager

   C department manager

Listening Paper Part 2: Exam skills

Part 2 consists of:

- one short telephone conversation, or possibly an answerphone message which you hear twice
- seven gaps in a form or set of notes where you must fill in information.

You practised similar skills in Unit 5 (page 30), Unit 7 (page 39) and Unit 9 (page 46).

This part of the Listening exam tests your ability to:

- understand factual information (especially dates, prices, telephone numbers, etc.)
- take down spellings of a name, company, address, etc.

Cue words

When listening for specific information, it is very important to listen for the cues or words which will introduce the information that you want. For example, if you need to know the price of something, listen for the cue word *price* or *cost* and be ready for the information you want to come immediately after this. If you are noting down specific information, try to decide what the cue word is likely to be for each one.

Suggested exam technique

1. **Use the pause** before you hear the recording to read the form and think what information you must put in each gap.
2. When you hear the recording, listen for the key words which introduce the information that you need. For example, if one question is 'discount offered', listen for the word *discount*. The information on the recording is in the same order as the questions.
3. For many of the questions, you will hear two numbers or two pieces of information and you will have to choose the right one, so don't just write down the first one that you hear.
4. Before you hear the recording for the second time, think where you must concentrate especially hard for any answers that you missed.

Exercises

1   (2)(11) You will hear a speaker giving some information about DHL, the express delivery service. Listen to the talk and fill in the correct numbers. (The speaker gives many more facts than you need so listen carefully to what the numbers refer to.)

Year in which the company started:	1 ....
Percentage of shares owned by Deutsche Post in 2001:	2 ....
Value of UK National Health Service contract:	3 ....
Total saving on National Health Service expenses:	4 ....
Number of trucks used for delivery of in-flight catering:	5 ....

2   (2)(12) People often confuse the names of the following letters in English: *A, C, E, G, I, J, R, S.* Listen to the recording and write these letters in the order that you hear them.

1	2	3	4 ....
5	6	7	8 ....

3   (2)(13) Listen to the following short conversations and complete the information. In each case, you need to write the correct spelling.

1   **Name:** Keith ....
     Address: 34, ... Close, Croydon
2   **Name:** ....
     Address: 62, ... Drive, London
     Postcode: ....
3   **Company:** ....
     Contact name: ....

4   (2)(14) Listen to four short conversations and write the correct numbers. In each case you will hear more than one number so be sure to choose the correct one. If you find this difficult, write down all the numbers you hear and then listen to the recording a second time to decide which is correct.

1   Contact phone number: ....
2   Time of arrival: ....
3   Discount: ....
4   Total number of staff: ....

To try a real exam task, go to page 160.

Listening Paper Part 2: Exam practice

② **15** Questions 9–15

- Look at the notes below.
- Some information is missing.
- You will hear a man giving information to his female colleague about a contract.
- For each question **9–15**, fill in the missing information in the numbered space using a **word**, **numbers** or **letters**.

You will hear the conversation twice.

Contract Details

Client:	Halls Construction
Item:	Sheet glass
Specifications:	
size of glass	750mm × **(9)** .... mm
thickness of glass	**(10)** .... mm
Quantity for first order:	**(11)** .... sheets
Delivery address:	**(12)** .... Estate
	(13) Unit ....
Delivery:	monthly
First delivery due:	**(14)** .... August
Total charge:	**(15)** £ ....

Listening Paper Part 3: Exam skills

Part 3 consists of:

- one monologue
- one form or set of notes with seven gaps.

You must fill the gaps using one or two words. One of the answers may be a date.

You practised similar skills in Unit 12 (page 60), Unit 14 (page 70), Unit 18 (page 87) and Unit 20 (page 94).

This section tests your ability to:

- listen for specific information
- take short notes.

Suggested exam technique

1 **Use the pause** before you hear the recording to read the notes carefully and think what kind of information could go in each gap. You may even be able to guess one or two of the answers before you hear the talk.
2 The speaker may say two or three possibilities for each question, so don't just write down the first that you hear. Listen carefully to decide which is correct.
3 The speaker will not use the same words as are used in the questions. Listen for the same idea expressed with an alternative word or phrase. Try to think of some in the pause before you hear the recording.
4 Use the pause before the first and the second listening to decide what questions you still need to concentrate on.
5 Use the second listening to check the answers you already have as well.

Exercises

1 a **Look at the following notes on items from a business news programme. Think about the questions in italics before you listen.**

> **Westcloud**
> The company opened their first Chinese store in
> **1** ....
> *(What kind of information could go in this gap?)*
> The biggest increase was in sales of **2** ....
> *(The company is described as a fashion and beauty retailer. What are some possible products?)*
> Reason for their success: **3** ....
> *(What could be some possible reasons?)*
> The company are planning to increase their **4** ....
> *(The company are doing well so what might they plan to increase?)*

b (2) 16 **Now listen and fill the gaps with one or two words or a date.**

2 a **Some words and phrases in the following questions are underlined. Find the words and phrases in the audioscript below with the same meaning.**

1 John Butler is a <u>previous head</u> of a ....
2 He is planning to <u>make an offer</u> for a ....
3 He is seeking <u>support</u> from a ....
4 There are <u>rumours</u> of a ....

> John Butler, the former chairman of TV West, is currently in talks to launch a bid for the cinema chain, Cineworld. Butler lost his position as chairman of the TV company last year after TV West merged with Tele40 to form a single independent television company. He is seeking backing for his offer from a number of investment banks. There is also speculation of a joint bid with Hans Muller, the owner of the private equity group Orbis. However, Mr Muller was not available for comment.

b **Now complete sentences 1–4, using one or two words.**

3 a **Listen to another news item. Before you listen, think about:**

- the kind of information that could go in the gaps in the notes below
- alternative words and phrases that the transcript could use. Use the questions in italics to help you with this.

> **Morton and Campbell Insurance**
> Division that the company plan to sell: **1** ....
> *(What are some other ways of saying 'plan to'?)*
>
> Reason for selling: **2** ....
> *(A reason is normally introduced with what word?)*
>
> An increased number of claims came from **3** ....
> *(What could be another way of saying 'an increased number')*
>
> According to the newspapers, an offer has been made by a/an **4** ....
> *(What is another way of saying 'the newspapers'?)*

b (2) 17 **Now listen to the news items and fill the gaps in the notes above with one or two words.**

To try a real exam task, go to page 162.

Listening Paper Part 3: Exam practice

②⑱ Questions 16–22

- Look at the notes below about flexible working arrangements.
- Some information is missing.
- You will hear part of a talk by a business expert called Tim Johnstone.
- For each question **16–22**, fill in the missing information in the numbered space using **one** or **two** words.
- You will hear the talk twice.
- You have 10 seconds to read through the notes.
- Now listen, and fill in the missing information.

FLEXIBLE WORKING ARRANGEMENTS

Background information

Powercom first introduced this scheme in the (16) .... industry in 1996.
The scheme allows employees to choose (17) .... and location.

Research findings

Main advantage to employers: they can reduce (18) ....
Main benefit to staff: (19) ....

Tim Johnstone's own firm

He works in an (20) .... which introduced flexible working.
Most employees work at home, using email
and mobile phones.
His company encourages a quiet and (21) .... working environment.
Messages are sent out at (22) .... and early evening each day.

Listening Paper Part 4: Exam skills

Listening Part 4 consists of:

- an interview or conversation between two or more speakers.
- eight multiple-choice questions. You must choose **A**, **B** or **C**.

You practised similar skills in Unit 19 (page 93), Unit 22 (page 107) and Unit 23 (page 111).

This part of the exam tests your ability to

- listen for gist (general meaning)
- understand the speakers' opinions
- pick out specific information.

> **Paraphrases**
> In the Listening paper, the speakers on the recording will not use the same words that you see in the question. The correct answer will often be expressed in different words (paraphrasing). When you read the questions, try to think of what different words might be used to express the same ideas.

Suggested exam technique

1 **Use the pause** between the instructions and listening to the recording to read each question and underline the most important words.

2 The speaker will probably say something about all three alternatives or something similar to them. Listen carefully to decide which is correct.

3 Remember that the speaker will not usually use the same words as in the questions. You must listen for the same idea expressed in different words.

4 If you find a question difficult, use the pause before listening the second time to read it again and think about what you have heard.

Exercises

1 a **(2)(19)** You will hear a woman being interviewed about working flexible hours. Choose the correct answer, A, B or C.

1 The majority of people recruited through Flexiwork are
  A women with young children.
  B men with large families.
  C people who care for relatives

2 According to the speaker, working from home is more efficient because
  A employees do not need their own desks.
  B employees do not waste time travelling.
  C employees use fewer company resources.

3 Employees who are offered flexible hours are more likely to
  A stay with the company.
  B do extra hours.
  C meet job targets.

b **Read the audioscript of the interview. Underline the phrases which give you the correct answers. How are they expressed?**

A So tell us something about Flexiwork.

B Well, we're a recruitment agency but we specialise in finding employment for people who want to work flexible hours.

A And who are your clients? Is it mainly working mothers who need to organise their work around childcare?

B No, not really. A great many men these days want more flexibility in their working hours, just because they want more control over when and where they work. Actually we find the most common reason for wanting more flexibility is that that person is looking after a parent or elderly member of the family.

A And how difficult is it for companies to offer flexible hours?

B It's becoming easier and easier really, and it's often much more efficient. Why do you need to do everything at your desk at work if you have a computer at home? You still have to go into work for some things but even then, you won't be forced to go during the rush hour. And that's a big saving of time. Just think of all those unproductive hours you spend on the train normally.

A Are there any benefits for companies?

B Yes certainly. Staff turnover among flexible workers tends to be much lower than among other employees, partly because it may not be easy to find this balance between work and family needs somewhere else. And if companies can hang on to their best workers by saying 'OK, because of your situation, we'll offer you flexible hours', then they're more likely to meet their targets.

2 a **(2)(20)** Listen to an interview with Luke Davey, the owner of a recruitment business. Listen to the first part of the interview and fill in the blanks. Then answer the multiple-choice question at the end.

A So Luke, you're now the owner of one of the largest recruitment companies in the country. Have you always worked in this field?

B No, not always. My father ran a successful **1** .... and he always wanted me to join the family business. But I wanted to make my own way, so I moved out and I actually went to a **2** .... to find work. The first place they found me was in a **3** ....

4 Luke's first job was in a
   A bakery
   B recruitment agency
   C hotel

b **(2)(21)** Now listen to the complete interview and choose the correct answers.

1 What did Luke enjoy most about working in the recruitment agency?
   A phoning companies.
   B analysing CVs.
   C interviewing candidates.

2 What did Luke use to finance his start-up?
   A his own savings.
   B a bank loan.
   C money from his family.

3 What does Luke think first attracted clients to his agency?
   A his marketing techniques.
   B his large premises.
   C his prestigious address.

4 Why did he decide to sell the trade magazine?
   A It cost too much to produce.
   B It took up too much time.
   C Its readership was declining.

5 How has the business changed since it was first set up?
   A They deal with different types of companies.
   B They manage the entire recruitment process.
   C They have a better quality of client.

c **(2)(21)** Listen to the interview again. Complete the extracts from the text below and answer the questions to help you check your answers to Exercise 2b.

1 Luke mentions all three activities but complete the following sentence to give the correct answer: 'I really loved doing the ....'

2 Luke says he was reluctant to do two of the alternatives. Complete the following extracts: 'I didn't want to pay interest on ....' 'I didn't feel I could ....' Which alternative remains?

3 Complete the extract: 'Having an .... was what brought in the clients'. Which alternative does this paraphrase?

4 Complete Luke's statement about the magazine. 'The readership ....' Which alternative does this contradict?

5 Complete the two sentences. 'The biggest difference is that our function ....' 'What we offer now is a .... of the recruitment activity.' Which alternative does this paraphrase?

To try a real exam task, go to page 165.

Listening Paper Part 4: Exam practice

(2)(22) Questions 23–30

- You will hear a radio interview with Penny Yates, director of executive training programmes at Middlebrook Management College.
- For each question **23–30**, mark one letter (**A**, **B** or **C**) for the correct answer.
- You will hear the interview twice.
- You will have 45 seconds to read through the questions.
- Now listen, and mark A, B or C.

23 Penny believes managers like attending training courses mainly because
   A   they like being away from the workplace.
   B   they see them as a reward for effort.
   C   they acquire new skills.

24 According to Penny, companies today need help with
   A   short-term strategies.
   B   new technology.
   C   management skills.

25 Nowadays, Middlebrook Management College's clients are mainly
   A   small local companies.
   B   well-known international companies.
   C   large national companies.

26 Penny says training is best done by colleges because companies
   A   can develop the right skills in a short space of time.
   B   find it cheaper than other methods.
   C   don't have appropriate trainers in-house.

27 How long is a typical programme at Penny's college?
   A   six weeks
   B   four months
   C   three years

28 What does Penny say is the main benefit of training programmes?
   A   promoting new investment in the company.
   B   persuading good staff to stay with the company.
   C   providing new opportunities for staff within the company.

29 Penny believes her training programmes can help large companies
   A   deal with change.
   B   introduce new leadership styles.
   C   improve communication within the company.

30 Where does Penny prefer to deliver training courses?
   A   at a convenient hotel
   B   at a conference centre
   C   at a client's office

Writing Paper Part 1: Exam skills

Writing Part 1 consists of:

- one short text of 30–40 words written to someone within the same company
- three key points which you must include.

You practised similar skills in Unit 2 (page 17), Unit 4 (page 24) and Unit 6 (page 35).

This part of the exam tests your ability to:

- cover all three key points in a short text
- use correct register (formal or informal)
- use correct grammar and vocabulary.

> **Register**
> The register you use will depend on:
> - the subject you are writing about
> - who you are writing to
>
> For example, if you are writing an email to a senior manager, the register will be quite formal, but if you are writing to a close colleague, you may use quite an informal register.

Suggested exam technique

1 Read the instructions carefully. The first one or two sentences explain the situation. Then you are given the three points to include. Underline the most important words in the situation and the key points, including who you are writing to. You will probably need to use a semi-formal style.
2 Write one sentence for each point.
3 Choose a suitable greeting and sign-off.
4 Read your answer and add any link words if you feel it is necessary.
5 Check for any mistakes in grammar or spelling (for example, 's' missing from the ends of words).
6 Check the number of words.
7 Write your answer on the answer sheet.

Exercises

1 a **Read the following writing task and underline the key words in the situation and the key points to include in the note.**

> You asked your secretary to photocopy some handouts for a presentation you are going to give. However, you now find that you will need ten extra copies of each one.
> Write a **note** to your secretary:
> - thanking her for doing the copies
> - asking her to do the extra ones
> - telling her where to leave them.

b **Below are three possible answers to this task. Which one do you think is the best?**

A
> Dear Sally,
> Thanks for doing the copies for me. More people are coming so you must make 10 extra of each one. Leave them at reception.
> Anna

B
> Sally,
> Mr Stevens has just told me that more people are coming to the presentation so I'm going to need extra copies of all the handouts. Please could you make me another 10 of each one?
> Thanks,
> Anna

C
> Sally,
> Thanks for doing these photocopies. However, the training manager has just told me that there will be extra people at the presentation. Please could you do another 10 copies of each handout and leave them for me at reception?
> Anna

c **Now match one of the following examiner's comments (1–3) to one of the answers above.**

1 The style is suitable but it does not cover all the key points.
2 All three points are covered and the style is good.
3 All three points are covered but they are not linked and the style is too direct. It is also too short.

2 a **You work for the finance department of a company. A customer has telephoned to say that you have charged her too much for an order.**

> Write an **email** to your assistant:
> - giving the customer's name
> - explaining why the customer thinks the amount is wrong
> - asking her to check the invoice and get back to you.

b Here is an answer to the question but it does not cover all the points well. What is missing?

> **To:** Helen Smith
> **From:** Philip Day
> **Re:** order
>
> Helen,
>
> A customer rang today at 10 o'clock. She has received her DVDs but says that the invoice is wrong because it includes two that she didn't order. Please could you check this out?
>
> Thanks,
>
> Philip

c Now write an improved version of the above memo.

3 a You have arranged for a new brochure to be printed for your company. However, it will now arrive later than you planned.

> Write a **memo** to all staff
> - apologising for the late arrival
> - giving the reason for the delay
> - saying when the brochure will arrive.

b The following answer covers all the three key points but it is too long. Rewrite the memo to keep it within the 30–40 words limit.

> **MEMO**
>
> **To:** all staff
> **From:** ....
> **Date:** 30 March
> **Re:** new brochure
>
> I'm sorry but our new brochure hasn't arrived yet. I realise that this is very inconvenient but there have been technical problems at the printer's. It will hopefully be with us in two weeks' time. Please carry on using the old brochure for the moment, and tell customers about any changes.

4 a You work in the Human Resources department and are going to interview some candidates for a new sales post. The best of the candidates has just emailed you to say he is no longer interested in the post.

> Write an email to the sales manager:
> - saying which candidate has withdrawn
> - explaining why he is no longer interested
> - suggesting a meeting time to discuss the remaining applications

b It is important to read your answer to check for errors. Look at the following answer and check it for missing 's' on the ends of words. You need to add 's' in two places.

> **To:** John Barrow
> **From:** Janice Jacobi
> **Re:** candidates
>
> Hi John
>
> Simon Dale, the best of our candidate, has emailed to withdraw his aplication. Unfortunatly he has eccepted a post elsewhere. Please could we meet at nine tomorrow to look again at the rest of the application?
>
> Janice

c Read the answer again, focussing on the spelling. Find and correct three spelling mistakes.

To try a real exam task, go to page 168.

Writing Paper Part 1: Exam practice

Question 46

- You are having problems with some equipment in your department.
- Write an **email** to the Finance Manager of your company:
  - describing the problems you are having
  - asking to buy new equipment
  - telling him how much this will cost.
- **Write between 30–40 words.**
- **Write on your Answer Sheet.**

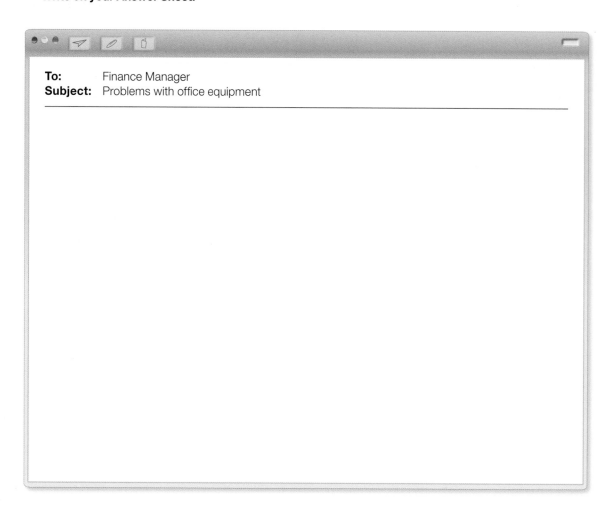

To: Finance Manager
Subject: Problems with office equipment

Writing Paper Part 2: Exam skills

Part 2 consists of:

- one short text such as part of a business letter. You must write a reply of 60–80 words.
- four key points which you must include.

You practised similar skills in Unit 12 (page 61), Unit 14 (page 71), Unit 16 (page 79) and Units 20, 21 and 23 (pages 96, 103 and 109).

This part of the exam tests your ability to:

- read and understand the purpose of a short text
- write a reply in the correct register which achieves your purpose
- use correct grammar and vocabulary.

Suggested exam technique

1 Read the text and the four key points carefully. Underline the most important words and phrases.
2 Write one sentence for each key point.
3 Add linking words and phrases, any extra information, and a suitable greeting, beginning and ending.
4 Read your answer through, thinking about the person who will read it. Will it have the right effect on the reader?
5 Check for any mistakes in grammar and spelling.
6 Check the number of words.
7 Write your answer on the answer sheet.

Exercises

1 a **Read the following part of a letter from Mr Steele, head of the business studies department in a college in your area. Underline the important words.**

> We have a large business studies department for students who are planning to work in companies such as yours. We are currently putting together a programme of talks by visiting speakers. We would like to ask if you would be willing to come and give a talk to the students on some aspect of your company before the end of the summer term, preferably on a Friday afternoon.

  b **Now read the task below.**

> Write a **letter** to Mr Steele
> - agreeing to give a talk
> - giving the subject of the talk
> - asking how long the talk should be
> - suggesting a possible date.

c **Put together the following phrases to make four complete sentences.**

> please could you tell me
> to come and give a talk at your college
> is a possible date for me
> I would like to outline
> I would be happy
> how long the talk should be?
> our company's product range and main markets
> Friday 16 April

d **Now match each of the sentences with one of the four key points in the task box in Exercise 1b.**

e **Study the following phrases and sentences.**

> Yours sincerely
> I look forward to hearing from you
> Thank you for your letter of 12 February
> Dear Mr Steele
> Please let me know if this date would be suitable.

f **Write the letter using the phrases and sentences from Exercises c and e.**

2 a **Read this online advertisement from a company which deals in second-hand equipment.**

> ## DELFORD EQUIPMENT
>
> ### We buy and sell second-hand equipment.
>
> With our good staff and good business knowledge, we aim to provide you with the best service and the most suitable equipment for your needs.
>
> Following the cost-reduction programme at Bolton Catering, we have recently acquired a range of equipment for the food and catering industry. Contact us for further details on www.delfordequip.com.

b **Read the task below and underline the most important points.**

> Write an **email** to Delford Equipment.
> - informing them what kind of business you own
> - saying what kind of equipment you are interested in
> - requesting a list of items in stock
> - asking about the guarantee.
>
> **Write 60–80 words.**

c   Read the following answer, then answer the questions.

> Dear Sir,
>
> I am writing with regard to your advertisement for food and catering equipment. I am one of the owners of a chain of juice bars. As we are currently expanding, we would be interested in purchasing a number of items of bar equipment, especially juicers and toasters. Please could you tell me how long the guarantee lasts on any purchase?
>
> I look forward to hearing from you.
>
> Yours faithfully,
>
> Ken May

1   Which phrase does the letter use to introduce the subject?
2   Which phrase is used to ask for information?
3   Which phrase is used to finish (and say you expect a reply)?

d   Although the letter is written in a suitable style, it would not get the maximum marks in the exam because not all the four points in the task are covered. Which one is missing?

e   Rewrite the letter so that it covers all four key points. To do this, you will have to make some of the other parts in the letter shorter.

3 a   Read the extract from a letter from Matthew Diskin, informing you that you have won an award.

> We are delighted to inform you that your company has won the award for Employer of the Year. We would like to invite you to a reception at 9pm on Friday 18 May at the Eldorado Hotel to receive the award.
>
> It is normal for all winners of this award to write a short article for our journal giving details of your company's human resources policy. Please could you let us know if you would be willing to contribute?

b   Read the task below and underline the important points.

> Write a letter to Matthew Diskin
> • accepting the invitation
> • requesting directions to the hotel
> • asking if other employees can attend
> • enquiring about the length of the article

c   Read the following answer to the task.

> Dear Mr Diskin,
>
> Many thanks for your letter with the news about the award. I will be delighted to attending the reception and would be greatful if you could give me some directions to the hotel. Please could you also told me if other employees can to attend?
>
> I would be happy to write a short article for your journal but I would like to now approximatly how long it should be.
>
> Yours sincerly,
>
> Martina Berezin

d   Read the answer again. Find and correct four wrong spellings.

e   Read the letter a third time. Find and correct three wrong verb forms.

To try a real exam task, go to page 171.

Writing Paper Part 2: Exam practice

Question 47

- Read this part of a letter from Martin Holmes, a university student.

> I am 23 years old and am studying business administration at university. As part of my course, I have to do three months' work experience this year. I would very much like to do this in your company. Please could you let me know if this would be possible and, if so, what kind of temporary work I might be able to do for you?

- Write a letter to Martin Holmes:
  - informing him when work experience is available in your company
  - giving details of the work experience you could offer to him
  - mentioning one skill that he will need to do this work
  - suggesting a date for an interview.

- **Write 60–80 words.**
- **Write on your Answer Sheet. Do not include any postal addresses.**

Dear Martin Holmes,

Speaking Paper Part 1: Exam skills

The speaking test takes about twelve minutes to complete. You are usually examined in pairs by two examiners. Only one examiner talks to the candidates.

In the test you are given marks for:

- **grammar and vocabulary.** You need to show that you have a good range of vocabulary and can use correct grammar. However, occasional small mistakes will not affect your mark.
- **discourse management.** You need to show that you can speak in a logical way about the subject and to speak for the right amount of time.
- **pronunciation.**
- **interactive communication.** You need to show that you can listen to the examiner and to your partner and give suitable answers.

In Part 1:

- the interviewer asks you general questions about yourself, your work, your free time, etc.
- the interviewer asks you questions on a business topic.

This part of the test takes about two minutes.

You practised similar skills in Unit 1 (page 12) and Unit 4 (page 25).

This part of the exam tests your ability:

- to talk about yourself
- talk about preferences
- agree
- disagree.

Suggested exam technique

1 Before you go into the exam make sure that you can answer questions about yourself and your job.
2 Don't answer the questions with just one or two words. Add reasons or an example.
3 Smile at the examiner, make eye contact and look confident.

Exercises

1 a Read these examples of possible test questions. Unfortunately, this candidate does not say very much!

Examiner	**Where are you from?**
Candidate	1 Turkey.
Examiner	**What work do you do?**
Candidate	2 I'm an accountant.
Examiner	**What do you like about your job?**
Candidate	3 My colleagues are nice.

Examiner	**Now I'm going to ask some questions about your place of work. Do you have a comfortable office at work?**
Candidate	4 Yes.
Examiner	**Is it important for you to have your own office?**
Candidate	5 Yes. It's important.
Examiner	**And would you like to have a bigger office?**
Candidate	6 Not really.

The candidate could gain a higher mark by adding a reason or an extra piece of information to these answers and saying more. This is more interesting for the examiner too!

b Below you will find some more information and ideas which the candidate could use (a–f). Match each one with one of the answers above to make longer answers.

a I work for a clothing firm in Istanbul.
b I've got several good friends among them.
c If you don't have your own office, people can interrupt you all the time. It can be difficult to concentrate.
d I was born in Ankara but now I live in Istanbul.
e There's plenty of space for all my files already.
f It's very light with nice furniture.

c (2)(23) Listen to the examiner's questions and answer them. Avoid answers of just one or two words. (If you are not yet working, answer about the place where you study.)

d Work in pairs. Take it turns to be the examiner and the candidate for the following questions.

Now I'm going to ask you some questions about telephoning.
- how important is it for you to have a mobile phone?
- what are the advantages of using text messages instead of speaking to people?
- are there any situations when it's better to talk to people face to face instead of telephoning?

Now I'm going to ask you some questions about foreign languages.
- is it important for business people to speak a foreign language?
- apart from English, which language is the most important in your area of work?
- do you think companies should give language training to their staff?

Speaking Paper Part 2: Exam skills

In Part 2:

- You are given a page with two topics printed on it. The topics consist of a question beginning *What is important ...?* followed by three alternatives. You must talk for about one minute on one of the topics.
- You must also listen to your partner's talk and briefly answer his or her *What is important ...?* question.

You practised similar skills in Unit 16 on page 79.

This part of the exam tests your ability to:

- speak for a longer time, as you might have to do in a business meeting or when giving a short presentation
- organise your ideas clearly and keep to the topic.

Interview nerves

It is natural to feel a little nervous about this part of the speaking test. Tell yourself:

- You have something interesting and important to say and the examiner wants to hear your ideas.
- He/she would be equally nervous is he/she had to give a talk in your language!
- Above all **keep speaking**. If you can't think of something to say, take a breath and start again. Don't worry if you repeat something you have already said.

Suggested exam technique

A You have **one minute** to prepare. Use it to:
1 Choose the topic which is easier for you.
2 Think about the three points and why they are important. Decide which one or two are the most important.
3 Think about examples you can give for the points you have chosen. Personal examples make the talk more interesting.
4 Note down some key words and ideas for each alternative to help you remember and organise your talk.

B When speaking:
1 Use your notes but look at the examiner.
2 Start by saying which question you have chosen.
3 Use linking words and phrases like *firstly, because, for example*. This will make your talk easier to follow.
4 Watch the time and try to finish with a short concluding sentence.
5 Keep speaking for the minute. If you run out of ideas, take a breath and begin again, even if you are repeating an idea you have talked about before.

Exercises

1 a **Look at the following question.**

What is important when giving a presentation?
- Using visuals
- Giving handouts
- Allowing time for audience questions

Below you will find an example of a talk that a candidate might give on this topic. Write the best linking word or phrase from the box in each gap.

also   because   but   firstly   for example
like   secondly   so   to conclude   this means that

Well, I've decided to talk about what is important when giving a presentation. **1** ...., I think it's important to use visuals like PowerPoint slides or things written on a flip chart **2** .... it's easier for the audience to concentrate when they have something to look at. Of course, there are some things which you can explain more clearly if you use visuals. **3** .... if you are talking about figures, you really need to show them to your audience on a graph of some kind.

4 ...., I think it's very important to give the people who are listening time to ask you questions at the end. **5** .... you can explain something to them again if it wasn't clear the first time. It **6** .... means that the audience can find out more about any part of the talk which interested them.

People usually give handouts, **7** .... copies of the PowerPoint slides, to the audience. This is nice **8** .... I'm not sure it's essential. People often prefer to make their own notes. I sometimes wonder if many people look at the handouts again after the talk. **9** ...., I think the most important things are using visuals and allowing the audience to ask questions at the end.

---

b **2 24 Now listen to the talk and check your answers. (More than one answer may be possible.)**

2 a When planning your talk, you do not have time to write full sentences. Just write down some key words and phrases so you do not forget your ideas when you are talking.

Look at the questions below. Match each of the notes to one of the bullet points.

1

> **What is important when meeting a new customer?**
> - Your knowledge of the product
> - Personal appearance
> - Meeting the customer on time

a people judge by appearances
b reason for meeting customer!
c being late = disrespectful
d gives impression of being organised
e first impressions important
f smart appearance = customer trusts you
g not knowing all the facts looks unprofessional/foolish
h customer can't decide without knowing facts
i customer may not be free later

2

> **What is important when employing a personal assistant?**
> - experience
> - IT skills
> - politeness

a always necessary today!
b needs to give good impression to visitors/clients
c will settle in more quickly
d less need for training
e need to type up documents, etc.
f part of good communication
g will be more aware of office systems
h business is lost through rudeness!
i needs to use office software

b Work in pairs. Decide in each case which is the least important of the three points.

c Choose one of the topics each and give your talk. Use the ideas in the notes in Exercise 2a, or add your own ideas if you prefer.

3 Work in pairs. Choose one of the topics below and take a minute to plan and make some notes. Then give your talk to your partner. Your partner should listen and make any suggestions for ideas you could add at the end.

> **What is important when attending a job interview?**
> - arriving on time
> - body language
> - enthusiasm about the job

> **What is important when choosing a supplier?**
> - location
> - delivery charges
> - reliability

To try a real exam task, go to page 175.

Speaking Paper Part 2: Exam practice

Task Card: Candidate's Copy

A: What is important when ...?

Deciding on a new product
- Demand from customers
- Ease of production
- Competition

Task Card: Examiner's Copy

A: What is important when ...?

Deciding on a new product
- Demand from customers
- Ease of production
- Competition

Is the **demand from customers** the most important thing to consider? (Why?/Why not?)

How important is it to consider **the ease of production**? (Why?/Why not?)

How important is the **competition**? (Why?/Why not?)

Task Card: Candidate's Copy

B: What is important when ...?

Planning a business meeting
- Venue
- Participants
- Agenda

Task Card: Examiner's Copy

B: What is important when ...?

Planning a business meeting
- Venue
- Participants
- Agenda

Is **the venue** the most important thing to consider? (Why?/Why not?)

Is it important to consider **all the participants**? (Why?/Why not?)

How important is it to consider the **agenda**? (Why?/Why not?)

Speaking Paper Part 3: Exam skills

In Part 3:
- The examiner describes a situation.
- You are given some suggestions for that situation, either pictures or notes. You must talk with your partner and decide together which would be best. You may be asked to choose one or more than one.
- The examiner will ask further questions after candidates have discussed the task.

You practised similar skills in Unit 14 (page 70), Unit 15 (page 74) and Unit 22 (page 105).

This part of the exam tests your ability to:
- give opinions
- agree
- disagree
- listen and respond to your partner.

Taking turns to speak

In this part of the speaking test, it is important not to take over the conversation. When you have said something, ask your partner what he/she thinks. Say things like: *What about you?* or *What do you think?* If your partner is speaking too much, interrupt politely by saying *Yes, but …* (if you disagree) or *Yes, and …* (if you agree).

Suggested exam technique

1 You have about thirty seconds to look at the suggestions before you begin. Use this time to think about the different ideas and the advantages or disadvantages of each one.
2 Begin by offering an opinion, and ask your partner if they agree.
3 Make sure you discuss all or most of the suggestions. If you are spending a long time on one, introduce another and ask your partner's opinion.
4 Watch the time and try to reach an agreement at the end of two minutes.
5 Don't let your partner do all the talking, but equally, don't do all the talking yourself. Listen to your partner's ideas and respond. Usually you should avoid interrupting your partner.

Exercises

1 Read the phrases (1–9) which you could use in this part of the test. Match each one with the correct purpose in the table below the phrases.

1	What do you think about ….?	2	How about….?
3	I think you're right.	4	I think…

5	Yes, that's true.	6	But don't you think…?
7	I'm not sure I agree.	8	My feeling is…
9	Maybe, but….		

Ask your partner's opinion	
Give your opinion	
Agree with your partner	
Disagree with your partner	
Persuade your partner	

2 a Work in pairs. Read the situation and the list of advertising media below. Decide which method of advertising to use in this situation.

You need to recruit a new member of staff to work as a marketing executive. Look at the following ways of advertising the post and decide which one would be the best.

- newspaper
- business magazine
- internet site
- recruitment agency

b Read the following conversation. Choose a phrase from Exercise 1 to put in each gap.

A 1 .... the best place to advertise is in a business magazine. If it's something that business people buy, there is more chance that the right sort of person will see it. It's probably cheaper than advertising in a national newspaper too.

B 2 .... I'm not sure how many people read business magazines. 3 .... the Internet? A lot of people look for jobs online these days.

A 4 .... Websites reach a lot of people as well. We might even get candidates from other countries.

B 5 .... using a recruitment agency?

A No, I don't think that's the best way. I'm not sure the best people usually go to agencies.

B It depends on the post, but 6 .... It's not a good idea for a post like this. So it's the Internet then?

A Yes, I think so.

c (2) 25 Now listen and compare your answers with the conversation on the recording.

To try a real exam task, go to page 177.

Speaking Paper Part 3: Exam practice

Collaborative task and discussion (about 5 minutes for 2 candidates; about 7 minutes for 3 candidates)

Task Card: Examiner's Copy

Now, in this part of the test you are going to talk about something together.

I'm going to describe a situation.

Your company is going to launch a new product. Talk together about what is important when advertising a new product and decide which three types of advertisement are most important.

Here are some ideas to help you.
- Newspapers
- Magazines
- Online
- Outdoor
- Television
- Radio
- Brochures

I'll describe the situation again.

Your company is going to launch a new product. Talk together about what is important when advertising a new product and decide which three types of advertisement are most important.

Now talk together. Please speak so that we can hear you.

*[Allow the candidates about * 2 minutes to complete the task without intervention. Prompt only if absolutely necessary.]*

*3 minutes [for 3 candidates]

[Select one or more of the following questions as appropriate, to redress any imbalance between candidates in Part 3, or to extend the discussion.]

Thank you. That is the end of the speaking test.

Answer key

UNIT 1

Getting started

2 Rosie   3 Alex   4 Gamal   5 Sveta   6 Daniel   7 John Paul
8 Marcelo   9 Jan   10 Ben

Company departments

Vocabulary

2 b   3 g   4 a   5 c   6 e

Personal assistants

Listening

2 taking phone calls, answering letters, taking notes in meetings, prioritising appointments, welcoming visitors, looking up information
3 1 do you do   2 does that involve   3 enjoy   4 What about
4 2 organised   3 stressful   4 friendly, helpful   5 reliable

Changing Places

Reading

2 Donald Eisner: paragraphs 2 and 4
  Alex Jennings: paragraphs 3 and 4
3 2 True   3 False   4 True   5 False   6 True   7 False   8 True

Grammar workshop

Present simple and present continuous

1 Present simple: usually, always, every month, each year, generally, never, often, sometimes, twice a month
  Present continuous: now, at the moment, currently, this month, today, this week
3 2 Our staff ~~are not understanding~~ our financial position. *do not understand*
  3 They are advertising for a new sales executive at the moment.
  4 I can't employ him because ~~he's having no~~ references. *he has no / doesn't have any*
  5 Don't disturb Richard just now because he's doing the payroll.
  6 ~~I'm thinking~~ this new system is a big mistake. *I think*
  7 I'm thinking of going on holiday next week.
  8 Some people ~~are still preferring~~ to use a flipchart instead of PowerPoint. *still prefer*
4 *think*. As a state verb 'I think' means 'this is my opinion' (like 'believe'). As an action verb, 'I am thinking' means 'I am using my mind' or (as here) 'I am planning'.

UNIT 2

Getting started

2 2 print   3 cut   4 attach   5 save   6 copy   7 highlight
3 2 download   3 log on   4 restart   5 crash   6 drag   7 post   8 upload

Digital media

Reading

3 2 Dave Carroll   3 Paul Patterson   4 Adam Brimo   5 United Airlines
4 2 B   3 C   4 B

Emails

Vocabulary

1 2 d   3 a   4 b   5 c   6 f
2 a word: com, org, biz, co, net
  separate letters: uk, us, ac
3 2 S   3 D   4 S   5 D   6 S   7 D   8 D
4 2 E   3 L   4 probably E (but a letter could be forwarded through the post)   5 E   6 B   7 E   8 E   9 E   10 B

Writing

1 2 c   3 f   4 a   5 j   6 h   7 e   8 d   9 g   10 b
2 Suggested answers:

Beginnings	Endings
2 Dear John	2 Kind regards
3 John	3 Best wishes
4 Hello John	4 All the best
5 Hi John	5 Bye for now

3 Suggested answers:

Requests:	Apologies:
1 I would be grateful if you could	1 We would like to offer our sincere apologies for
2 Please could you	2 Please accept our apologies for
3 Could you	3 We are sorry about
4 Can you	4 Sorry about

4

Formal	Informal
Dear Mr Morris, I would like to arrange a meeting to discuss the schedule for training day My diary is very full for next week but perhaps you could suggest a suitable time for the week after Looking forward to your reply Susan Jackson	Hi Andy, Can we get together sometime to talk about the schedule for training day I'm pretty booked up next week but I could manage the week after. let me know Sue

5 Sample answer:
Dear James

I'm sorry but I can't now meet at 10 o'clock tomorrow. My manger is meeting a possible new client and wants me to attend too. Could you make Thursday afternoon instead?

Yours

Martin

UNIT 3

Getting started

1b; Samsung   2f; Toyota   3a; Google   4d; Sony   5c; Ford
6e; Virgin

Haier

Reading

1 2 e   3 g   4 b   5 d   6 a   7 f
3 2 enterprise   3 keen   4 substandard   5 smash   6 broadened   7 acquired
4 2 No, they didn't decide to carry them. It was Mr Zhang's decision.
  3 No, they didn't smash them accidentally / they smashed them on purpose.
  4 No, they didn't only sell fridges / they also sold other electrical goods.
  5 No, they didn't. Haier produced more fridges than Whirlpool.

Grammar workshop 1

Past simple

1 1 and 3 are correct

2 1 It just adds 'd' e.g. *realised*.
  2 The 'y' changes to 'i' before -ed e.g. *carried*
  3 The final consonant doubles e.g. *planned*
  4 The final consonant does not double e.g. *broadened*

3 began, became, told, grew, overtook

4 2 I ~~heared~~ the news about the merger yesterday. heard
  3 I think we ~~payed~~ too much for that new equipment. paid
  4 He ~~red~~ business studies at university. read
  5 He ~~toke~~ a taxi across town to vist the factory. took
  6 He ~~choosed~~ not to go into the family business. chose

5 Suggested answers:
  2 What did it make?
  3 How much money did the founder have?
  4 How many people did it employ?
  5 What were their first electrical products?
  6 When did they acquire an air conditioning company?

Growing pains

Listening

1 Headline A

3 2 T 3 F 4 F 5 T 6 F

4 2 market research 3 profitable 4 special

Speaking

2 Suggested answer: B

Business ideas

Reading

2 A 3 B 1 C 2

3 2 founder 3 empire 4 stuck 5 combine

Grammar workshop 2

Past continuous

1 1 B 2 A 3 C

2 when, while

3 2 was pushing 3 was wearing 4 rang 5 needed 6 had
  7 hit 8 launched

UNIT 4

Vocabulary

1 2 fix a time 3 keep up with the times 4 take on challenges
  5 plan a strategy

2 1 standard procedures 2 serious risk
  follow standard procedures **take** a serious risk

3 1 reduce: the risk, costs, prices
  2 set up: a system, a business, a meeting
  3 build up: a good relationship, your confidence, a business
  4 meet: your needs, a deadline
  5 cut: costs, prices

4 2 closely 3 build up 4 effective 5 take on 6 run 7 wide
  8 heavily 9 reduce 10 set up

5 Suggested collocations: manage a system, deal with clients, bring benefits, promote growth, improve local markets, provide support

6 2 make 3 doing 4 have 5 made 6 do 7 make

Describing changes

Listening

1 Correct order: the company culture, possibilities for promotion, staff benefits

2 Company culture:
When he joined: friendly, supportive, they looked after customers
Now: focussed on targets
Possibilities for promotion:
When he joined: less competition
Now: people are more competitive, they don't trust each other
Staff benefits:
When he joined: smaller bonuses
Now: good insurance package, long holidays, generous bonuses

Writing

2 1; 2 d 3; 4 b 5 c; a
Sample answer:
The management are planning to make some changes to our working hours. I would like to set up a meeting to discuss this on Tuesday at 12.30. I think we need to make our feelings about this clear as soon as possible.

Speaking

Question A	Question B
What's the name of your company?	Who do you work for?
What's your job?	What do you do?
What do you hope to do in the future?	What are your plans for the future?
What time do you start and finish work?	What are your working hours?
What exactly do you do?	What does your job involve?

Questions which do not form a pair: What are you studying? What do you enjoy about your job/studies? Do you do many different things in your work/studies? Do you travel much in your job?

3 2 d 3 f 4 c 5 b 6 a

GRAMMAR WORKSHOP 1

Present simple and present continuous

1 2 are / 're having 3 am / 'm working 4 need 5 are getting
  6 finds 7 tell 8 expect 9 am / 'm looking

2 2 have 3 are having 4 have 5 have 6 are all having
  7 have 8 is having

Position of time phrases

2 She is never in the office on Mondays.

3 They often promote people from within the company.

4 We have a shareholders meeting twice a year.

5 My PA doesn't usually deal with matters like this.

6 He comes to the board meeting every week.

7 They never use artificial flavourings in their products.

8 Those suppliers aren't always very reliable.

9 The hotel is often fully booked in July.

10 We are currently reviewing a number of our policies.

Past simple and past continuous

1 Suggested answers:
  2 Where did he set up his first clothing business?
  3 When did they begin producing the trousers/ new design? When did the two men go into partnership?
  4 When did they stop using the name overalls? / When did they start calling the trousers 'jeans'?
  5 When did they make their first TV commercial?
  6 Why did the company grow so rapidly?

2 2 went, was sitting 3 were wearing, knew 4 was living, met
  5 was writing, froze 6 didn't/did not send, wasn't/was not working

3 2 I am writing with regard to your advertisement which I ~~was reading~~ in *Business Chronicle*. *read*
  3 The refreshments arrived while he was giving the presentation. CORRECT
  4 I couldn't print the document because the printer ~~was falling~~ on the floor. *fell*
  5 They were locking up when the manager phoned to say she was still in the building. CORRECT
  6 I ~~was working~~ in the same department for six years so after that I was ready for a change. *worked*
4 2 I am ~~writting~~ to confirm the conference room booking. *writing*
  3 We stopped making that model two years ago. CORRECT
  4 Profits ~~droped~~ in the second half of the year. *dropped*
  5 Two new clients are ~~comming~~ this afternoon. *coming*
  6 You can get the information by ~~refering~~ to the website. *referring*
  7 Our company is ~~planing~~ to make a video. *planning*
  8 They delivered the order this morning. CORRECT

UNIT 5

Getting started
2 j 3 d 4 k 5 f 6 h 7 g 8 i 9 a 10 e 11 b

Describing objects
Vocabulary
2 2 a 3 h 4 e 5 c 6 f 7 d 8 g
3

Materials		Shape adjectives	
metal	paper	circular	square
plastic	glass	rectangular	
steel	rubber		

Dimensions
Listening
1 Item one no, item two probably yes.
2 1 width 2 depth 3 height 4 length
3 1 180 cm 2 40 cm 3 112 cm 4 320 cm
4 2 480, 500 3 black 4 £96 5 19 July

Problems with equipment
Vocabulary
1 2 a 3 c 4 b 5 e

Reading
1 a 3 b 4 c 2, 6
2 2 Murat Yuzgun 3 projector 4 seminar room 2 5 bulb needs changing 6 Richard Parker 7 10 April

The gizmo game
Listening
2 2;3 pliers, scissors (in either order) 4 handles 5 ring 6 round
3 2 c 3 f 4 a 5 d 6 e
4 Speaker 1: to make holes in belts and leather
  Speaker 2: to hold pieces of metal in place when building aeroplanes
  Speaker 3: to make cuts in wood, especially on violins
5 Speaker 2 is telling the truth.

UNIT 6

Getting started
1 1 life cycle 2 lifespan

2 2 cut 3 put 4 removed 5 shredded 6 recycled 7 assembled 8 distributed 9 purchased 10 thrown away 11 dismantled
3 2 F 3 F 4 T

Grammar workshop
The passive
2

The original company S **Karhu skis** _S__ They ____S__ **The picture of a bear_S_**	still produces V **are still produced** _V__ use __V___ **is used __V__**	Karhu skis. O **by the original company.** _O__ the picture of a bear _O__	on their products.

3 1 the verb *be*, past participle 2 *by*
4 1 is tested 2 are used 3 are taken
5 2 are built 3 is tested 4 are sold 5 are exported 6 are bought
6 2 Staff do not feel that they are ~~payed~~ enough. *paid*
  3 Meetings are always ~~hold~~ in the production department. *held*
  4 Invoices are always ~~send~~ with the order. *sent*
  5 Protective gloves are always worn in the workshop. CORRECT
  6 Some of the money is ~~spend~~ on staff travel. *spent*

Chanel No. 5
Vocabulary
2 are loaded / are put 3 are transported 4 are weighed 5 are put / are loaded 6 is added 7 are washed 8 are removed 9 is evaporated 10 is required

Listening
1 and **2** Check your answers against the transcript.

Outsourcing
Reading
3 a 2 b 3 c 4
4

Disadvantages of outsourcing to other companies in Sydney	suppliers not meeting deadlines
Disadvantages of in-house production	high staff costs difficulties with recruitment
Advantages of outsourcing to companies abroad	low staff costs access to new techniques

Short texts
Reading
1 1 Protective clothing **is** kept
  2 Counterfeit banknotes **are** believed
  3 candidates **are** given first interview, successful candidates **are** interviewed again
2 2 h 3 g 4 a 5 e 6 b

Writing
Sample answer:

Dear Bettina,
I'm sorry but I can't attend the training on Monday because I booked a week's annual leave to start that day. Could one of my colleagues take me through the new system when I return?
Yours,

UNIT 7

Grammar workshop
Modal verbs of obligation

1

Verb is used to say that	Example
1 an action is necessary (an obligation)	*have to / must*
2 an action is a good idea (advice)	*should*
3 an action is not a good idea (advice not to do something)	*shouldn't*
4 an action is possible	*can*
5 an action is not possible (because it is against the rules or for another reason)	*can't*
6 an action is not necessary (there is no obligation)	*don't have to*

2　2 have to　3 mustn't　4 not　5 can't　6 can't
3　2 should　3 must/have to　4 don't have to　5 mustn't
　　6 should　7 can/should
4　2 A　3 B　4 C　5 A

Selling overseas
Reading

1　legal issues: IP protection, patent, insurance, customs
　　marketing: packaging, price, label
　　overseas contacts: sales agent, distributor, embassy
　　transport: lorry/truck, ship, airfreight
2　marketing, overseas contacts, transport, legal issues
3　b 2　c not in the text　d 5　e 3　f 3　g 1　h 2

Telephoning
Listening 1

2 A　3 C　4 B

Chasing an order
Listening 2

2　2 ZS431　3 car paint A535　4 19 April　5 20 May
　　6 375　7 Macpherson

UNIT 8

Getting started

3　2 c　3 g　4 b

Marketing
Vocabulary

1　2 logo　3 slogan　4 campaign　5 market share
　　6 market leader　7 sponsor
2　2 f　3 a　4 d　5 b　6 e

Speaking

1　Coca-Cola
2　2 associated　3 support(s)　4 sponsor　5 logo　6 slogans

Singapore Airlines
Reading

1　2 and 4
2　1　strong brand management
　　2　no domestic flights
3　in order to
4　2 a　3 c　4 b
5　2 so　3 This means that　4 as a result

6　a 7　b 5　c 2, 6　d 3, 4
7　2 with　3 a　4 the　5 who　6 on　7 its

A promotional letter
Writing

2　exciting, great, fabulous, brilliant, brand
3　Sample answer:
　　To our customers,
　　We're writing to give you some news about our new product.
　　We're bringing out a new hands-free transmitter to help you
　　enjoy your iPod in the car. It's a compact, easy-to-use device and
　　it's available online or in all good computer stores from March
　　1st. It's a must-have for any iPod user. What's more, if you make
　　your purchase in March, you can enter our lottery to win a stylish
　　leather iPod case.
　　(adjectives: compact, easy-to-use)

GRAMMAR WORKSHOP 2

Passive forms

1　2　The invoices are kept in the filing cabinet.
　　3　Most of their products are sold over the Internet.
　　4　Their staff are taught basic accounting skills.
　　5　Staff are not / aren't allowed to smoke in here
2　7　Simsons may be acquired by an American company.
　　8　The purchase can't be authorised by the secretary.
　　9　Your CV should not / shouldn't be written by your friend.
　　10　These expenses must be met by your company.
3　2 is imported　3 agree　4 apologise　5 be held
　　6 concentrate　7 be reduced　8 is scheduled　9 explains
4　2　Payments are never sent by courier.
　　3　Meetings are always held in the boardroom.
　　4　Deliveries should never be left in the corridor.
　　5　Claim forms must always be signed by the manager.
　　6　Discounts are usually offered on large orders.

Modal verbs

1　2 don't have to　3 shouldn't　4 can　5 mustn't
　　6 don't have to　7 can't　8 should
2　2　I think we should ~~to have~~ at least a 10 per cent discount. *have*
　　3　The successful candidate must ~~has~~ good computer skills. *have*
　　4　Everyone at the conference ~~will must~~ wear a name badge. *must*
　　5　All staff have to have a parking permit. CORRECT
　　6　I am afraid the company cannot ~~sent~~ payment until next week
　　　　send
3　2 mustn't/can't　3 should　4 don't have to　5 can
　　6 can't/mustn't

because and *so*

2　I was off sick so I couldn't send you the information last week.
3　The sales manager is coming because he wants to check the
　　figures.
4　Because the service was so unsatisfactory, we do not intend to use
　　your company again.
5　Interviews are taking place in our usual room so we will have to
　　meet in room 10.

UNIT 9

A company visit
Listening

1 Hong Kong　2 14th　3 SQ341　4 7.30

Grammar workshop 1

Present continuous for future arrangements

1 1 's (not) arriving   2 's arriving   3 Are you (still) meeting
2 2 is not/isn't having   3 is/'s meeting   4 is/'s presenting
   5 is/'s visiting   6 is not/ isn't doing   7 is/'s flying

Making an appointment

Listening 1

1 Day: Thursday   Time: 2 o'clock
2 2 suit   3 manage   4 available   5 arranged   6 booked up
   7 do   8 make
3 2 C   3 C   4 A

Listening 2

2 A   3 A   4 A

Grammar workshop 2

will and going to future forms

1 a 3   b 1   c 4   d 2
2 2 am/'m going to type   3 will be   4 I'll call
3 1 decision made at the moment of speaking, a prediction based on
   an opinion
   2 a decision made before the moment of speaking
   3 an offer or request for instructions
4 2 C   3 B   4 B
5 2 I'll answer   3 Shall I make   4 will grow   5 I'll give
   6 I'm seeing

UNIT 10

Getting started

3 Suggested answers:
   Advantages of flying: quicker for long distances, more comfortable
   Advantages of travelling by train: usually cheaper, takes you to the
   city centre, more space to work

Air travel

Vocabulary

1 2 hold luggage   3 boarding card/pass   4 passport control
   5 departure lounge   6 duty free shop   7 information desk
3 2 a   3 f   4 c   5 b   6 e
4 Suggested collocations:
   1 catch a flight/plane   2 miss a flight/plane
   3 get off a plane/flight   4 board a plane/flight
   5 get on a plane/flight   6 pass through customs
   7 book a flight   8 swap seats   9 cancel a flight
   10 reschedule a flight   11 go through customs   12 reserve seats

Reading

2 C   3 B   4 B   5 A

Train travel

Reading

1 1 B   2 B   3 A
3 2 1 hour 20 minutes   3 1882   4 15 million   5 40 m   6 £99
   7 1986   8 50 km
5 1 However   2 whereas   3 despite
6 1 however   2 despite   3 although, despite and whereas
7 2 We will be happy to give the session at your premises but the
   maximum number of trainees must still be sixteen.
   3 That airline is usually rather expensive. However, the customer
   service is better.

4 The training day was very well organised although the breaks
   were too short.
5 Driving to work can be very stressful, whereas the train journey
   is much more relaxing. CORRECT
6 We hoped our TV advertisement would increase sales.
   However, the results have been disappointing.

Bicycle share schemes

Writing

3 Dear Ms Costa,
   Many thanks for your invitation to the roadshow. Mr Groves will
   be very happy to attend and give a short talk. Please could you let
   us know how long this should be.
   I can also confirm we have three employees who will take part in
   the race. However, all three are keen cyclists and so they would
   prefer to wear their own cycling clothes. We look forward to
   seeing you at the roadshow.
   Yours sincerely,

UNIT 11

Half holidays

Listening

1 1 a rush to finish everything before you go, difficult to switch off
      completely
   2 going away on holiday but taking work with you and keeping
      in contact with the office
2 2 far busier than   3 even worse   4 bigger problem than
   5 more relaxing   6 less stressful   7 much longer than

Grammar workshop 1

Comparatives

1 2 with 'more' before the adjective: more relaxing
   3 the y changes to i and then we add er: busier
   4 the last consonant doubles: bigger
   5 less   6 than   7 far, much, even   8 better, worse
2 2 tidier   3 more expensive   4 larger   5 hotter
   6 more important   7 further
3 2 longer   3 smaller   4 more flexible   5 further
   6 better   7 easier

Netflix

Reading

1 They have no policy. Staff can take as much holiday as they want,
   when they want.
2 2 monitor, track   3 assembly line   4 innovation
3 2 They work at home solving problems and answering emails.
   3 No one tracks their annual leave.
   4 It operates in the US and a number of other countries.
   5 According to the writer, it has become less important than in
      the past.

Grammar workshop 2

as … as structures

1 1 a   2 b
2 2 is not as fast as   3 is not as easy as
   4 are not as expensive as   5 doesn't … as early as
3 Suggested answers:
   2 as much as you want / like
   3 as much as we can / as much as possible
   4 as long as you want/like
   5 as close as we can / as close as possible
   6 as far as I can go

Offsite meetings
Reading
1 Suggested answers:
there are fewer interruptions, there are no office politics, it is easier to concentrate
2 1 They spent the four days in a small boat in the Arctic Circle.
2 They made key decisions about the group's structure.
3 2 A 3 C 4 B 5 B 6 A 7 C

UNIT 12
Getting started
2 b lecture c venue d delegates e plenary f floor
g case study h webinars

Choosing a venue for a conference
Listening
2 2 biggest 3 best 4 larger 5 biggest 6 smaller
7 least suitable 8 further

Grammar workshop
Superlatives
1 2 with *the most* before the adjective 3 the
4 the best, the worst 5 the least
2 Suggested answers:
Telepresent is the most expensive package.
Only Connect is the easiest package to use.
Roco Webinars is the most secure.
Telepresent has the highest speaker capacity.
Telepresent has the greatest number of features.
Roco Webinars is the cheapest package.
Roco Webinars is the most difficult to use.

A welcome speech
Listening
2 mobile phone app 3 West Room 4 main theatre
5 coffee shop 6 (digital) clock 7 Sales Talk

Feedback comments
Reading
2 A 3 B 4 B 5 A 6 B

grateful and *pleased*
Writing
2 2 grateful 3 pleased 4 X 5 grateful 6 X 7 grateful 8 X
3 Suggested answers:
4 (most) helpful, convenient,
5 useful, helpful, (more informally) great, nice
6 helpful, useful
5 1 I would be very grateful if you could
2 If possible we would prefer 3 Please could you tell me
6 Sample answer:
Dear Mr Kospanos
Many thanks for your email. I have now completed the booking form for 4 March. Please could you tell me what the catering arrangements are and if we need to fill in a separate form for this? If possible, we would prefer a buffet lunch.
I would be very grateful if you could suggest a time when we could come and view the centre, if possible at least one week before the event.
Yours sincerely

GRAMMAR WORKSHOP 3
Future forms
2 I'll call 3 I'm leaving 4 shall we 5 Are you going to ask
6 Shall I see 7 he's coming 8 will fall

Contrast words
1 2 Although 3 whereas 4 although 5 despite 6 whereas
7 Despite 8 However
2 2 We need a hotel with a good business centre ~~but~~ and if possible wifi access in the rooms. *but*
3 I am afraid ~~but~~ we cannot offer you a discount. *but*
4 Although the hotel prices are low now ~~but~~ they will start to go up next month. *but*
or: ~~Although~~ the hotel prices are low now but they will start to go up next month. *although*
5 I am sorry but I cannot agree to your request. CORRECT
6 She is a good manager ~~however~~ but she has little experience of this field. *however* **or**: She is a good manager. However, she has little experience of this field.
7 ~~Although~~ the plane left on time, despite the bad weather. *although*
8 Although the talk was interesting, ~~and~~ it didn't relate to my area of work. *and*

Comparatives and superlatives
1 2 cheaper 3 widest 4 greater 5 lighter 6 heaviest
7 more attractive 8 best
2 2 I was wondering if you could start the job a week ~~earlyer~~ than we planned. *earlier*
3 Of all the hotels the Marquis has the ~~bigest~~ conference room. *biggest*
4 Your desk is looking tidier than I ever remember. CORRECT
5 We need one large conference room and another ~~smaler~~ room. *smaller*
6 We need to find a fairer way of giving bonus payments. CORRECT
7 This is one of the ~~busyest~~ airports in the world. *busiest*

Text completion
1 2 the 3 and 4 takes/is 5 than 6 as 7 is 8 much / far
9 but 10 longer
        are
2 2 We ^ going to organise a training day next month.
        as
3 We must send in our report ^ soon as possible.
        for
4 I would be very grateful ^ your advice in this matter.
        to
5 We are pleased ^ confirm your booking for the conference centre.
6 You may have to leave some parts blank, but complete as much
        as
of the form ^ you can.
        could
7 I would be grateful if you ^ send me some information.
        it
8 I was looking forward to the talk but I found ^ disappointing
        to
9 Please complete the form in order ^ confirm your booking.

UNIT 13

The career doctor

Reading 1

2 2 B   3 A   4 C   5 C   6 A   7 C   8 A

Grammar workshop 1

Present perfect

1 1 a   2 d   3 c   4 b   5 d

2 *just/already/ever/never*: after the auxiliary verb *have*
   yet: this is usually put at the end of the sentence

3 2 have...met   3 have not/haven't told   4 has / 's...been
   5 sold out   6 have / 've forgotten   7 has / 's...read   8 has fallen

4 Suggested answers:
   2   Do you know Mr Miyasaki?
   3   He doesn't know the news.
   4   She doesn't know what New York is like / She isn't familiar
       with New York.
   5   We don't have that model.
   6   I don't know the telephone number.
   7   He knows the information in the sales report.
   8   The share price is lower than it was before.

Reading 2

3 2 field   3 hasty   4 turn out   5 concerned   6 settle in
   7 get on better

Grammar workshop 2

Present perfect and past simple

1 1 you've...worked   2 I worked...I had   3 I've felt   4 I left, told

2 Possible answers:
   1   before, for the last 5 years, since 2010
   2   already, just, recently
   3   last month, in 2010, three years ago
   4   as soon as I left school, last month, in 2010, three years ago,
       when I was eighteen
   5   yet
   6   before, recently

A career change

Listening

2 1 d   2 a   3 b   4 c

3 1   after university
   2   10 years
   3   travelling to lots of new places, meeting lots of people
   4   feeling lonely when away from home
   5   having to work intensively and get on with groups of new
       people

4 2   've learnt   3 has been   4 've realised   5 've wasted

5 1   past simple
   2   present perfect
   3   Exercise 3 is about the jobs he did before his current job,
       Exercise 4 is about the job he still does now

UNIT 14

Getting started

1 5 and 8 do not collocate

Promotional gifts

Reading

3 a, b, e, f

Grammar workshop 1

Countable and uncountable nouns

1

Countable (singular)	Countable (plural)	Uncountable
idea	items	time
survey	people	stuff
cover	documents	room
prize	consumables	rain
	goods	stationery
		food
		chocolate
		equipment
		glassware
		rubber

2 1   No singular form: consumables, goods.
       Irregular plural: people
   2   time (uncountable) = minutes and hours
       a time (countable) = an occasion
       room (uncountable) = space
       a room (countable) = a part of a building
       chocolate (uncountable) = the food or the drink
       a chocolate (countable) = a small sweet covered in chocolate

3 2 some   3 a   4 some   5 some   6 an   7 a   8 some

4 2   Members of staff will be happy to answer your questions and to
       give ~~advices~~ advice on products.
   3   I am afraid that your ideas were not accepted by the board.
       CORRECT
   4   Please can you confirm that the ~~equipments~~ equipment we
       requested ~~are~~ is available.
   5   All electrical devices need to be checked regularly. CORRECT
   6   The company spent a lot of money on ~~travels~~ travel last year.
   7   We have managed to save the business but I'm afraid the ~~works~~
       ~~have~~ work has only just begun.
   8   We can provide ~~transports~~ transport to and from the airport.
   9   What are your responsibilities in the new job? CORRECT
   10 It's only a weekend trip so I don't need to take ~~many~~ much
       luggage.

Cultural awareness

Listening

2 a

3 a: agrees because it needs to be meaningful/ special
   b: disagrees because it could be embarrassing if the host feels they
      have to give something expensive back
   c: disagrees because it confuses showing someone you value the
      relationship with wanting them to advertise for you
   d: disagrees because it could be rude if other people in the
      company don't receive anything
   e: disagrees because presents often have to reflect the person's
      rank in the company

4 2 July (Ochugen)   3 department store   4 fruit   5 white paper
   6 in private   7 both hands   8 death

Grammar workshop 2

Articles

1 2 a, extract b   3 the, extract f   4 the, extract c   5 no article,
   extract e   6 no article, extract a

2 2 a   3 no article   4 a   5 an   6 no article   7 the
   8 no article   9 no article   10 a   11 no article   12 the
   13 the   14 no article   15 no article

Saying thank you

Writing

2 2 h 3 c 4 f 5 e 6 i 7 d 8 g 9 a

UNIT 15

Team-building

Reading

1 b 4 c 5 d 1 e 2

2 2 10 minutes, 15 seconds 3 50 4 3 hours 5 bells, shakers
6 hats and protective clothing 7 Scheuble Hotel
8 Scandinavia 9 plastic walls and trees 10 70

3 b 3, 4 c 5 d 1

4 1 break the ice 2 break down barriers (in either order)

Suffixes

Vocabulary

1 N: tion, ity, ment
A: ive, ous, ful, al, y

3 2 improvement 3 equipment 4 achievement 5 instruction
6 familiarity 7 availability
Added to verbs: -tion, -ment
Added to adjectives: -ity

4 2 successful 3 famous 4 musical 5 wonderful
6 mysterious 7 messy 8 practical 9 protective
10 interactive 11 creative 12 co-operative
Added to nouns: -ful, -al, -ous, -y
Added to verbs: -ive

Teamwork

Listening

2 1 F 2 F 3 F 4 T 5 F

3 Check your answers against the transcript.

Kaizen

Reading

1 paragraph 1: d
paragraph 7: c

3 a 3 b 5 c 7 d 1 e 2 f 6 g 4

4 ii e iii a iv b v c

UNIT 16

Global HR management

Reading

1 1 3, 4 2 5 3 2

2 2 C 3 B 4 A 5 C 6 C 7 A 8 A

Grammar workshop

Quantity expressions

1

For countable nouns	For uncountable nouns	For both
not many a few a large number of several	not much a little how much	a lot of lots of

2 2 many 3 how much 4 much 5 a little 6 how many
7 several

3 2 We have invested ~~much~~ money in this market. *a lot of / a great deal of*
3 There hasn't been much interest in the new position. CORRECT
4 He has ~~much~~ experience in this area. *a lot of /lots of / a great deal of*
5 Do you have many Chinese customers? CORRECT
6 There isn't much space to store the new furniture. CORRECT
7 There are ~~many~~ spare copies of the form in that cupboard. *a lot of / lots of / a great many*
8 Their employees need ~~much~~ training in health and safety procedures *a lot of /lots of / a great deal of*

International teams

Listening

3 2 f 3 a 4 b

Global management

Vocabulary

2 B 3 D 4 A 5 B 6 D 7 A 8 C

Requesting information

Writing

3 1 c, f 2 a, d 3 e, h 4 b, g

4 Sample answer:
Dear Mr Leman,
We are a Swedish company who makes novelty furniture. We are interested in opening up a branch in the USA as we already have a number of regular American customers. Please could you tell me what kind of help your organisation can provide for this project? I would also be grateful if you could give me contact details for any of your partners who are located in Sweden.
I look forward to hearing from you.
Yours sincerely,

GRAMMAR WORKSHOP 4

Present perfect and past simple

1 2 have / 've just finished 3 have...been 4 moved 5 had to
6 were not / weren't 7 arrived 8 have not / haven't unpacked

2 2 launched 3 have / 've...started 4 have not / haven't finished
5 have / 've sent 6 has been 7 have / 've had 8 saw
9 have / 've cost 10 did, started

a/an and *some*

2 some 3 a 4 some 5 some 6 a 7 some 8 a 9 some
10 some

Articles

2 an 3 no article 4 no article 5 the 6 the
7 no article 8 a 9 the 10 the 11 The 12 the

Quantity expressions

2 A 3 C 4 A 5 B 6 B

Word types

1 2 The sales figures showed a small ~~improving~~ last month. *improvement*
3 We have made a few changes to the seminar programme. CORRECT
4 Ms Baker is a new member of our ~~designing~~ team. *design*
5 Please let me know if you have any questions or ~~suggests~~. *suggestions*
6 I am pleased to announce the ~~arrive~~ of a new colleague. *arrival*
7 He will be ~~responsibility~~ for all data systems. *responsible*
8 You have made an excellent contribution to the department. CORRECT

9 You can check the ~~depart~~ time of your flight on the website.
departure

10 I would like to express my ~~appreciate~~ for your help last week.
appreciation

2 2 c   3 a   4 b

3 2 She felt very ~~nerveous~~ before the job interview. *nervous*

3 I would like to talk about our ~~achievments~~ over the past year.
achievements

4 I would be ~~gratefull~~ if you could send me some information.
grateful

5 Using the machines without protective clothing can be dangerous. CORRECT

6 We have a number of plans for staff ~~developement~~.
development

7 The report that you sent me was very useful. CORRECT

8 The product has been very ~~succesful~~ in our overseas markets.
successful

9 We would ~~definitly~~ like to see some samples of your products.
definitely

10 It is not ~~adviseable~~ to buy the cheapest equipment you can find.
advisable

UNIT 17

Getting started

1 1 B   2 C   3 A; Chart C shows changes over a period of time, Charts A and B show the situation at one point in time.

2 2 T   3 T   4 F   5 F

Describing trends

Vocabulary

1 1 v   2 ii   3 vi   4 iv   5 i   6 iii

2 2 a   3 f   4 d   5 b   6 e

3 2 at   3 Between, from, to

4 **to** 200 pence means that 200 pence is the final figure.
by 200 pence means that there is a difference of 200 pence between the first and last figures. We don't know what the actual figures are.

Grammar workshop

Adjectives and adverbs

1

Verb	Noun
to rise	a rise
to fall	a fall
to increase	an increase
to decrease	a decrease
to dip	a dip
to fluctuate	(a) fluctuation
to recover	a recovery

2

Adjective	Adverb
slight	slightly
sharp	sharply
gradual	gradually
steady	steadily
dramatic	dramatically
noticeable	noticeably

3 2 dramatic rise   3 fell sharply   4 fluctuated slightly   5 slight dip

Reporting figures

Writing

Sample answers:
Student A:
In the first week the price of silver stood at about 35 dollars per ounce. It fell slightly in week two and also in week three to about 29 dollars. Then it levelled off but it experienced another slight dip in week five. However, after that, the price started to recover. It rose to around 30 dollars in week six, levelled off in week seven and increased again to about 40 dollars in week eight.
Student B:
In the first week, the price of gold stood at about 1650 dollars per ounce. In the second week it fell to about 1600 dollars and then experienced a more dramatic fall to 1400 in week three. In week four it rose again to about 1580 dollars and then decreased slightly in week five. It remained around this level until week six when there was another slight fall.

Statistics

Listening

2 C   3 B   4 A   5 B

Reading

1 2 e   3 b   4 f   5 d

2 Sample answer:
Although revenue from sales increased dramatically in the second year, in the third year it fell back to the same level as Year 1. Revenue from after-sales service increased steadily throughout the period.

UNIT 18

Finance

Vocabulary

1 2 d   3 k   4 c   5 e   6 a   7 h   8 i   9 f   10 j   11 g

2 1 break even   2 go bankrupt   3 revenue

3 1 pays off a debt   2 chases payment   3 writes off a debt

4 2 C   3 A   4 A   5 B

Working in finance

Listening

1 2 KPMG   3 (chartered) accountant

2 2 T   3 T   4 F (you can have a degree in any subject)
5 F (he has worked with many types of businesses, e.g. hotels, care homes, retail businesses, a golf course, manufacturing industries, printing …)

3 2 confidential   3 the truth   4 fraud   5 hide information

4 2 positive   3 profitable   4 money   5 jobs

Café Coffee Day

Reading

2 2 is not mentioned

3 2 B   3 A   4 A   5 C   6 C

4 (ii) B   (iii) B   (iv) B   (v) A   (vi) A   (vii) A

5 2 bait   3 sideline   4 median   5 outlets
6 depreciation   7 boost

UNIT 19

The stock exchange

Vocabulary

2 b   3 c   4 f   5 g   6 a   7 d

Financial news

Reading

1 1 b   2 d   3 g
2 2 stake   3 float   4 flotation   5 bond   6 bull market   7 equities
8 dividend yield

Men and women's investments

Reading

2 1 women   2 women trade their stocks less often than men
3 a 2   b 5   c 6   d 3   f 4
4 2 A   3 A   4 B   5 B

Working in investor relations

Vocabulary

2 B   3 D   4 B   5 A

Listening

1 a 5   b 2   c 6   d 3   e 4
2 2 B   3 B   4 A   5 C
Sample answers:
3 1 investor relations involves taking clients to possible investors,
public relations involves spreading the story of the company
through media, like newspapers, radio and TV and especially to
current shareholders
2 in two ways: where they are listed on the stock exchange and
where their assets are
3 very risky and capital intensive, but the rewards can be huge
4 the majority are based in Sydney

UNIT 20

Getting started

(possible answers)
1 premises costs: work from home, sell via the Internet
legal costs: ask a lawyer friend to do the paperwork for you
utilities (e.g. electricity bills), insurance, stock: compare prices via
the Internet and choose a cheap provider
advertising: use your website and /or rely on word of mouth
staff costs: use freelance staff, so you don't need to worry about
some costs like pensions.
2 use your savings, borrow from friends and family, take out a bank
loan, find a business angel

Business support

Listening

1 2 provide funding/capital   3 secure a loan   4 asset   5 cashflow
2 five (use own savings, borrow from family/friends, bank loan,
venture capital firm, business angel)
3 2 marketing   3 financial   4 own money / savings / from family
and friends   5 business plan   6 cashflow   7 house
8 equipment   9 venture capital   10 successful business
person   11 angel investment networks

Teenage entrepreneurs

Reading

1 Text A
1 father died when he was young, moved to a house with no
electricity or water
2 setting up a borehole in order to provide clean water for the
village
3 when he needed money for school fees and decided to use the
rain to get drinking water
4 borrowed it from a rich farmer

5 now sells thousands of bottles per month, employs five
workers, water is also sold in Uganda
Text B
1 suffered from dyslexia and left school
2 making chocolate cakes for family and friends
3 after he moved on to making chocolates
4 borrowed it from his grandparents
5 now supplies major stores, planning to open outlets in Mexico

Grammar workshop

Which/who/that/where clauses

1 2 who   3 where   4 in object relative clauses
5 Subject relative clause: he decided to create a new borehole
which could provide the people in the village ... / he bought a
water purifier which could be used for rainwater
Object relative clause: he took the money that he was planning to
use for his high school fees ...
He moved on to making chocolates, which were so successful he
decided to start his own business.
2 2 We were given your name by Ms Tina Furlan who we believe is
one of your regular customers.
3 We enclose a complete product list and three pastries which we
hope you will enjoy.
4 They are made from high quality ingredients which we import
from Greece.
5 We began selling our products six months ago at a local market
where they proved to be very popular.
3   which/that
2 This figure is a reduction in the amount ^ was spent last year.
3 I would like to demonstrate a new product we have launched.
CORRECT
                                                           who /that
4 The training is for members of staff ^ work in the customer
services department.
5 I am writing to complain about the service I received.
CORRECT
                                                     which /that
6 There was a short delay ^ occurred because of a computer
failure.

Writing

Sample answer:
Dear Mr and Mrs Niarchos,
Thank you for your letter of 9 November and the samples. We would
be very interested in increasing our product range as we are planning
to open a new branch. Would you be free to meet in the afternoon of
Friday 17 November?
I would also like to enquire if you are willing to offer a discount on
larger orders. Perhaps we could discuss this on Friday?
I look forward to meeting you.
Yours,
Isabella Tanzi

Funding

Reading

2 An employer might do this if they were interested in using the
services or products of the new company. Paragraph 3 gives the
reason.
3 3 a   4 f   5 d   6 b   (heading *e* is not needed)

Time and money

Vocabulary

1 2 save   3 invest   4 waste
2 1 on   2 on   3 in
3 Underline verbs: pumped / tap into
4 2 flooded   3 tap into   4 dried up

GRAMMAR WORKSHOP 5

Adjectives and adverbs

2 declined gradually   3 a sharp rise   4 increases suddenly
5 (a) real improvement   6 a dramatic recovery
7 have fluctuated considerably

Reference words

2 it   3 This   4 these   5 them   6 This   7 one   8 these

Which, what and *that*

1 2 which   3 Which   4 what   5 which   6 which
2 2 that   3 what   4 that   5 what   6 that

Prepositions

2 with   3 in   4 on   5 on   6 on   7 in   8 with

Grammar and spelling revision

1 2 A   3 C   4 A   5 B   6 B   7 A   8 A   9 C   10 B
2 2 Sales rose in the autumn and reached a ~~pick~~ in December. *peak*
   3 The new data management system is a big ~~improvment~~ on the old one. *improvement*
   4 There are a number of ~~diffrent~~ software packages you can buy. *different*
   5 They have invested ~~heavyly~~ in their marketing campaign. *heavily*
   6 We have still not ~~recieved~~ payment for the last invoice. *received*
   7 Their raw materials can all be purchased ~~localy~~. *locally*
   8 When would be a ~~convient~~ time for the conference call? *convenient*

UNIT 21

Getting started

2 2 b   3 f   4 c   5 h   6 g   7 d   8 a
3 Suggested order:
   b 5   c 4   d 6   e 8   f 7   g 3   h 2

Writing CVs

Reading

1 His CV does not contain a career profile.
2 2 ✓   3 ✗ (not necessary to include marital status)
   4 ✗ (do not include elementary school)   5 ✓
   6 ✗ (too exaggerated and no reference to any evidence)   7 ✓

Careers advice

Listening

2 2 A   3 B   4 A   5 C   6 B   7 C   8 A   9 A
3 2 mirror   3 skills   4 formatting   5 banking   6 university
   7 conferences   8 programming languages

Corresponding with applicants

Writing

1 a 2   c 4   d 3   e 5
3 2 I am pleased to inform you that
   3 We would like you to
   4 Please let us know
   5 We look forward to meeting you
4 2 and 4 are stronger
5 a 2   b 3   c 1

6 Sample answer:
   Dear Ms Balabanovic
   Thank you for your application for the post of IT project manager. I am sorry to tell you that you were not shortlisted for the post. Although you clearly have relevant experience, it was felt that a candidate with more experience of managing people in a large company was necessary for this post. However, please accept our good wishes for your future career.
   Yours sincerely,

UNIT 22

Getting started

1 2 resign   3 redundant   4 dismiss
2 2 dismissal   3 redundancy   4 resignation
3 2 a   3 b   4 c   5 a   6 d   7 c

Grammar workshop 1

First conditional

1 1 company website   2 your own CV
3

Cause	Effect
If you spend some time doing this homework	the interview is much more likely to be successful.
If you are well informed	you will look better than many other applicants.
If the interviewer asks about these (facts about your place of work)	you'll be prepared.
If you arrive late and out of breath	you will make a very poor impression.

4 1 present simple   2 *will* future
5 2 ask   3 will be   4 do not / don't write   5 will/'ll forget   6 feel
   7 will hear

Interview questions

Reading

1 C
2 c 4   d 1   e 3 (you do not need heading b.)
3 2 estimate   3 prioritise   4 track record   5 odd   6 give the impression   7 alienate

Grammar workshop 2

Second conditional

1 1 no   2 no   3 would
2 If you had only six months to live, how would you spend them?
   If you were an animal, what animal would you be?

A recuitment agency

Listening

1 2 a   3 d   4 c
2 2 B   3 A   4 B   5 C   6 A

Writing

Sample answer:

We are a leading e-commerce company who currently needs to recruit a new network administrator. This will be a permanent post with a salary of around £36,000 a year. I would be grateful if you could call me on 0207 57390405 before 5pm today or tomorrow between 9 and 11 am so that we could discuss our requirements further. Please could you also give me some information about your fees?

Kind regards,

UNIT 23

Training

Reading 1

3 2 d 3 c 4 b 5 a 6 a 7 d

Reading 2

2 Helen Kadera 3 sales 4 25–27 May 5 £230

Writing

Sample answer:

Dear Sir/Madam,

I would like to book places for four members of staff on the 'Psychology of Selling' course. Please could you send a booking form to the above email address? Ideally, the trainees should attend the course in May if there are still places available. Please could you let me know if we qualify for the corporate group rate?

I look forward to hearing from you.

Sport and business

Reading

3 2 B 3 A 4 C 5 A 6 C

Vocabulary

1 2 football/baseball 3 chess 4 baseball 5 athletics
2 2 d 3 c 4 a 5 b

Giving and receiving feedback

Vocabulary

1 appraiser 2 appraisee
Other examples: trainer/trainee; interviewer/interviewee

Listening

1 *360 degree feedback* is feedback from everyone an employee has contact with.
2 1 anyone who comes into contact with the employee
   2 the employee (and the manager if the employee wants this)
3 2 C 3 B 4 B 5 B 6 C 7 A

UNIT 24

Getting started

2 producer 3 production 4 productive
5 unproductive 6 productivity

A meeting

Listening

1 to ask the staff their opinions about the current technology and if they need any extra equipment and send in a report
2 2 issuing 3 providing 4 to show 5 to make sure 6 playing
   7 to bring forward 8 spending

Grammar workshop

Infinitives and -ing forms

1 infinitives: 1,4,5,7
   -ing forms: 2,3,6,8
2 2 -ing form 3 infinitive 4 -ing form 5 -ing form 6 infinitive
3 2 to be 3 concentrating 4 to relax 5 giving 6 to see
   7 chatting 8 taking 9 to think
4 2 to call 3 to suggest 4 meeting 5 to increase/ increase (it is possible to use infinitive without 'to' after 'help'.)
   6 to accept 7 working 8 seeing

5

Verbs followed by infinitives	Verbs followed by -ing forms
hope hesitate would like help agree	look forward to enjoy stop

6 Possible answers:
   2 to make the office look nice, to clean the air, to improve the environment
   3 to cut the string on parcels, to open letters, to cut up your lunch
   4 to save time, to lose weight
   5 to save electricity, to see a DVD/film, to focus on the computer screen better, to give someone a birthday surprise
   6 Microsoft used a rubber chicken to decide who should speak during meetings. You could only speak if you were holding the chicken. When you finished speaking, you threw it to someone else. Another company used a rubber chicken to punish staff who did not follow health and safety rules. If you broke the rules, you had to wear the chicken round your neck. You could only give it away when you saw someone else break the rules.

A report

Writing

1 1 in the first two sentences
   2 their opinions on the current situations and their ideas for improvements
   3 to say what the company should do next
2 1 In general staff liked the idea of having smartphones, which they felt would be very useful. However, two members of staff were concerned that if they had smartphones, the company would call them at weekends. For this reason, they wanted to agree on times when the phones could be switched off.
   2 Several requests were made for new presentation software which could be an alternative to PowerPoint. James and Anisa agreed to research the price of other software packages and to get back to me after two weeks with some figures.

Older employees

Reading

2 2 A 3 B 4 A 5 C 6 B 7 B 8 C 9 C 10 B

Listening

2 h 3 b 4 a 5 f

GRAMMAR WORKSHOP 6

Conditionals

1 2 cannot 3 were 4 agree 5 felt 6 have 7 order, will receive 8 held
2 2 I would appreciate it if all of you ~~can~~ *could* attend a meeting at 3 pm.
   3 I ~~am~~ *would be* very glad if you could change the date of the meeting.

4 I would be grateful if you could book me a standard room. CORRECT

5 It ~~will~~ *would* be helpful if you could contact the sales department about this matter.

6 I would be delighted if you ~~are~~ *were* able to attend our meeting on 14 June.

7 I would appreciate it if you could send a company car to the airport. CORRECT

8 I would be very much obliged if you ~~can~~ *could* raise this issue in your meeting.

Infinitive and -*ing* forms

1 2 to inform 3 to invite 4 to come 5 to complete
6 attending 7 to contact 8 seeing

2 2 We are interested ~~to arrange~~ *in arranging* a training course for our staff.

3 We are pleased to inform you that you have been selected for the post. CORRECT

4 She will be responsible ~~to create~~ *for creating* our new range of bracelets.

5 Many thanks ~~to choose~~ *for choosing* our company to give this talk.

6 My talk will be about the importance ~~to prepare~~ *of preparing* a development programme for staff.

7 Would it be convenient to hold the meeting at 12 o'clock? CORRECT

8 Please accept my apologies for the delay ~~to complete~~ *in completing* this project.

Grammar and spelling revision

1 2 B 3 B 4 B 5 A 6 A 7 C 8 A 9 A 10 C 11 B 12 A

2 2 about 3 if 4 give/create 5 raise 6 but 7 to 8 for
9 instead 10 have 11 need/want/ought 12 are 13 many
14 to

3 2 applicant 3 resignation 4 dismissal 5 impression
6 redundancy

4 2 One of your colleagues made a very ~~usefull~~ suggestion. *useful*

3 The price of the ~~hole~~ package is just under 100 dollars, ~~wich~~ is very reasonable. *whole, which*

4 We really need to find cheaper premises ~~then~~ these. *than*

5 The new product is not very ~~diffrent~~ from the old one, despite the higher price. *different*

6 A great many customers ~~complaint~~ about the poor service. *complained/complain*

7 All applications need to be sent to the ~~personal~~ manager before the end of the month. *personnel*

8 Please could you ~~advice~~ all your staff about the changes to the system. *advise*

WRITING REFERENCE

Levels of formality

1 1 I 2 F 3 F but it can depend on the company
4 F but it can depend on the company

2 1 i 2 d 3 e 4 a 5 b 6 f 7 h 8 c 9 g 10 j

3 Email A: more informal Email B: more formal

4 A: Beginnings: Hi Louise; Dear Louise; Louise
endings: Thanks; Cheers
B: Beginnings: Dear Mr Ford
endings: Yours sincerely; Kind regards; Many thanks

5 More informal:
Hi Sam,
Please could you drop me a line and let me know how things are going with the data management project? Do you think you'll finish on time or do we need to look at the deadline again?

More formal:
Dear Sam,
I would be grateful if you could send me a short progress report on the data management project. Please could you let me know whether you are likely to finish on time or if the deadline needs to be revised?

6 Possible signs offs:
Informal email: Thanks; Cheers; All the best
Formal email: Many thanks; Kind regards; Best wishes

Emails

1 T 2 T 3 T Sometimes people do write like this to close colleagues and friends but it is best to avoid it. 4 T
5 F This is the equivalent of shouting at someone.
6 F Emails do not usually use these. Again, some people might use some of them in emails to close colleagues and friends but you should avoid it.

Emails: Requests

1 1 c 2 a 3 b

2 Could you …; I wonder if you could …; I would be grateful if you could …; Please could you …

3 More formal: I would be grateful if you could …; The request is to someone the writer does not know.
I wonder if you could …; The request is not part of the person's job and they could refuse more easily.

4 1 Thank you for your enquiry 2 We would be happy
3 Please call our office 4 I can confirm 5 I also attach
6 We would be grateful if you could

Emails: Invitations

1 1 b 2 e 3 a 4 d 5 c

2 1 b 2 d 3 a 4 c

Emails: Enquiries

1 1 I am writing with reference to
2 I am especially interested in
3 However, I also notice that
4 I would definitely like to
5 Please could you send me
6 I would also like to enquire

2 1 b 2 e 3 a 4 c 5 d

Emails: Other functions

1 1 B 2 A 3 C

2 1 A 2 C 3 B

Memos

1 1 e 2 a 3 b 4 d 5 c

2 1 because 2 in order to 3 but 4 so that 5 and

3 1 please note that 2 hopefully; with luck 3 re
4 I am sorry to say 5 I am happy to tell you

Notes

1 1 T 2 F 3 T 4 T

2 1 phoned 2 let his line manager know 3 mind 4 cheers
5 call 6 going on

4 *Sample answer:*
Koji – pls can you call Paul asap? He needs to check figures on your spreadsheet. Thanx Rina.

Letters and more formal emails

1 1 c 2 g 3 f 4 e (although nowadays some people use *Yours sincerely* here as well) 5 b 6 d 7 a

2 b

3 1 on behalf of   2 We look forward to hearing from you
3 thank you in advance   4 Yours sincerely   5 Anna Furlan
6 Course Director
4 1 b   2 d   3 a   4 e   5 f   6 c
5 1 top right hand   2 on the left   3 below   4 below   5 below
6   59 Cranmore Street
Manchester
M39 8GW

12.2.13

Personnel Department
Boltons Electronics
New Road
Salford
M47 2EB
Dear Mr Campbell,
I would like to apply for the post of Customer Service Officer
which you are advertising on jobsearch.com.
You will see from my CV that I have a degree in English and
economics. I have also completed a course in IT applications
including spreadsheets. I have good communication skills and a
wide knowledge of electronic goods, as I previously worked at
weekends in an electronics store.
I am available for interview at any time and look forward to
hearing from you.
Yours sincerely,
Martin Hope

Statistics and reports

1 1 stood at   2 reach   3 high   4 lower   5 increased   6 slight
7 decline   8 lowest   9 decreased   10 However   11 slightly
2 1 T   2 F   3 T   4 T   5 F   6 T
3 1 d   2 e   3 a   4 b   5 c

EXAMS SKILLS AND EXAM PRACTICE

Reading Paper Part 1: Exam skills

1 1   B   is not correct because this is only an advantage, not
essential.
C   is not correct because this is the date they must receive the
application, not the start date for the job.
2   A   is not correct because it is only valid for new subscriptions,
not renewals.
B   is not correct because this is the closing date for the offer.
3   A   is not correct because she works in marketing now.
C   is not correct because Claire is going on leave not Julia (and
'going on leave' does not mean 'leaving the company').
2 1   B   (held up = delayed)
2   A   (engaged = in use)

Reading Paper Part 1: Exam practice

1 C   2 A   3 C   4 C   5 B

Reading Paper Part 2: Exam skills

1b 1   green products, reduce pollution, magazine D
2   loan, interest rate, property, magazine B
3   buffet, set menu, magazine E
2c 1 B   2 E   3 C
3 1 D   2 E   3 B   4 F

Reading Paper Part 2: Exam practice

6 G   7 E   8 C   9 D   10 F

Reading Paper Part 3: Exam skills

1 1 B   2 C   3 A
2 1 D   2 B   3 E

Reading Paper Part 3: Exam practice

11 G   12 C   13 H   14 D   15 B

Reading Paper Part 4: Exam skills

1 1   A = R, B = DS, C = W
2   A = DS, B = R, C = W
3   A = W, B = DS, C = R
4   A = DS, B = R, C = W
5   A = R, B = DS, C = W
6   A = W, B = R, C = DS
7   A = W, B = DS, C = R
8   A = R, B = W, C = DS
2 1 W   2 DS   3 R

Reading Paper Part 4: Exam practice

16 A   17 C   18 A   19 B   20 C   21 A   22 B

Reading Paper Part 5: Exam skills

1a The text talks about a, b, e and f.
1b 1   (i he felt sure that he could; ii before) B
2   (i reluctant; ii because) C
3   (ii results) C
4   (i property; ii before) A
2b i 1   ii 3   iii 2
2c 1 A   2 C   3 B   4 B

Reading Paper Part 5: Exam practice

23 A   24 B   25 C   26 A   27 C   28 C

Reading Paper Part 6: Exam skills

1 1 C   2 A   3 B   4 A
2 1 B   2 B   3 C   4 A   5 C
3 1 B   2 C   3 A   4 C   5 C   6 A   7 A   8 C   9 A   10 B   11 C   12 C

Reading Paper Part 6: Exam practice

29 A   30 B   31 A   32 B   33 B   34 C   35 B   36 B   37 C   38 C
39 C   40 A

Reading Paper Part 7: Exam skills

1 1 Daniel Musser   2 Mahbub Dharmen   3 Maureen Kirk
2 1 day delegate   2 vegetarian   3 150

Reading Paper Part 7: Exam practice

41 1(st) November; Nov(ember) 1(st);1/11   42 large (size) stand
43 Phillips   44 (manufacturers of) (fine) Furniture   45 Jane Wright

Listening Paper Part 1: Exam skills

1 1 Monday   2 Thursday
3 Friday. A. They are going to meet on Monday.
2   1 60   2 30   3 10. B. She is going to interview about 30
candidates.
2 1 C   2 C
3 1 C   2 A

Listening Paper Part 1: Exam practice

1 B   2 A   3 B   4 A   5 B   6 B   7 C   8 A

Listening Paper Part 2: Exam skills

1 1 1969   2 51%   3 £1.6 billion   4 £200 million   5 38
2 1 I   2 A   3 R   4 E   5 S   6 C   7 J   8 G
3 1   Name: Keith Caraballo
Address: 34, Harries Close, Croydon

2 Name: <u>Ciro Romano</u>
   Address: 62, <u>Leigh Hunt</u> Drive
   Postcode: NW14 8EC
3 Company: <u>Harrow Wells</u>
   Contact name: <u>Jariya Kroksamrang</u>
4 1 (029)3491485 2 12.45 3 8 per cent 4 320

Listening Paper Part 2: Exam practice

9 340 10 6 11 950 12 Gilwray 13 28 14 15th 15 2118

Listening Paper Part 3: Exam skills

1b 1 2009 2 perfume 3 advertising campaign 4 retail space
2a 1 former chairman 2 launch a bid 3 backing 4 speculation
2b 1 television company 2 cinema chain 3 investment bank
    4 joint bid
3b 1 life insurance 2 low profits 3 (the) USA
    4 investment company

Listening Paper Part 3: Exam practice

16 tele(-)com(m)unication(s) (industry) 17 (both) timetable
18 (office) costs (reduction/reduce (in) (the)(office(s) cost(s)
19 job satisfaction 20 (insurance) company
21 stres(s)(-)free / stressless / unstressful / not stressful 22 (only)
midday/12.00/noon

Listening Paper Part 4: Exam skills

1a 1 C 2 B 3 A
1b 1 'the most common reason for wanting more flexibility is that
    that person is looking after a parent or elderly member of the
    family.'
    2 'you won't be forced to go during the rush hour. And that's a
    big saving of time. Just think of all those unproductive hours
    you spend on the train normally.'
    3 'Staff turnover among flexible workers tends to be much lower
    than among other employees.'
2a 1 bakery 2 recruitment agency 3 hotel 4 C
2b 1C 2 A 3 C 4 B 5 B
2c 1 interviewing 2 a bank loan; ask my father. These contradict B
    and C 3 upmarket location. This paraphrases C
    4 was still growing. This contradicts C.
    5 has changed; full outsourcing. This paraphrases B.

Listening Paper Part 4: Exam practice

23 B 24 A 25 C 26 A 27 B 28 B 29 C 30 B

Writing Paper Part 1: Exam skills

1b C is probably the best as it covers all the key points and is the most
polite.
1c 1B 2C 3A
2b The memo does not give the customer's name and does not make
it clear that the assistant is to report back to Philip.
2c Sample answer:
    To: Helen Smith
    From: Philip Day
    Re: order
    Helen,
    Mrs Janet Conway rang today. She has received her DVDs order
    number 2334, but says the invoice includes two she didn't order.
    Please could you check this out and get back to me by tomorrow?
    Thanks,
    Philip

3b Sample answer:
    To: All staff
    From:
    Date: 30 March
    Re: new brochure
    I'm afraid our new brochure hasn't arrived yet. Sorry for the
    inconvenience but there have been technical problems at the
    printer's. It will hopefully be with us in two weeks, so please be
    patient.
4b Simon Dale, the best of our <u>candidates</u>, has emailed to withdraw
his *aplication*. *Unfortunaly* he has *eccepted* a post elsewhere.
Please could we meet at 9 tomorrow to look again at the rest of the
<u>applications</u>?
4c application, unfortunately, accepted

Writing Paper Part 1: Exam practice

Dear Matt,
I'm afraid we have problems with our printer and scanner, which
keeps jamming. It's quite old so please could we replace it? You can
get a similar model for about £90.

Many thanks,

Austin

Writing Paper Part 2: Exam skills

1c I would be happy to come and give a talk at your college.
    I would like to outline our company's product range and main
    markets.
    Please could you tell me how long the talk should be?
    Friday 16 April is a possible date for me.
1f Sample answer:
    Dear Mr Steele,
    Thank you for your letter of 12 February. I would be happy to
    come and give a talk at your college. I would like to outline our
    company's product range and main markets. Please could you tell
    me how long the talk should be?
    Friday 16 April is a possible date for me. Please let me know if this
    date would be suitable. I look forward to hearing from you.
    Yours sincerely,
2c 1 I am writing with regard to … 2 Please could you tell me …
    3 I look forward to hearing from you.
2d point not covered: requesting a list of items in stock.
2e Sample answer:
    Dear Sir,
    I am one of the owners of a chain of juice bars. We would be
    interested in purchasing a number of items of equipment,
    especially juicers and toasters. Please could you send me a list of
    items that you have in stock? I would also like to enquire how long
    the guarantee lasts.
    I look forward to hearing from you.
    Yours faithfully,
    Ken May
3d grateful, know (now), approximately, sincerely
    Dear Mr Diskin,
    Many thanks for your letter with the news about the award. I will
    be delighted <u>to attending</u> the reception and would be *grateful* if
    you could give me some directions to the hotel. Please could <u>you
    also told me</u> if other employees <u>can to attend</u>?
    I would be happy to write a short article for your journal but I
    would like to *know approximately* how long it should be.
    Yours *sincerely*,
    Martina Berezin
3e I will be delighted to attend, Please could you also tell, if other
    employees can attend

Writing Paper Part 2: Exam practice

Dear Martin Holmes,

Thank you for your letter. We can offer you work experience in the new financial year, from May to September. This normally involves helping to audit local businesses by calculating total revenue and expenses, and you will need to be able to work with spreadsheets. If you are interested, we would like to invite you for an interview on 29 March.

Yours sincerely,

Amit Sharma

Speaking Paper Part 1: Exam skills

1b 1 d   2 a   3 b   4 f   5 c   6 e

Speaking Paper Part 2: Exam skills

1a 1 Firstly   2 because   3 For example   4 Secondly   5 This means that   6 also   7 like   8 but   9 So to conclude

2a 1   Your knowledge of the product: b, g, h
Personal appearance: a, e, f
Meeting the customer on time: c, d, i

2   *These are just suggested answers. Other answers are possible.*
experience: c, d, g
IT skills: a, e, i
politeness: b, f, h

Speaking Paper Part 3: Exam skills

1

Ask your partner's opinion	1 What do you think about …? 2 How about …?
Give your opinion	4 I think … 8 My feeling is …
Agree with your partner	5 Yes that's true 3 I think you're right.
Disagree with your partner	9 Maybe, but … 7 I'm not sure I agree.
Persuade your partner	6 But don't you think …?

2b 1 I think /My feeling is … In my opinion …   2 I'm not sure I agree … / Maybe, but …   3 How about …/ What do you think about …   4 Yes that's true/ I think you're right.   5 What do you think about …/How about …   6 I think you're right.

Transcripts

UNIT 1

(1) 02 Listening, page 11, Exercises 2, 3 and 5

I = Interviewer; S = Sally

I: So what do you do, Sally?
S: Well, I'm a PA for the director of CF TV.
I: Oh really? So what does that involve?
S: Oh …all sorts of things. The first thing I do when I get to work is check my email. There are always lots of requests for meetings with Richard, my boss. I'm in charge of prioritising these and fitting them into Richard's diary, around all his other appointments. A lot of the time he needs information before a meeting, so I end up looking things up for him online. And when visitors arrive, it's my job to welcome them to the office. A lot of the rest is like secretarial work. I attend meetings and take notes, deal with phone calls, that sort of thing. And I'm responsible for answering all the correspondence.
I: It sounds very busy.
S: Oh it is. There's always loads of people coming and going.
I: So do you enjoy your job?
S: Yes, most of the time. The most important thing for a PA, you know, is to be organised. The part I don't like is when there are just too many things going on. Sometimes it can get a bit stressful. But if you've got the right systems set up on computer and the right software, it's not too difficult to keep track of everything.
I: And what about the people you work with?
S: Oh, they're great. Most of them are really friendly and helpful.
I: That's what makes the difference, isn't it? I hope your boss is nice as well.
S: Oh yes, he's fine. We have a good working relationship on the whole. He knows I'm reliable and that's important because he's out of the office a lot. I'm quite often left in charge to deal with things when he's away.

UNIT 2

(1) 03 Vocabulary, page 16, Exercise 2

com   uk   org   biz   us   ac   co   net

(1) 04 Vocabulary, page 16, Exercise 3

1   G Brent, that's G-B-R-E-N-T 39 at g mail dot com
2   sales at taylormills, that's T-A-Y-L-O-R-M-I-L-L-S dot co dot E-S
3   Ben D Murphy, that's B-E-N-D underscore M-U-R-P-H-Y at hotmail dot com
4   Natalie Omar, that's N-A-T-A-L-I-E-O-M-A-R at blogspot dot com
5   W-W-W dot G-L-F dot com forward slash products
6   Mary-Ann Perkins, that's Mary hyphen Ann dot Perkins, spelt P-E-R-K-I-N-S at Copeland, that's C-O-P-E-L-A-N-D dot org dot U-K
7   W-W-W dot Gaskell hyphen training dot biz
8   S dot Denham, that's D-E-N-H-A-M, at D-U-R dot co dot UK

UNIT 3

(1) 05   (1) 06   (1) 07 Listening, page 20, Exercises 1, 3 and 4

I = Interviewer; A = Adrian

I: It was confirmed yesterday that Spectrum, the well-known chain of sandwich bars, is facing collapse. For the first few years, the company showed spectacular growth, but about three years ago things started to go wrong. Profits began to fall and it seems they've never recovered. With me I have our business consultant, Adrian Gifford, to talk about what's gone wrong. Adrian, hi.
A: Hello.
I: So, is this the end for Spectrum?
A: Not necessarily, no. It's possible that they'll find a buyer. I believe that one or two companies have expressed interest. But if they want to buy the chain, they'll have to make the move very soon. The deadline for offers is getting close.
I: So what exactly went wrong? Five years ago they seemed such a strong brand. I think many people will wonder how they ended up like this.
A: Well, I think it's a classic example of trying to do too much. Their first shop was really successful. People really liked the novelty fillings and because the product was good, they didn't mind paying a fairly high price for it. So then Spectrum's response was to try and open more and more branches. Three years ago they opened over twenty new branches in one year. They just expanded too quickly.
I: But surely expansion is a good thing? It's what all successful businesses want to do.
A: Of course, yes, but it needs thought and planning. Quite often a company will try and launch a new product on the back of some previous success, but it doesn't always work. I think Spectrum did this when they started offering pizzas. There's so much competition from big pizza restaurants. It was very unlikely to succeed.
I: But it wasn't just because of one unsuccessful product, was it? They really seemed to lose custom in general.
A: Yes, because another thing that happens when a company expands too quickly is that the quality suffers, and they lose that attention to detail. For example, in this case, I think one big mistake was that they started to use frozen ingredients in the pizzas and even in some of the other products. One of their selling points before that was 'we only use fresh ingredients' and that was why people liked them.
I: Right.
A: This is a mistake that even really big companies can make. Remember the famous case of Toyota in 2010 when they had to recall several million vehicles? That happened because the company focussed on expansion and didn't pay enough attention to quality control. They actually admitted that.
I: Hmm. So what advice would you give to a company that wanted to expand?
A: I'd say, it's best to expand slowly and carefully and plan every step. Don't try to break into a new area without doing proper market research. Before you open a new branch, make sure all your current branches are profitable. And when you plan to open a new branch, always remember what makes your company special.
I: Good advice, Adrian.
A: Thank you.

UNIT 4

① 08 Listening, page 24

A = Adam; M = Marisa

A: Hello?

M: Hello, can I speak to Adam Musser please?

A: Speaking.

M: Hello, Adam, it's Marisa here. I'm a friend of Geoff. You might remember me? We met at his birthday party last year.

A: Oh yes. Hello, Marisa.

M: I hope you don't mind, but I'm ringing because I know you work for National Bank.

A: Yes, that's right. I've been with them for the last six years.

M: Well, I'm thinking of applying for a job there. I wonder if you could tell me a bit about it. Is it a good place to work?

A: Well, it depends. It was rather different when I started there six years ago. I don't know if you know, but two years ago, there was a merger.

M: Yes, I remember. So did the place change after that?

A: Well yes, I think it changed the culture rather a lot. When I started there it was quite friendly and supportive and they really looked after their customers too. Now they're much more focussed on targets. I mean …well, don't quote me on this, but there's always a lot of pressure to make a sale, even if you feel it's not really right for the customer.

M: So it's very target driven?

A: Yes, very.

M: I see. Are there good possibilities for promotion?

A: Well, there are for some people. But that's changed as well. When I first joined, there was a lot less competition for places. But now people have become much more competitive. They don't really trust each other, especially if they're applying for the same post.

M: Hmm … The package that they're offering seems very good though. It's better than my current salary.

A: Oh yes, that's true. You get a lot of benefits that you don't find in many other companies. They offer a good insurance package, and quite long holidays. They're very generous with bonuses too. They were much smaller a few years ago. But it is tough. I don't think it's a good place to work if you want a caring management style.

M: Right. I'll need to think about whether I really want to apply now. Anyway thanks for that, Adam, it's very useful.

A: You're welcome. And if you apply for the job, good luck. And let me know if you want to know anything else.

M: Thank you.

UNIT 5

① 09 Listening, page 29

M = Man; W = Woman

M: I think something like this would be good.

W: Yes, I like the style.

M: Perhaps two of them along the back wall?

W: Is there enough space?

M: I think so. The room's about 450cm wide and this is only 180cm.

W: I didn't just mean the width though. Remember we've got to have enough space in the room for all the clothes hangers. I think this might stick out too much.

M: The depth is 40cm? I think it'll be fine.

W: I still wonder if shelves on the wall would be better. It won't look so funky I know, but you could display a lot more. How big are those cubes?

M: 180 divided by five, so I guess that's, er … each one is 36cm across. And the total height of the unit is 112cm, so if you divide that by three…

W: We could still display a lot more on shelves, you know.

M: Yes …

W: We want something like this to display the poster in the window.

M: How does it work?

W: Well, there are two cables that you run from the top to the bottom and then you attach the posters to it.

M: Ah. How long are the cables?

W: Each one is 320cm.

M: The window can't be that big though. It can't be more than about 250cm.

W: No, no, but they're adjustable. You can adjust them to whatever length you want.

① 10 Listening, page 30

M = Man; W = Woman

M: Good morning, Perry's Workshop Goods.

W: Hello, I'm calling about an order that we made last week for some tool storage boxes. I'd like to add something to the order.

M: OK. What was the name please?

W: Routledge. That's R-O-U-T-L-E-D-G-E.

M: Ah yes. It was for two JNV 106 storage boxes, wasn't it?

W: Yes, that's right. We'd still like those, but we'd also like one of the smaller model as well.

M: Which one? There are two other models.

W: Oh, I didn't notice. Well, the one we want is 480mm by 800mm.

M: And 500mm high, yes? That's the JNV 90.

W: Yes.

M: OK, that's no problem. Same colour as the others?

W: I didn't know there was more than one colour. I thought they only came in black.

M: No, if you look on the website, there's actually a drop-down menu under 'colour'. They can be black or grey.

W: Oh, we'll stick with the same colour.

M: Fine, so that's an extra £96 to your order making a total of £345 in all.

W: How soon can you deliver?

M: Mm. Well, we can send your original order within the next day or so, so you could get that by the 15th of July. The only thing is the JNV 90 isn't in stock so it will take a bit longer. It would be the week beginning the 19th of July.

W: OK, well, you can deliver them all together. That'll be fine.

M: OK, I'll just process this additional order and we'll send it all when the JNV 90 comes in.

W: Thank you.

① 11 Listening, page 31

1 = Speaker 1; 2 = Speaker 2; 3 = Speaker 3

1: This is a tool which you use to make the holes in belts and leather goods. You put the belt between the two parts of the tool and then press the handles together. The circular piece of metal cuts a small hole in the leather. Of course people don't use this tool much nowadays, because you can make holes in leather by machine, but some traditional craftsmen still use cutters like these.

2: This is actually a tool used by engineers who build aeroplanes. When you assemble an aeroplane wing, you have to fasten the pieces of metal together with rivets. But you also need something to hold the pieces of metal in place while you do this. This tool holds the metal sheets still before the permanent rivets are put in.

3: No, no, this is really a tool used by people who make wooden musical instruments, especially violin makers. You use the semicircular ring to make cuts in the top of the violin. They don't change the sound, they're just for decoration. You then either fill these cuts with paint or you can fit different coloured pieces of wood inside them.

UNIT 6

① ⑫ Listening, page 34

I = Interviewer; D = Director of operations

I: Welcome to the programme today and I am delighted to have here in the studio, director of operations for the world famous Chanel perfumes. Hello there.

D: Hello. It's nice to be here.

I: Can you tell us a bit about how you actually make Chanel No. 5, your most famous perfume?

D: Yes, of course. Well the roses on our farm are in season from April to June and the jasmine from August to September. Firstly, the flowers are picked on the farm and the petals are put into sacks. Then they are transported to the production plant to be weighed. At some farms, the petals may wait a day before they are treated, but at Chanel, freshness is considered very important, and the petals reach the plant within half an hour. The next stage is to extract the natural oils and resins. In the past, this was done with cold fat which was spread on the petals but nowadays we use extraction solvents like ethanol. The petals are washed three times in over 2,000 litres of this solvent and the perfumed oils dissolve into it. In the next stage, the flowers are removed from the vats and the solvent is eliminated by a process of evaporation. This leaves a solid which is known in the trade as the *concrete*. This can be stored for several years. When the perfume is required, it is extracted from the concrete with alcohol. If we then evaporate this alcohol, we are left with a very pure form of flower perfume which we call the *absolute*. Different absolutes are then blended to create different perfumes.

I: Great, well, thank you, that really does give us a great insight …

UNIT 7

① ⑬ Listening 1, page 39

M = Man; W = Woman

1 W: Hello, this is Diane Campbell from Healey's. I'm just phoning to ask about your order. How would you like us to transport it to you?

M: Oh. What are the options?

W: Well, we usually use road or rail freight unless it's urgent, in which case we can send it by air.

M: No, it's not that urgent. I'm not really near a rail depot though so it's probably best if you just send it by road.

W: OK, we'll get that off to you this week.

2 Good morning, this is David Harrison from Jutes Office Supplies. I'm just phoning to let you know that we now have the three digital projectors that you ordered. We've looked at our delivery schedules again and we'll actually be able to deliver them to you this afternoon, not tomorrow morning as we said earlier. We haven't heard anything about the laser pointers yet, but hopefully they'll be with you next week.

3 Hello, this is Zakia Haddy from Yellands. I'm phoning about the stationery order that we placed about two weeks ago. We received one delivery last week but some of the items like the ink cartridges were missing. We received another parcel today containing ink cartridges and windowed envelopes, but the invoice also lists address labels, and they weren't included. I presume that's a mistake so could you get back to me today please and let me know when you can deliver the rest? Thanks.

4 *W1 = Woman 1; W2 = Woman 2*

W1: Good afternoon, Celia Jewellery.

W2: Good afternoon, this is Hilde Ringo from Holgesson in Oslo. I'm phoning about the order that we made for one hundred watches in the new starburst design. We've just received a phone call to say that they're stuck in customs. Apparently the packing list isn't correct and they won't let them through.

W1: Oh. I don't know what's happened there. We'll have to get on to our freight forwarding agent as they're looking after that side of things. Let me follow this up here and I'll get back to you as soon as I can.

W2: Thank you.

① ⑭ Listening 2, page 39

K = Kerry; S = Selina

K: Sales department.

S: Good morning. My name's Selina and I'm phoning from Khalil. We placed an order over three weeks ago for some industrial paint but we've not heard anything since. I'm just phoning to check you received the order?

K: Right. What was your company's name again?

S: Khalil. That's K-H-A-L-I-L.

K: Do you know your account reference number?

S: Well the one I've got here on a previous invoice is ZS431.

K: What exactly did you order?

S: It was the new heavy duty car paint that's advertised in your catalogue, colour number A535.

K: And when did you place the order?

S: Well, we phoned on the 18th of April and the order form is dated the 19th. As far as I know it was sent to you that same day.

K: OK, hold the line please and I'll see if I can trace the order. One moment...mm.....hello?

S: Yes?

K: We did receive the order. Apparently there have been a few problems with the supply of that colour, so we've had a backlog of orders. However, that has all been resolved now and the paint should arrive next week.

S: So we should get it on Monday the 18th?

K: Well more like mid-week. It should certainly be with you by Wednesday the 20th of May. Could I have your extension number please, just in case there are any more problems?

S: It's 375. And if I'm not here you can call John Cooper on 398.

K: And sorry, what's your surname?

S: Oh, it's Selina Macpherson. That's M-A-C-P-H-E-R-S-O-N. Thanks for sorting this out.

K: You're welcome.

UNIT 8

① ⑮ Speaking, page 41

I think all types of consumer buy this product but it targets young people in particular, maybe from the age of about eight to about mid-30s. It's a very international brand, you can see it pretty much everywhere. I'd say it's associated with being young and active because the company support a lot of sports events. In fact, I think they always sponsor the Olympic Games.

Its logo is very famous. It shows the name of the product and it's red and white, usually white letters on a red background. I don't think it's changed much since the product began back in the 1880s. They've used a lot of different slogans over the years and some of them have become quite famous.

UNIT 9

① 16 Listening, page 46

Hi Jeannette, it's Paul. Sorry about the late call. I've just received an email from Mr Gavino. Apparently there have been delays to his journey and he's missed his connecting flight from Hong Kong. So he's not arriving tomorrow after all, he's arriving on the 14th at 6.20am instead. He's given me the flight number, it's SQ341. Could you please let the hotel know and could you also book a taxi for him for the 14th? We're going to have to change the programme a bit now. I've already left a message for Jason, so are you still going to meet him tomorrow morning? Maybe you could use some of that time to revise the programme. Oh, and could you please ring the restaurant as well, cancel the booking for tomorrow and rebook for the day after? Same time, 7.30, OK?

Nothing goes smoothly does it? OK, I'll see you tomorrow morning. Call me at home if there are any problems. Bye.

① 17 Listening 1, page 47

C = Carmen; S = Stefano

C: Hello, this is Carmen Vanegas from Medica. I was wondering if we could fix a time to meet next week?

S: Yes of course. What time would suit you?

C: Well, I was wondering if you could manage Tuesday afternoon.

S: Sorry, I'm not available at any time on Tuesday as I've arranged to be at our other branch all day.

C: How about…er…Wednesday afternoon?

S: I'm booked up Wednesday afternoon as well, but I could do Wednesday morning or I'm free all day on Thursday.

C: Could you make Thursday at two o'clock?

S: That would be fine, yes.

C: OK, so let's confirm that then. Thursday at two o'clock.

① 18 Listening 2, page 48

W = Woman; P = Peter; M = Man

W: Peter, could you see if you could change my flight on Thursday? I've got an appointment at 11.30 so I really won't be able to leave until mid afternoon.

P: What time do you have to get there?

W: Well, I'd like to be there by 6.30 if I could.

P: Mm …Shall I see if I can get you onto the 4.20 flight?

W: That would be great. Thank you.

M: Miss Casale's train gets in at ten past two, so could you drive down to the station after lunch and pick her up?

W: The problem is I'm seeing Simon at two o'clock to discuss the programme. She could get a taxi couldn't she? Or she could even walk if you gave her directions.

M: What, carrying a heavy bag? No. Anyway, Simon isn't here today.

W: Isn't he?

M: No, he phoned in sick earlier on.

W: Oh, OK. I'll pick her up then.

M: We have a visitor arriving on the 26th, so could you please arrange a meet and greet at the airport? It's KLM flight number 459.

W: What name is it?

M: Well, I'm not quite sure how you pronounce it but it's spelt B-U-L-K-I-E-W-I-C-Z.

W: One moment, that's B-U-L-K-E-I-W-I-C-Z.

M: No, K-I-E not E-I.

W: OK.

M: Per Jonsson, the chief executive at Misson Credit, the merchant bank, has announced his retirement. His place will be taken up by Yolande Haisman, currently chief financial officer.

① 19 Grammar workshop 2

A = Announcer; M = Man; W = Woman

1 A: One
W: I need to get to the airport by 6.30.
M: Shall I book you a taxi?

2 A: Two
W: What are you doing with those files, Roger?
M: I'm going to type up the sales figures for Mr Durand.

3 A: Three
The Bank of Canada have announced that economic growth will be relatively slow this year.

4 A: Four
M: I've tried to set up the room for the presentation but the microphone isn't working.
W: I'll call the technician. I've got the number somewhere here.

① 20 Grammar workshop 2, page 49

A = Announcer; M = Man; W = Woman

1 A: One
W: I need to get to the airport by 6.30.
M: Shall I book you a taxi?
W: Yes please. For about 5.45, I think.
M: Shall I make it 5.30? I think there might be a lot of traffic around at that time.
W: Yes, good idea.

2 A: Two
W: What are you doing with those files, Roger?
M: I'm going to type up the sales figures for Mr Durand.
W: Can I ask you to scan these documents for me as well and send them to our Frankfurt branch? They're quite urgent.
M: Could I do the typing first? Mr Durand wants them by three at the latest, otherwise he can't finish his report.
W: Yes, as long as you send them off by the end of the day.
M: Yes, I will.

3 A: Three
The Bank of Canada have announced that economic growth will be relatively slow this year. This is because of weak demand from Japan and parts of Europe. Their forecast for Canadian growth is now 2.4% compared with the 2.8% they predicted just three months ago. They have, however, rejected the suggestion that growth could drop below 2%.

4 A: Four
M: I've tried to set up the room for the presentation but the microphone isn't working.
W: I'll call the technician. I've got the number somewhere here.
M: I've already called him. I left a message but I don't know if he'll get it in time. I was wondering if you could come and have a look at it. You're better at these things than I am.
W: I don't know about that. What about the hand-held microphone? Couldn't he use that?
M: I'm not sure where it is. Could you see if you could fix the one that's there and I'll see if I can find the hand-held one?
W: OK.

UNIT 10

① 21 Vocabulary, page 50

The last time I came to this airport, I lost my passport. I was nice and early, so there were no queues at the check-in desk. I checked in my hold luggage, got my boarding card and went through passport control all very quickly. Then, just because I had so much time, instead of just sitting in the departure lounge, I decided to do some shopping. I wanted to get a present, so I was trying all the different perfumes in the duty-free shop. I don't know how it happened but I must have dropped my passport there. I went to the gate to board the plane and then I realised that I couldn't find my passport. At that moment, they called me over the loudspeaker. 'Will passenger Martinez travelling to Madrid please contact the information desk.' I felt so embarrassed.

UNIT 11

1 22 Listening, page 54

M = Man; W = Woman

M: So you're off on holiday next week?

W: That's right.

M: Are you going anywhere nice?

W: Yes, we're going to spend a few days down by the sea. But it'll be a working holiday really. I'm going to take some work with me and I've agreed to check my BlackBerry every day.

M: Oh, that's awful. That's not really a break. People expect you to be available 24/7 these days. It was much better in the past when people didn't have BlackBerries.

W: Well, I'm not sure actually. When you take a complete break, you're always under pressure to finish off everything in time and organise everything for when you'll be away. The last two or three days before you go are far busier than normal, so you start your holiday feeling really stressed.

M: I know what you mean. Actually, coming back to work is even worse. There's always a backlog of work to do and hundreds of emails to answer.

W: That's right. I sometimes think organising three weeks away is a bigger problem than staying in the office. But if you take a sort of half holiday like this, you set aside a couple of hours a day for work and you check your email to make sure everything is going along OK. Then the rest of the time you can walk along the beach and do all the things you enjoy. And the really good thing is there's no rush to finish everything before you go. I actually think that's more relaxing.

M: Yes, it certainly makes your last day less stressful. But you still want to switch off completely, don't you? I think people need a complete break sometimes.

W: I'm not sure I do. I find it quite hard to switch off completely, especially for a short break like this. Maybe we need to rethink our ideas about holidays.

M: So wouldn't you want to have any complete days off?

W: Oh I think we should keep single days like Christmas and bank holidays. But the rest of the time could be divided into times when you have to go into the office and work full capacity, and half holidays like this when you just keep in touch and work a little bit out of the office.

M: You'd like that?

W: Yes I would. And just think, the half holidays could be much longer than the holidays people take now. You could take four or five months a year.

M: Hmm. You almost convince me.

UNIT 12

1 23 Listening, page 58

M1 = Man 1; M2 = Man 2

M1: The most convenient is the Avilon. It's only two kilometres from the airport.

M2: But it's too small. The biggest conference room only holds 40 people. I think the best place is the Flamenco.

M1: It certainly has a larger conference room than the Avilon. But actually our rooms don't need to be as big as that.

M2: But that's just the room with the biggest capacity. I expect they have some smaller rooms as well. The only thing is, it's 25 kilometres from the airport.

M1: Rydes Vale sounds nice.

M2: But I think that's the least suitable of the three. It's even further from the airport than the Flamenco. We don't want to be right out in the countryside.

1 24 Listening, page 60

Good morning, ladies and gentlemen and a very warm welcome to this, Utilita's third annual conference.

Promoting a product or service is becoming more challenging and exciting every year, so we have decided to share our experience and take 'social media' as the topic of our conference this year.

First of all, there are one or two changes to the programme that I'd like to draw your attention to. Unfortunately, Mr John Pineda can't be with us today. So instead of his session on measuring TV audiences, Ms Stefania Volksmann will be giving a talk on mobile phone app advertising. The other main change is that Mr Tim Shi's talk on 'The consumer as boss' has been moved from the Green Room downstairs and will now take place in the West Room.

Our final session tomorrow afternoon will be a discussion panel with our key speakers. That will be here in the main theatre at two o'clock. We are expecting a large audience so I advise you to make your way from the main hall as soon as lunch is finished.

Inside your welcome pack you'll find a short feedback questionnaire. I'd be grateful if you could fill it in at the end of the conference and drop it into the box by the coffee shop. If you need a new feedback form, then you can get one from the stand next to the reception. That's where you can also get your free souvenir, which this year is a very nice digital clock for your desk. Put it next to the mousemat that we had last year.

Last but not least, we intend to make a contribution to the literature available on social media marketing by publishing this year's conference proceedings in a book. This should be available in June and will be called *Sales Talk*. We also intend to publish shortened versions of some of the presentations before that online. You'll be able to find these on our website hopefully from April. Just click on the link entitled *Conference papers*.

Ladies and gentlemen, I'd now like to hand you over to our first speaker, Dieter Pietsch, and once again, thank you all for coming here today …

UNIT 13

1 25 Listening, page 67, Exercise 3

I = Interviewer; M = Matt

I: You just mentioned just now that you started off as a professional classical singer. Erm, when did you start your singing career?

M: Erm, I sang from very early on, but I suppose, as a career, I sang at university a bit more than I actually did my degree, to be perfectly honest. Er, but officially to call it a career, I'd say after university. I started working professionally, doing regular concerts, at the same time as studying as a postgraduate at music college in London. Er, I did that for four years, actually, studying as a postgraduate, er, at the same time as working, and then went into the opera world as an opera soloist, and ended up singing around the world, which was fantastic, but particularly opera houses in Europe.

I: So how long did you work as, er, an opera singer?

M: I'd say I worked about 10 years in the end, er, including the time I studied; so really my early twenties to early thirties.

I: What did you most enjoy about singing?

M: Singing had lots of fabulous things about it. Erm, I saw a lot of the world from singing, which I really wouldn't have seen, went on tours all over the place, and that was fantastic. Er, and also

I got to meet lots of people, every couple of months I would be, er, starting a new opera, a completely different set of people who you had to work very intensively with for, er, a few weeks, and for those few weeks you'd become the best of friends, though you wouldn't necessarily, er, call them ever again once the opera had finished, that's the nature of the thing. But, no, I think that's it, meeting lots of people and, and getting to see lots of places.

I: And was there anything that you didn't particularly like about it?

M: Er, the, the reverse side of the coin to travelling around the world is that you're away from home, and, er, it can be very lonely.

I: And, erm, what made you finally decide to change course and work at Fortbridge? I mean, did you actually go out looking for it, or did it come to you?

M: It came to me. Er, I had a quick transition. I decided to stop singing without actually deciding what I wanted to do, and did a couple of years in the wine industry, strangely enough. Erm, realised the wine industry wasn't quite for me, not that I regret the couple of years, they were fantastic; I know a lot about wine, and I think any experience is, is great. And then Bill Kemmery, the, the managing director of this company, came up to me and wanted somebody he could trust to open his London office, and we talked about it and I decided to jump in feet first. It was, it was a bit experimental because I didn't really know the industry, and it was a very steep learning curve but it's been, been well, well worth it.

I: Do you think you bring skills from singing to working for Fortbridge?

M: I don't think there's, yes, there's not much overlap but, er, the one thing I would say, is that talking as we did earlier about meeting a new group of people every couple of months, and having to work very intensively with them, you do develop a way of getting on with people in very many different ways. You can either be very personable, or, or you can be very bossy, or, you know, demanding – as, as opera singers famously are – but, I think I brought those skills of, of getting on with people, but also knowing the moments when you need to put your foot down and say 'no, this, this can't happen,' or 'no, I don't feel comfortable with that.' Those, those are hard life skills to obtain, I think, sometimes, and hard, definitely hard ones to balance.

① 26 Listening, page 67, Exercise 4

I = Interviewer; M = Matt

I: And has the job changed at all since you started?

M: The job has changed enormously simply because I've learnt what the job involves. Erm, this has been part of the fun of the whole thing in that I, I jumped in, and had to learn jumping in the deep end, and whilst I've been on the job I've realised what's important, what's, what I need to concentrate on, and what I've wasted a bit of time on. It's all been good learning, but now I'm much more sure about what I need to be working on and what I can leave.

UNIT 14

① 27 Listening, page 70

I = Interviewer; T = Tara

I: I have with me Tara Brandon from Business Companions, a consultancy which trains business executives in cultural issues. Tara, perhaps first of all you could tell us a little about the kind of training you give?

T: Well, basically we deal with cultural awareness. It covers obvious things like when holiday periods are in different countries, but also attitudes to time, dress and all those things

which will help you make a good impression when you're dealing with clients or colleagues in another country.

I: And gift-giving is part of that?

T: Gift-giving is a very important part of that. It's one of those things which can make or break a business relationship.

I: So what advice would you give about choosing presents for, say, a fairly new overseas contact who you're hoping will become a business partner?

T: It's difficult to generalise, but obviously, if it's an overseas partner, you want to try and give them something that they can't find at home. If it's something they can find on sale in their country, then it won't seem very special.

I: So are you saying the present needs to be expensive?

T: No, not necessarily. It could actually be embarrassing for your host if they feel they have to give you something just as expensive in return. That might be a problem for them if they have a tight budget. The important thing is that it's carefully chosen.

I: Right. Anything else?

T: Well, another thing I'd say is a definite no-no is giving something with your company logo on it. That confuses gift-giving with wanting someone to advertise your company. A present should really only be to say to people how much you value your relationship with them.

I: OK.

T: You also need to think as well about who the present is for. It's usually best to give something the whole company can share. It could be very rude to give a present to your contact person, or one person in a group, and nothing to the others. Or you could take lots of different gifts for different people. In that case though, in many countries you'll need to think about people's positions in the company. Make sure that the most important present goes to the person with the highest rank.

I: So you don't give the same present to the director and the van driver?

T: That's right. But for anything more specific than that, I think you just have to do a bit of research and find out what people are likely to appreciate in that country. And of course, whether it's really expected that you'll give a gift at all. Some cultures place a very high value on gift-giving whereas for others it's not so important.

I: So give us an example of a country where gift-giving is really important.

T: Well, the one which is very often top of the list is Japan.

① 28 Listening, page 70

I = Interviewer; T = Tara

I: So tell us about Japan.

T: Well, the main times of the year when people give presents in Japan are in December, just before New Year, and for what's called Ochugen, normally in July. That's when companies might give presents to good customers or partners. And of course if you're doing business in Japan at these times, then you really need to take a present for your hosts.

I: What kind of things should you take?

T: Something from a well-known, high-quality department store like Harrods, I would say. Another thing which is often appreciated is good quality fruit. But one very important thing is that presents in Japan are always wrapped. You need to do it very carefully so it looks beautiful. Of course that can be a problem if you're bringing a present through customs so it's probably best to wrap the present when you're there. Actually, quite a lot of hotels will do it for you. And you shouldn't use white paper to wrap it. Light blue paper or some other pastel colour is the best choice.

I: Ah. Anything else?

T: Well traditionally in Japan, you don't open the present immediately in front of the giver. You open it in private. If your host does suggest that you open your present, then you need to do it carefully. You mustn't just tear the paper like we might do in Europe.

I: So that shows your respect and appreciation for the gift as well.

T: Yes that's right. And there are one or two other rules. Firstly, gifts should be given and taken with both hands, and the other one is, don't give four pieces of anything as a present. That's because the Japanese word for 'four' sounds like the word for 'death'.

I: Really interesting. Thanks for talking to us.

UNIT 15

① ㉙ Listening, page 74

… So if we all agree that good teamwork is the key to success, we need to ask, what makes a good team? Because we all know of course, that you can't be sure that people are going to work well together, however talented they might be as separate people.

First of all, a team needs a good leader. This needs to be someone who is committed to the team and its aims, someone who is calm in a crisis and most of all someone who trusts their team members and listens to them. The leader doesn't have to be the most intelligent member of their team; in fact, it's often best if they're not. Very intelligent team leaders sometimes use arguments that other team members don't understand and they can also dominate a situation. A team leader who is of average intelligence but has the right personality is better.

Most teams need someone who can think of new ideas and new ways to solve problems. This is the creative, original thinker, a very important team member. But it's a mistake to think that teams with lots of people like this will do well. In fact, you'll probably get a lot of fights and arguments that way because creative, imaginative people are not always good at understanding or working with other people's creative ideas. Ideally, you need just one person like this and different types of people for the rest of the team.

This brings me on to the most important principle of team-building. You need a balance of different personalities. Just think about when you're launching a new product. You need the creative thinker or designer who has first thought of the idea. You need the enthusiastic salesperson with great communication skills who can go out there and sell it. But you also need the careful, thoughtful person who pays attention to all the details, and who makes sure all the checks and tests are done and the product is ready for the market.

It would be nice to think, wouldn't it, that if teams need all these different types of people, that everyone could be a good team member of some type. Unfortunately, studies suggest that this isn't true. There are some people who just don't work well in any team. Something in their personality is against it … is against team spirit. What's more, people who can't fit into any team sometimes reach quite high positions in business.

So, how can we use this knowledge we have about teamwork? Firstly, when choosing someone to join a management team, we need to think about the balance or mix of the team as a whole. It's a mistake just to choose someone similar to the people you already have, because that probably won't make the most effective team. Secondly, people often get jobs because of their previous experience. They're given a job just because they've done something like it before, even if they weren't very good at it. I would argue in favour of using a personality test and choosing the right person from the results of this, rather than just looking at previous experience. If you look at your handouts, you'll see an example of the kind of test that I mean …

UNIT 16

① ㉚ Listening, page 78

1 Last year I was appointed to lead the marketing group for a new international agricultural product. The company wanted to create a team who knew about our different target markets so they brought in a whole variety of people, all from different countries. The challenge was to get them to work well together. We started off with a training day when we gave them questionnaires to get them talking about different cultural issues, and then went on to how we might relate these to our marketing strategy. It went well and we had a really successful product launch.

2 We have to work with people who are based in different countries so we often end up as part of a virtual team. We communicate through conference calls and video conferencing. I know some of my colleagues have found virtual teams like this a really positive experience but for the two teams I've worked on it's been disappointing. It was always difficult to contact people when you really needed to and people often didn't seem to know what the rest of the team were doing.

3 We've just acquired a well-established company in Trinidad, which we're all quite excited about. We want to recruit some of the new staff locally if we can. The most important thing for us is to find someone local to be in charge of personnel. We feel they'll be able to recruit more local talent than someone who is just relocated from this country.

4 There are lots of opportunities for working overseas in my company and so last year they introduced a new way of evaluating the management team. All the usual criteria for performance are still there but they also rank you according to how willing you are to move. So at the top you have people who are happy to relocate overseas, even for a long period, then people who will do it only for a short period, and then at the bottom people who don't want to move from their home base. So now, when a new overseas opportunity comes up, management know immediately who might be able to take it.

UNIT 17

① ㉛ Listening, page 84

1 Anyway, here are the figures for this month. Sales of ladies' handbags are down on last month, but executive products like briefcases are still doing very well. I have to say I'm very disappointed with our new range of leather jackets. We don't seem to have been able to reach the right market there.

2 Our sales showed a strong performance in the last quarter. They dropped slightly in January, after the Christmas rush, but recovered in February and as we can see, that upward trend continued until the end of March.

3 So, turning now to our markets, we can see that there has been a sharp increase in our sales in Asia over the past five years. It now makes up about 35% of the total, so it has not quite overtaken Europe, which is still the best performing region, but we have definitely made big inroads. However, sales in America remain well below the other two regions.

4 M: This isn't really what I expected. I thought the peak would be around mid-morning on Saturdays.

W: But actually it's later, around two or three in the afternoon.

M: Yes. Late afternoon is a slow period but then things seem to pick up again at around seven o'clock.

5 M: So what were the sales figures like for October?

W: Still not very good, I'm afraid. It's worrying. We usually see a big increase after August.

M: Isn't there any improvement at all?

W: Yes, they are slightly higher than September but it really isn't good enough.

UNIT 18

(1) 32 (1) 33 Listening, page 87, Exercises 1 and 2

I = Interviewer; S = Steve

S: My name's Steve Keley, and I work for KPMG. I work in their restructuring practice, and I'm a manager in that practice. So we work with stressed, distressed and failing businesses, trying to advise those businesses to either, er, save and turn them around, or, if that's not possible, to make the best of the situation that exists.

I: And is this something that you'd always thought you'd ... did you train as an accountant?

S: Yes, I'm a chartered accountant.

I: I think it must be very interesting, especially in the recession, that, er, you know: you're having to be quite helpful and creative with, with people, aren't you?

S: Yes. I mean, because I work in restructuring, given the recession recently, we have been very busy. Erm, our, our team's expanded somewhat, and, er, the flow of work is fairly constant.

I: That's quite nice to be in something that is actually growing and, and expanding in that way.

S: It's always very difficult to talk about our industry as nice, because obviously it's companies that are in trouble; so, the fact it's, it's expanding – it's not generally good news.

I: Yes, and what particularly attracted you to KPMG, to this company?

S: KPMG is one of the biggest accounting companies, so clearly it has a fantastic reputation and standing in, in the market place. It's one of the big four, as they're known, so it's, it's very prestigious. It's a very strong brand, it's a good name to have on your CV and to be associated with as an individual, and kind of, in going forward in your career.

I: And anyone who's listening to this – what qualifications or training is necessary for someone who wants to work in this field?

S: Well, in the broader sense of accountancy, er, in the UK you don't specifically need a degree in accountancy – you can come into the firm with a degree in any discipline and the firm will actually provide all your accountancy training as you become a chartered accountant, which takes about three years, and there's various exams. More specifically to restructuring, you don't have to be a chartered accountant, but it's highly beneficial, so we do have people that work in restructuring from a very broad spectrum of backgrounds and areas.

I: What kind of companies do you work with in your job, in your role?

S: Because I work in the mid-market practice, erm, we're not sector-specific, so I work with a very broad range of businesses, and it, it very much varies as to what companies happen to be in distress at the time. I mean, over recent years I've worked with hotels, with care homes, with retail businesses, with, er, a golf course, so the spread is quite broad. Manufacturing industries, er, printing ... it is quite a broad spectrum.

(1) 34 Listening, page 87, Exercise 3

I = Interviewer; S = Steve

I: Do you have to be very careful about confidentiality of companies that are showing you their figures, or is that just a given?

S: There's very clear guidance around ethics and independence, so it's very clear that you have to be objective, and professional; and issues like confidentiality are issues that we take for granted day in, day out, that there'll be information, we are, er, made aware of that is confidential to the business interests, not for talking about down the pub, for example.

I: No, no, quite, or: 'Oh, yes, I know someone who worked there, and blah, blah, blah ...' No, I'm sure that's the case. And, do you think, erm, companies always tell you the truth?

S: Well, it's always individuals rather than companies, and individuals – truth can be a, er, a very much a – shades of grey, subjective issue. Certainly there are instances when people do not tell the truth, and that's unsurprising given the sector and space I work in. So, because companies are in trouble ... you come across companies in distress and this isn't, certainly not all the time – but there are times when we come across businesses where fraud has taken place, and therefore you get directors that are trying to be, er, obstructive, and are not trying to be helpful.

I: But, I would think that would be pretty transparent, wouldn't it? And, you'd be able to tell that there was something that you weren't being told?

S: You'd be amazed at, er, the way that, erm, individuals and companies could hide information if they wanted to. I mean, you've got the classic example over the past few years of businesses like Enron and WorldCom that were committing fairly major frauds.

(1) 35 Listening, page 87, Exercise 4

I = Interviewer; S = Steve

I: What do you find most satisfying about your job?

S: The most satisfying thing is probably when a job goes really well, and a business that, when you first take it on is in trouble, you work alongside the management and the lenders, and come to a positive outcome, and the business is returned to a positive, profitable cash generative state, and goes forward, and therefore no one loses any money, or the individuals involved don't lose their jobs, and the owners don't lose their livelihoods, etc., etc. Those kind of positive stories are the most, most satisfying.

UNIT 19

(1) 36 Listening, page 93

I = Interviewer; M = Matthew

I: And, er, can you tell me a bit about your job?

M: My job, sounds more complicated I'd imagine than it is, it's investor relations and public relations for mining companies. The investor relations part involves taking clients to people who are potentially interested in financing their operations; er, so it's simply getting those two groups to meet up and hopefully come to an agreement. The other side is public relations, which is more media focussed: spreading the story of the companies, the clients, er, through newspapers, through trade journals, television, radio, er, trying to get a positive message about the company across, and also, most importantly, getting it across to the shareholders of that company: the people who have already invested in the company, er, they want to hear that things are progressing, they want to hear what's happening in the future, so that they know that their investment is safe, and potentially maybe invest a little bit more.

I: And, are your clients, er, are they global clients, international clients?

M: The clients are global in two ways: first of all we categorise them by where they're listed on the stock exchange, so they might be listed, er, on the London stock exchange, or Australian, Johannesburg, er, across the world, but also where their assets are, where ... these are mining companies so they'll have exploration licences or mines anywhere from Mongolia to Mozambique, to Chile.

I: That's really interesting. So you're dealing in fact with lots of different people from lots of different cultures.

M: Yes, that's why it's been very important for us to have a company that is global. We have offices dotted around the world, er, for example in Beijing and myself here in London. The point is to be able to bring a global approach to companies that are often listed in one part of the world, they have their office in another part of the world, and they have their mine in yet another part of the world.

I: And what do you like about your job, particularly?

M: I, as we've discussed, do find the industry very interesting. Mining is incredibly capital intensive, you need a lot of money before you even dig anything up. Er, and at the same time it's very risky, it's very hard to tell what you have under the ground and it takes a lot of money to take what is an educated guess, but the rewards can also be huge. And the other part of it is that I, in effect, manage my own company; I'm part of a larger company but I run the office here in London, and it's very exciting and interesting to be your own boss.

I: And is there anything you don't like about it?

M: I, at present, am working on my own here. The majority of the people working in the company are based in Sydney, in Australia, er, so literally the other side of the world, and I do like to have people around me just for social purposes, and I always think it's good to have a good social atmosphere at work, which of course I don't have at the moment. But, I work from home, which is a much bigger advantage than the disadvantage of not having co-workers.

UNIT 20

① 37 Listening, page 94

I = Interviewer; T = Tara

I: I have with me Tara Ganesh, the marketing director of Entrepreneur, a business support service. Tara, hello.

T: Hello.

I: Perhaps you could begin by just explaining briefly what Entrepreneur does.

T: Well, we are a service which offers advice and support for people who run their own business, especially people who are just starting up. We have a lawyer who can give legal advice, and a marketing adviser who they can consult. And quite importantly actually, we offer financial advice about all areas of business.

I: OK, so I've got this new idea for a product that I think is going to make my fortune. How do I raise the capital to get started? What are my options?

T: Even today, I think the most common way to set up a new business is with your own money. People use their savings and if they don't have enough, they borrow from family and friends.

I: Hmm. And that's still the best way, is it?

T: In many ways, because it is so simple. But if family or friends are involved you need to be very clear about what will happen if things go wrong and how you'll pay the money back. Even if it's someone close to you, you should still draw up a written contract.

I: Yes I can imagine there have been a lot of broken friendships over this sort of thing. But what if I can't provide the money myself? What's the best option, a bank loan?

T: For the small business, yes, it's probably the best choice. But your bank manager will need to see a detailed business plan. And if you're not experienced in writing business plans, you'll need to get some professional help, like we provide at Entrepreneur.

I: What kinds of things are the bank looking for?

T: In the business? Well, realistic targets, steady growth, not necessarily dramatic at first, and a strong cashflow. Essentially what the bank are interested in is whether you'll be able to pay off the debts. And for that reason, your bank loan will have to be secured against an asset.

I: What kind of asset?

T: Well it could be your house or some equipment you own for the business. You know, so that if your business doesn't pay back the loan, the bank can claim that asset instead.

I: What other sources of capital are there?

T: Well there are companies who provide start-up capital in return for a stake in the business. These are so-called venture capital firms. But they get lots of applications for loans, so there is usually tough competition. They tend to fund businesses which are involved in new technology and they'll want to see a very high growth rate on your plan, 20% at least. Or you might find a business angel to provide the money.

I: A what, sorry?

T: A business angel. It's just someone who will invest in a start-up company in return for a share in it. Usually it's someone who has already been successful with a company of their own.

I: And how do I go about finding a business angel?

T: It can be difficult. They don't usually advertise because they don't want to be flooded with applications. But there are angel investment networks you can go through.

I: Tara Ganesh, thank you very much.

UNIT 21

② 01 Listening, page 102

I = Interviewer; J = Jacqui

2 I: So Jacqui, basically your job is giving students advice on how to prepare their CVs.

J: Yes, though there's a bit more to it than that. I also organise careers education programmes, and advise people on how they can gain work experience and so on.

I: So if we think about the English-speaking world, do you think there are differences in how CVs are written in English-speaking countries? Take for example the UK and the USA?

J: Yes, definitely. One difference is the length. If you've just recently graduated from university in the US, you usually have a one-page résumé. That's different from here in the UK where the normal length is two pages. Obviously, if it's been five or six years since you graduated, then it can be a little longer.

I: Any other differences?

J: Yes, in the US they give more importance to research projects. So if you don't have any experience in the field you're applying for, then you might have a section on your CV about any research projects you've carried out instead. In the UK, there's more emphasis given to skills you can bring to the new job. So you emphasise any work that you've done and the skills that you can transfer.

I: Like, for example?

J: Like for example being a waiter, where you had to work under pressure or deal with complaints.

I: And what about in the non-English-speaking world? How might CVs be different in, say, India or China?

J: Well there again there's much less emphasis on transferable skills, and they tend to be quite academically focussed. There's more importance given to things like academic awards, scholarships, that kind of thing.

I: Any other differences?

J: How different countries deal with references is another

thing. In the US, you often put details of your three referees on a separate piece of paper so they almost don't form part of the CV itself. In Asia you might actually include letters of reference with the CV when you send it off. In the UK, you tend to put two referees on the bottom of your CV.

I: Or not put them at all. On my CV I just put 'References available on request.'

J: Yes, that's quite common here as well. There are some countries where they might not say anything about referees on the CV.

②02 Listening, page 102, Exercise 3

I = Interviewer; J = Jacqui

3 I: So when a client comes to you, what are the most common things that need to be changed about the way they've written their CV?

J: I think the most important thing to get across to them is that the CV isn't a history of your education or your work experience. You have to see it as a marketing tool. That means you have to look at the job description and all the specifications and then write the CV as a mirror for it. That can be quite a new idea for people in the UK and perhaps even more for overseas graduates.

I: So what is often wrong about the CVs that you see?

J: Well they're often too long. And there's often too much about their academic achievement or what jobs they've done instead of focussing on the skills that they've gained. Or quite often when I see a CV that a client brings me, another thing that is not suitable is the formatting, like they may have used lots of tables and boxes for things like exam results.

I: And if we think about different areas of business or different professions, are there differences in the way that CVs are intended to look?

J: Yes, certainly. Again if we're talking about the UK, your CV should be just one page long if you want to work in banking. For other fields, it can be up to two pages, and it can be longer if you're applying for a university job as a lecturer or something like that. And you need to reorder and retitle things and give different information according to what sector you are applying for.

I: What different information?

J: Well for example, if you are applying for an academic job, you might have a section on conferences. Or in some fields you might need different sections for technical information. So if you're applying to work in IT, you'd need a section saying what programming languages you know.

I: So you certainly shouldn't just have a standard CV that you send out to all jobs you apply for?

J: No, certainly not. It needs to be changed each time to make it match the job description as closely as possible.

UNIT 22

②03 Listening, page 107

I = Interviewer; S = Simon

I: So Simon, how many full-time or part-time staff positions do you deal with?

S: That's quite a complicated question because part of our client base is large consultancies, and they might want about one hundred people placed in total during the year. So that's where the majority of our people go. But I also work on specialist vacancies in smaller companies, which could be anything from IT support jobs to supervising the whole IT team.

I: And what's the female to male ratio?

S: That's quite a difficult question as well because things are changing. There's a big movement at the moment towards more diversity which partly involves bringing in more female employees. There's lots of advantages to that, of course, as it means that businesses can tap into a wider pool of talent. It's certainly had an effect as there are definitely more women now than, say, 10 years ago. I don't know, maybe it's now up to about 40 per cent.

I: And what's the age range of your candidates?

S: Quite wide. We have people who are in their early twenties, twenty-three, or twenty-four, right up to clients in their late fifties. And we have placed one or two who were sixty-one or sixty-two. So it's quite broad. I think we do better here than many other organisations who just tend to attract younger people.

I: And what level of qualifications do your clients need? Degrees, I suppose?

S: One of my clients absolutely requires degrees. Most of them though, aim to get people with degrees but they're actually a bit more flexible and if someone is really good but doesn't have a degree, they will take them. And of course to some clients a vocational qualification in IT can be just as good as a degree.

I: And are all the people who come to register with you British or do you get people from outside the UK?

S: Oh yes, certainly. Most of them are either British or Indian. We have a lot of Indian IT specialists. I think that's mainly because India produces loads of computer graduates, far more than we do. And of course we have got a big Indian community in this country, which I suppose can draw them towards looking for employment with a UK-based company.

I: Right. And do you think things are changing in your field?

S: In IT?

I: Or in recruitment. I mean, yes, IT is changing of course, but is the method of recruitment changing?

S: Well, yes, I do think it's changed. When it was a new industry, there was perhaps relatively little control over how agencies operated and there were a lot of small agencies all in competition with each other. There were organisations which tried to place people into jobs they weren't suited to and did various things which gave the industry a bad name. I suppose there are still some organisations like that. But I think we've improved on the whole and we've become much more professional. I'd like to think so anyway.

UNIT 23

②04 Listening, page 111

I = Interviewer; Y = Yvonne

I: So, Yvonne, what exactly is 360 degree feedback?

Y: Well, it's a way of helping staff to develop. It means that you don't just receive comments and feedback from your manager. Instead, you get it from your manager, your colleagues, people who work under you, even customers and suppliers. Anyone really who comes in contact with you and has an opinion.

I: And who chooses these people who are going to give the feedback?

Y: The employee's manager has to choose some. That's a rule. But I think it can be nice to make it a shared process, and let the employee choose one or two colleagues or customers as well.

I: How is the feedback given? Do you actually meet all of these people and talk about your performance?

Y: No, not necessarily. The feedback is on a form which lists the skills needed for your job. Appraisers give you a grade for each one. There's a space for them to write their opinion as well, which is often more helpful than just giving a number. And the important thing is, the employee gives himself or herself grades as well.

I: What, for the same skills?

Y: That's right. You assess yourself using the same form. Then when the feedback comes in, you can see if there's a difference between how you see yourself and how others see you. That can be an eye-opener.

I: Yes. I must say it sounds quite frightening as well, though. Er, could the results of this feedback be related to the employee's pay? You know, if the feedback is good, they get a pay rise?

Y: No, I'm not at all keen on that idea. I won't say it's never happened but it isn't normal and it isn't really what 360 degree is about. It's to help staff develop.

I: So what happens to the feedback then?

Y: Well, one thing that makes it less frightening is that the appraisee owns the feedback. Other members of the organisation don't see it and you don't even have to show it to your manager.

I: So what's the point of it then?

Y: Well, the employee uses their feedback to write a development plan for training they would like to receive. The manager has to see this plan, so this gives the manager an idea about the feedback. But I think if employees really feel that the manager is concerned with staff development, they will usually share the feedback as well.

I: Does the employee know who the feedback is from?

Y: That depends on the person or the organisation. Some people prefer giving feedback anonymously and it can make it easier for the employee to deal with any criticism. I do feel though that you get more benefit when people write their names on the feedback. In the right institution, people should be able to cope with this.

I: So are you saying that there is such a thing as a wrong institution? Are there any companies where you wouldn't recommend it?

Y: Well, as I've said, I think it's a very powerful way of helping staff to develop. But yes, of course it can be used as a weapon. So if you are working in an organisation where there's a lot of mistrust and bad feeling, then no, it isn't suitable. And you shouldn't use it at a time when there are big changes going on, like a merger or something. What you have to do is to work on the culture of your institution and try to create the sort of atmosphere where 360 degree feedback will be used to everyone's benefit.

I: I see.

Y: And funnily enough, the process of preparing for 360 degree is often more beneficial than the feedback itself. I've seen many cases where the culture of an institution has really changed, not because of the feedback but because of what was done in preparation for it. When it was time for the feedback, most of the important changes had already happened.

I: Interesting.

UNIT 24

(2) 05 Listening, page 112

A and B = Men; C and D = Women

A: I'm sure that one thing we have to do is to improve our equipment. The internet connection is quite slow and it often goes down.

B: Well, we are planning to upgrade the system next year.

A: But isn't there anything we can do to improve things now? How about issuing the staff with smartphones?

C: Hmm. You know, providing people with a lot of gadgets isn't always a good idea. Quite often it doesn't improve productivity at all. They're just a distraction.

A: But I think people would feel more motivated if they had really good state-of-the-art equipment. I do think we have to do something to show staff that we support them in their work.

C: It's difficult to make sure people use smartphones properly. They might just waste more time. How do you stop people playing games on them?

A: I think you can block access to certain sites.

B: Well I think I agree with Paul. Smartphones would help people to do their work more efficiently. And it might be possible to bring forward the date of the system upgrade if staff really are feeling frustrated. But before spending a lot of money on new equipment, we should find out how people really feel. Marina, could you do a bit of research on this for us? Find out how they feel about the present system and ask if there's any extra equipment they think would help them. No guarantees, mind.

D: OK, I'll send round an email, and possibly see if people want to meet up to talk about things.

B: Send me a short report on people's opinions by the end of next week if you can.

D: OK.

(2) 06 Listening, page 115

1 I'm 62. I lost my job about two years ago but I'm a surveyor and there don't seem to be many young people going into my field of work. There were lots of places going and I managed to find a new job quite quickly.

2 I accepted early retirement from my bank about six years ago. I've done some temporary work since then but nothing for very long. I feel a bit frustrated and annoyed at not being able to use my skills but I shouldn't complain really, I suppose. It would be much worse if I was short of money.

3 I work as an executive PA at the moment but I'd really like to move on. The trouble is, I'm 54 and I can't even get an interview. As soon as I put in my CV with my age on it, I just seem to get a straight 'no'.

4 Things haven't been very easy since I was made redundant. I found a job in another company but I'm not very keen on it. The new company will only give me a monthly contract. I won't reach retirement age for another four years, so I really need a more reliable source of income, something with more of a guarantee.

5 I'm 58 and I'm the manager of an IT department. There's a lot of stereotypes about people in IT all being really young, but it's certainly not true in my department. I'm not in a minority at all, there are lots of people like me.

Exam Skills and Exam practice

(2) 07 Listening Paper Part 1, Skills Exercise 1, page 156

M = Man; W = Woman

1 M: Do you want to meet sometime to discuss the market research survey? I could do next Monday morning.

W: Yes, I could as well, but I was hoping we could meet earlier than that. How about Thursday this week, or Friday morning?

M: Sorry, I can't make either of those. I'm in meetings both days.

W: OK, then, next week it is.

2 M: Has there been much interest in the new post?

W: Yes, we've had about 60 applicants, some very good ones too. I'm choosing them for interview at the moment and it looks like I'll be seeing about 30 of them.

M: So we should probably always advertise in that paper from now on. When we put the advert online, only about 10 people contacted us.

1 A: I'd like to book a room for Friday the 23rd of May please.
   B: That's £140 for a standard room and £175 for a suite.
   A: I just want the standard room. And I'm from Mason's. We usually get a discount.
   B: Oh, sorry. That will be £125 then.
2 A: Where are you taking Mr Sullivan for lunch?
   B: Well, it would be nice to take him to that new Greek restaurant but I just don't think there's going to be time. He has to catch the early afternoon train. It will have to be the staff canteen.
   A: You could take him to the steak bar. That's very near the station.
   B: No, he has to go back to the hotel and pick up his bag.

1 A: So have they finalised all these changes to the packaging for our chocolate drops?
   B: Well, they've decided not to go ahead with a lot of the changes. The design for the square tube was rejected, so it's still going to be round and they're still going to have plastic lids. The lettering on the packet will be the same as well but we are losing the blue background.
   A: After all that discussion!
2 W: What did you think of the presentation?
   M: I didn't think it was very interesting at all actually. I've heard that sort of thing so many times before.
   W: Oh, it was quite new for me. The only thing was, he spoke a bit too fast.
   M: Yes, I couldn't always catch what he said either.

Part 1: Questions 1–8

A = Announcer; M = Man; W = Woman

A: Here is an example: Who is Emily going to write to?
M: Emily, that supplier we use has become very unreliable, and we've decided to look for another one.
W: Seems a good idea.
M: We don't need to inform our clients, but could you send a note round to all our departments when we've decided who to replace the supplier with?
W: Yes, of course.
A: The answer is A. Now we are ready to start. You will hear the eight recordings twice.
A: One. What time will Jim's flight be?
W: Jim, I can't get you on the usual flight to Basle at 6.30 on Monday morning. It's full. Do you want to go on the 8.45, or would you prefer to fly out on Sunday night?
M: Mmm … what time is the Sunday flight?
W: There's one at 18.15 and one at 21.45 …
M: I'll take the earlier one on Sunday then … thanks.
A: Two. When will the sales conference take place?
M: Is the sales conference still going to be in September as usual this year? Someone told me they were thinking about moving it to October.
W: No, actually, they did consider November as that was a convenient time for our South American managers. But no, they've finally decided not to make any changes this year.
A: Three. Which graph is correct?
M: And now, manufacturing industries. Although the value of exports was greater than the value of imports at the beginning of the period, imports had exceeded exports by the end. However, over the whole period the value of both had risen.
A: Four. What does the woman say about the staff's telephone skills?
W: Whenever I call that company, it takes ages before anyone picks up the phone. And when I do finally get to ask my question, they politely say they have to pass me on to someone else who can tell me the right answer.
A: Five. Where should the presenter go first tomorrow?
M: John, the presentation you're giving tomorrow is in the Conference room rather than the Board room as originally planned. Can you make your way there? There's no point in going to the secretary's office first because she's on leave tomorrow. Call me if you need help setting up.
A: Six. What is the main problem with the new product components?
W: We've got a problem with the new components. We used the stronger plastic so they don't break as easily as the old ones and we've got the colour correct this time. However, they don't seem to fit into the old machines.
A: Seven. Which chart shows the company's expected sales figures?
M: … the company have announced they've seen a return to growth in the current quarter. Total sales are up, so they've increased their forecast and they're expecting further growth in the next quarter with an even stronger recovery after that.
A: Eight. Which job will the man apply for?
M: I'm thinking of applying for one of these jobs in the company magazine.
W: Let's see. Which one, the department manager's job?
M: Oh, is there one? I'm more interested in this area manager vacancy.
W: Shouldn't you try for a branch manager's job first to get more experience?
M: Probably, but there isn't one available.

Good morning. I'm going to talk to you today about some of the key challenges which DHL face over the next decade, and particularly how we can remain a world market leader in mail services while still keeping our commitment to reduce our impact on the environment. First of all, however, I'd just like to give you a few facts and figures about DHL.

I think it's pretty much beyond doubt that we are the world's most widely-known express delivery service. DHL was founded in 1969, but it expanded very quickly. We had an especially rapid period of growth in the early 80s, when we added 30 new countries to our list of possible destinations in just one year. Then in the 1990s, Deutsche Post started to purchase shares in DHL. In 2001 they acquired 51 % of the company shares and then the remaining 49 % the following year. This led to the launch of the new DHL and the expansion of our brand to a number of other Deutsche Post business units.

One of our most recent successes in the UK has been winning a contract with the National Health Service. This contract is worth £1.6 billion and means that we run the supply chain of health care products to their hospitals. It's estimated that through our efficient management of this delivery we have saved the average hospital up to 10 per cent in product costs. That's a total of over £200 million since we began the contract. Another success is our delivery of in-flight catering for British Airways, from the Flight Assembly Centre to the airport terminals. We have 38 trucks going back and forth delivering the catering to about 200 flights each day.

I've no doubt these successes will continue and that there will be more to come. But looking at the decade ahead, we also face new challenges …

(2) 12 Listening Paper Part 2, Skills Exercise 2, page 159

I, A, R, E, S, C, J, G

(2) 13 Listening Paper Part 2, Skills Exercise 3, page 159

1   W: Can I have your name please?
     M: Yes, it's Keith Caraballo. You spell that C-A-R-A-B-A-L-L-O.
     W: And the address?
     M: 34, Harries Close. That's H-A-R-R-I-E-S. Croydon.
2   W: Your name please?
     M: Well, it's an Italian name. Ciro Romano. You spell that C-I-R-O then R-O-M-A-N-O.
     W: And the address please?
     M: 62, Leigh Hunt Drive. That's L-E-I-G-H new word H-U-N-T. London. And the postcode is NW14 8EC.
3   M: Can I just check the spelling of your company?
     W: Harrow Wells. That's H-A-R-R-O-W then new word W-E-L-L-S.
     M: And what is the contact name for the order?
     W: You can use my name, Jariya Kroksamrang. That's J-A-R-I-Y-A and surname K-R-O-K-S-A-M-R-A-N-G.

(2) 14 Listening Paper Part 2, Skills Exercise 4, page 159

1   A: Can I just check the phone number? The one I've got is 029 3491 double 52.
     B: No, I think it's better if you use my direct line. That's 3491485.
2   A: What time is Mr Fenton coming?
     B: He was going to catch the train that gets in at 10.30, but now he says he can't make it. He should be arriving at 12.45.
3   A: What discount did you agree on?
     B: Well, we finally fixed on 8%. They wanted 12% at first, but I said we couldn't accept that. I know we don't usually give more than 5% but I think we're likely to get a lot more orders from them.
4   A: So how many members of staff do you have in total?
     B: Well the current figure is about 220, sorry, I mean 320. We took on another 40 people or so this year.

(2) 15 Listening Paper Part 2, Exam practice, page 160

Part 2: Questions 9–15

J = Jeff; C = Carla

J: Hello Carla, Jeff here. I've got the information we need for the contract with Halls Construction.
C: OK.
J: They just want us to supply sheets of standard quality glass.
C: What size? Seven-fifty millimetres by three-fifty?
J: Actually they want seven-fifty by three-forty.
C: OK. And how thick do they want it?
J: They want six this time rather than the usual four millimetres. They're fitting office windows. We'll have to change the programme on two of the machines.
C: How many sheets do they need?
J: They're going to start with 950.
C: OK. I think I've got the address already …
J: Are you sure? They've only just moved to the Gilwray Estate, that's G-I-L-W-R-A-Y.
C: Oh. And what's the unit number?
J: 27 I think … let me check … oh, it's 28, sorry.

C: Right. Got that.
J: Now, they've asked for monthly deliveries starting a week today, so that'll be August the 16th …
C: Actually, it's the 15th.
J: Right.
C: Have you agreed the price with them?
J: Yes. Including two thousand and fifteen for materials it'll be £2118. That includes £103 for insurance too.
C: OK Jeff. I'll do the contract right away.
J: Thanks a lot.

(2) 16 Listening Paper Part 3, Skills Exercise 1b, page 161

Good afternoon and welcome to today's business news. The fashion and beauty retailer, Westcloud, has enjoyed a rapid rise in sales over the last year. Performance has been especially strong in new markets, such as China and Latin America. The company opened their first store in China in 2009 but since then they have expanded rapidly and another five new stores were opened last year. Although clothing and accessories still account for the greater part of its product mix, by far the biggest rise over the past year has been in sales of perfume. Much of this success is believed to be the result of their advertising campaign, which successfully targeted the growing Chinese demand for luxury goods. The group have further plans for expansion in the coming year with a projected increase in retail space of 15%.

(2) 17 Listening Paper Part 3, Skills Exercise 3b, page 161

The insurance firm, Morton and Campbell, have announced that they intend to sell their life insurance division. In future they will concentrate only on their general insurance business. This is because of low profits. The company were hit last year especially, by a rise in the number of claims from the USA. According to the press, an investment company has offered to buy their life insurance unit in a deal worth £600 million. However, Morton and Campbell have not named the company.

(2) 18 Listening Paper Part 3, Exam practice, page 162

Part 3: Questions 16–22

Good evening everyone, my name's Tim Johnstone. As you probably know, the change to more flexible working arrangements, including working from home, began more than ten years ago. These arrangements were first introduced by companies able to take advantage of the enormous technological developments of the 1980s. And in fact, the first company to bring in this kind of work scheme was Powercom, a big name in the telecommunications industry, who introduced it in 1996.

Nowadays, almost a third of their workforce is involved in flexible working, and their staff have a choice of both timetable and location. In fact, about 10% of these employees have decided to work from home, with the remaining 90% working from a variety of different branch offices, moving around as it suits them.

Obviously employers realise that such arrangements improve their ability to attract staff, but research has shown that they consider the main benefit to be the reduction in office costs, with increases in staff productivity being the second most important. For staff, these schemes rarely result in a salary increase; according to a recent survey, the main advantage to them is job satisfaction. But, as you can see, it's a system which suits everybody.

So, understandably, flexible working has now spread to smaller firms, including my own – it's an insurance company – where we introduced flexible working a year ago. 45 of our 50 staff actually work from home now. Our clients contact the main office, and external staff are contacted through email and mobile phones, which have to be switched on from 8am to 6pm. We try to promote a quiet and stress-free environment, as staff can work more efficiently if left alone, and any non-urgent calls are therefore held back by our receptionist, with messages being delivered only at midday and early evening.

Now we're going to move on to look at schemes operated by other companies…

② ⑲ Listening Paper Part 4, Skills Exercise 1a, page 163

The transcript can be found on page 163.

② ⑳ ② ㉑ Listening Paper Part 4, Skills Exercises 2a, 2b and 2c, page 164

A: So Luke, you're now the owner of one of the largest recruitment companies in the country. Have you always worked in this field?

B: No, not always. My father ran a successful bakery and he always wanted me to join the family business. But I wanted to make my own way, so I moved out and I actually went to a recruitment agency to find work. The first place they found me was in a hotel.

A: And how long did you work there?

B: Not very long. I did other odd jobs for about a year or so and then I actually got a job in a recruitment agency called Hordens. I had to phone companies to see if they had any vacancies and then we advertised the post and interviewed the candidates for them. And I really liked it. I got quite good at reading people's CVs and spotting possible candidates, and I really loved doing the interviewing. I just enjoy talking to people, I suppose.

A: And then you started your own agency?

B: Then I started my own agency. It was a few years before I made the move because I needed to save up enough money. I didn't want to pay interest on a bank loan and I didn't feel I could ask my father for help. He was still a bit disappointed I wasn't following him into the family business.

A: So tell us how you went about setting up.

B: Well I'd already decided my main market was going to be financial services, so I think my biggest challenge was finding premises, because I wanted to be somewhere really central, near the City. I eventually found somewhere in one of the most expensive parts of London. It was tiny of course, because I couldn't afford anything very large in that area. But I do think that having an upmarket location was what brought in the clients and made us seem like a serious agency. And we grew from there. We moved into a larger premises after two years and a few years later we launched our trade magazine, Global Placements.

A: And you still run that as well?

B: No, actually. We decided to sell it in 2009. I was sorry to see it go because the readership was still growing, but big changes were taking place at that time, really exciting ones, and trying to put together and edit the magazines as well was just too much. Something had to go.

A: And how has the business changed since you started?

B: Well, the biggest difference is that our function has changed. Our market is still pretty much the same, and over half of our clients are still in financial services. But what we offer now is a full outsourcing of the recruitment activity. It's not just finding employees any more. We work in partnership with our clients to oversee the whole of the recruitment process and improve it in any way we can.

A: And is that how you see …

② ㉒ Listening Paper Part 4, Exam practice, page 165

Part 4: Questions 23–30

I = Interviewer; P = Penny

I: And today we welcome Penny Yates of Middlebrook Management College, to talk about recent developments in executive training programmes. Why are training courses popular with managers, Penny?

P: Well, I suppose for a few people getting away from the pressures and problems of the office can be a big attraction. But personally I think all managers see training courses as something they receive because they've worked hard. Learning new skills is much less important to them.

I: And do companies want different types of courses these days?

P: They do. Until recently executive training was very general: for example, to keep up to date with new developments in technology, or improve the management skills of particular individuals. But the business environment today is changing so quickly that what's needed is specially designed courses to help companies with the strategies they need to solve much more short-term problems.

I: So what kind of courses do you run, and who are your chief clients?

P: Well, our courses can be on anything from developing an e-business to managing a crisis. In the past our clients were always small local firms, but now they're much more likely to be the big national names. In the future, of course, we hope to attract some of the famous international corporations.

I: But isn't it better for a large company to recruit its own suitably-trained staff, rather than send managers away on courses?

P: Not at all. Obviously it's possible to recruit new senior staff, but they rarely have exactly the skills you need. Business schools have become much quicker at designing, developing and delivering special programmes. My college can deliver a special programme fast, and train a number of people at the same time. Designing an in-house scheme would take much longer, and it would only be slightly cheaper in the end.

I: And how long do your college's training programmes last?

P: Well, we can provide complete courses in just six weeks, though the more usual length is four months, possibly five. And many of our programmes are continuous. For one client, we've designed special courses over a period of more than three years now, and we've trained about a thousand staff in that time.

I: And what would you say is the main benefit to companies of your courses?

P: Well, of course, it is one way to show staff that you're making a commitment to them and investing in them. But the most important thing is that they encourage experienced individuals to stay in a company. Otherwise, they might look outside for new job opportunities.

I: Do training needs vary according to the size of the company?

P: Very much so. Small companies often have problems as they develop, and need advice on how to deal with change effectively when they only have a relatively small staff. Larger organisations often need help setting up effective systems for discussing issues that affect offices in different regions. We aim this sort of programme at middle managers, as top business leaders generally have their own management style, and prefer one-to-one coaching.

I: And what would you say is the perfect training environment?

P: Well, of course we sometimes go to the client's offices and that can work well. But usually I find that courses work best at a specialised conference centre, especially one which is equipped with the latest educational technology. We find managers are freer to think creatively there. But if that's not possible, we can meet at another convenient location, like a hotel.

I: Thank you Penny. If you're interested in finding out more, you can speak to Penny Yates on … *(fade)*

(2)(23) Speaking Paper Part 1, Skills Exercise 1c, page 172

Examiner: Where are you from?
Examiner: What work do you do?
Examiner: What do you like about your job?
Examiner: Now I'm going to ask some questions about your place of work. Do you have a comfortable office at work?
Examiner: Is it important for you to have your own office?
Examiner: And would you like to have a bigger office?

(2)(24) Speaking Paper Part 2, Skills exercise 1b, page 173

Well, I've decided to talk about what is important when giving a presentation. Firstly, I think it's important to use visuals like PowerPoint slides or things written on a flip chart because it's easier for the audience to concentrate when they have something to look at. Of course, there are some things which you can explain more clearly if you use visuals. For example, if you are talking about figures, you really need to show them to your audience on a graph of some kind.

Secondly, I think it's very important to give the people who are listening time to ask you questions at the end. This means that you can explain something to them again if it wasn't clear the first time. It also means that the audience can find out more about any part of the talk which interested them.

People usually give handouts like copies of the PowerPoint slides to the audience. This is nice but I'm not sure it's essential. People often prefer to make their own notes. I sometimes wonder if many people look at the handouts again after the talk.

So to conclude, I think the most important things are using visuals and allowing the audience to ask questions at the end.

(2)(25) Speaking Paper Part 3, Skills exercise 2c, page 176

A: I think the best place to advertise is in a business magazine. If it's something that business people buy, there is more chance that the right sort of person will see it. It's probably cheaper than advertising in a national newspaper too.

B: Maybe but I'm not sure how many people read business magazines. How about the Internet? A lot of people look for jobs online these days.

A: Yes, that's true. Websites reach a lot of people as well. We might even get candidates from other countries.

B: What do you think about using a recruitment agency?

A: No, I don't think that's the best way. I'm not sure the best people usually go to agencies.

B: It depends on the post, but I think you're right. It's not a good idea for a post like this. So it's the Internet then?

A: Yes, I think so.